IMAGINE THE GOD OF HEAVEN

A masterpiece! This book is a treasure trove of wisdom about God's love for you and all of humanity. John Burke's connection of God in the Bible with God in NDEs is brilliant and gripping. *Imagine the God of Heaven* provides powerful evidence that allows *anyone* to have a better rational understanding of this very personal God. You won't want to miss this vitally important book! It's easy to read and enthusiastically recommended.

JEFFREY LONG, MD, *New York Times* bestselling author of *Evidence of the Afterlife* and *God and the Afterlife*

Do you picture God as a cold, distant, and disinterested entity? If so, reading this book will shatter that false image and enchant your imagination with the wondrous glory of who God really is. My friend John Burke skillfully weaves captivating stories of near-death experiences with biblical principles to demonstrate an incredible truth: God is far more amazing than we ever imagined!

LEE STROBEL, *New York Times* bestselling author of *The Case for Christ*; founder of the Lee Strobel Center for Evangelism and Applied Apologetics, Colorado Christian University

As a science-based spinal surgeon, I didn't believe near-death experiences were real until my own NDE changed my life forever. This book reveals the God of endless compassion and kindness whose presence I never wanted to leave.

MARY C. NEAL, MD, *New York Times* bestselling author of *To Heaven and Back* and *7 Lessons from Heaven*

No one does a better job than John Burke in integrating near-death experiences with the Scriptures and the Christian faith. *Imagine the God of Heaven* is a must-read for Christians and a fantastic introduction to the Christian faith for skeptics. Your mind will soar in new directions and your heart will open even wider to the reality of God's goodness, grace, and promises.

CAREY NIEUWHOF, bestselling author of *At Your Best*; founder of The Art of Leadership Academy

As a medical doctor who has studied NDEs for more than thirty-five years, I've written extensively about the convincing evidence that there is a continuity of consciousness after the death of our body. John Burke first refers to the existing research on NDEs in the past forty years, and then he explores important questions as to what we can know about the image of God as was mentioned by many near-death experiencers. Though these questions go beyond the scope of scientific research, they are the truly important questions of life. I highly recommend this book.

PIM VAN LOMMEL, cardiologist; NDE researcher; author of *Consciousness beyond Life*

In *Imagine the God of Heaven*, John Burke shares an explosion of new insights of God's unconditional love for us and the many awesome ways that he wants to enrich our lives. It is a wonderful spiritual "road map" to deepen our relationship with God!

WALTER BRADLEY, PhD in materials science; contributing author of *The Mystery of Life's Origin*

Most of us wonder what awaits us beyond the grave, which is why the reports of those who survive near-death experiences hold such fascination for so many. In his conversations with numerous people who have returned from clinical death, John Burke has discovered several commonalities that align with Scripture. His latest book takes a look at the most important theme that runs through these accounts: the unfathomable, unfailing, all-consuming love of God for his children. John's insights provide tremendous encouragement as we await the day when we'll finally meet our Savior face-to-face.

JIM DALY, president of Focus on the Family

If you enjoyed John Burke's *New York Times* bestseller *Imagine Heaven*, then be prepared for another round of blessings with his new volume, *Imagine the God of Heaven*. Written in the same fashion, his second book on this topic should likewise thrill your soul with convictions of peace, assurance, and security. Do not wait—get a copy now!

GARY R. HABERMAS, PʜD, Distinguished Research Professor of Apologetics and Philosophy, Liberty University

Imagine the God of Heaven contains nearly seventy carefully vetted NDE accounts from all over the world. That alone makes this book worth reading. But the unique and exceptional feature of *Imagine the God of Heaven* is the picture of God it presents and the evidence Burke uses to support that picture. Drawing from history and detailed investigation of NDE experiences from numerous countries, cultures, and religions, Burke convincingly shows that a common core in this plurality of NDE experiences is a presentation of who God is, along with what his program for history is all about. All of this is consistent with the biblical God and not the alleged deities of other religions. In an age in which religious pluralism prevails, Burke's book simply must be read and studied by Jesus' followers.

J. P. MORELAND, Distinguished Professor of Philosophy, Talbot School of Theology, Biola University; author of *A Simple Guide to Experience Miracles*

Before reading John Burke and meeting him via radio, I was largely skeptical of the idea of near-death experiences. I can now see why God chose John for this message. He, too, was a skeptic with an engineer's brain. Then he came face-to-face with many who had more to lose by sharing their experiences than by keeping quiet. Yet they came forward anyway. John's research of Scripture and documented accounts of NDEs have revived hearts and renewed perspectives on God's majesty and goodness. My own sister found immense comfort in reading John's books while her husband passed from this life to the next. John Burke has given us a beautiful gift in this book. It's time for the church to wake up and live like eternity is as real and exciting as it is!

SUSIE LARSON, bestselling author; national speaker; talk radio host

JOHN BURKE

IMAGINE
THE
GOD
OF
HEAVEN

NEAR-DEATH EXPERIENCES,
GOD'S REVELATION, AND THE LOVE
YOU'VE ALWAYS WANTED

TYNDALE
elevate
ask. seek. find.

Visit Tyndale online at tyndale.com.

Tyndale and Tyndale's quill logo are registered trademarks of Tyndale House Ministries. *Tyndale Elevate* and the Tyndale Elevate logo are trademarks of Tyndale House Ministries. Tyndale Elevate is a nonfiction imprint of Tyndale House Publishers, Carol Stream, Illinois.

Imagine the God of Heaven: Near-Death Experiences, God's Revelation, and the Love You've Always Wanted

Cover designed by Dean H. Renninger

Edited by Christine M. Anderson

Published in association with Don Gates of the literary agency The Gates Group; www.the-gates-group.com.

For information about special discounts for bulk purchases, please contact Tyndale House Publishers at csresponse@tyndale.com, or call 1-855-277-9400.

Library of Congress Cataloging-in-Publication Data

A catalog record for this book is available from the Library of Congress.

ISBN 978-1-4964-7990-7

Printed in the United States of America

29	28	27	26	25	24	23
7	6	5	4	3	2	

To the One who has been my Father to the fatherless,
sovereign Lord, gracious Savior, and faithful Friend.

Contents

WHY IMAGINE GOD?

WE ALL IMAGINE GOD. Some imagine God as a myth or a fairy tale. Others imagine God as distant and scary, like a harsh judge or demanding parent. Still others imagine God as the most beautiful, loving, benevolent being in the universe. How you and I imagine God matters because it influences us, for better or worse, more than anything else we can think about.[1] It shapes how we view ourselves, others, and our very purpose for existing.

My journey of learning to imagine God started many years ago when my dad was dying of cancer. Someone gave him a book reporting the first research on what are now known as near-death experiences (NDEs). I read it in one night, and I was shocked. Here were people who clinically died—had no heartbeat or brain waves—yet modern medicine (or miracle) brought them back to life. When they revived, they claimed to have felt more alive than ever in an exhilarating world beyond our earthly space-time dimensions. Many of them also said they encountered God. I was an agnostic at the time and remember thinking, *Could this be real evidence of God's existence?*

I've always been a very analytical, skeptical person. I studied science and engineering and worked as an engineer. I never liked the "blind faith" idea. I needed to have reasons to believe. NDEs opened my skeptical mind to the possibility of God being real, yet I still had my doubts. How do I know these NDEs are not just wishful thinking, or a trick the brain plays as a person is grasping to hold on to life? What about hallucinations, or the effects of anesthesia, drugs, or other chemicals flooding the brain? I wrestled with all these questions and alternate explanations, as you will see.

As I researched over the last three decades, I discovered that millions have had NDEs, and thousands have been scientifically studied. I've studied the commonalities of over one thousand people who have clinically died, been resuscitated, and claimed to have experienced life after death. Many skeptical medical doctors have been persuaded by the same evidence I found. I became convinced that God is definitely real. Even more than that, God is relatable, and he is good!

In 2015, I wrote *Imagine Heaven* to share what I'd learned about the exhilarating life to come, showing how NDErs experience the same heaven revealed in Scripture. The response was overwhelming. Since *Imagine Heaven* was published,[2] numerous people have contacted me from all over the world, courageously sharing their near-death experiences. Of all the spectacular wonders of heaven people describe, the most consistent comment by far is that nothing comes close to the magnificent presence of God. That's when I realized I needed to write another book, this time focusing on the most important thing we can think about regarding heaven and earth: *God*.

In *Imagine the God of Heaven,* my goal is to present a thorough and thrilling understanding of who God is—from proof of his existence in history and his awe-inspiring attributes, to his intriguing story and unconditional love for all people today. I hope what I'll share with you in this book sheds light on the most important questions of life: Who created me? For what purpose? What really matters? What is God like? What does God want with me?

I'll also share the fascinating things I've discovered not only from researching NDEs, but also from studying the world's religions and history and seeking to understand how it all fits together. I hope to show how God's self-revelation in history aligns with what NDErs experience today. I have chosen to use BCE and CE (rather than BC and AD) as historical references, as I am writing to reach a global audience who may be more familiar with those designations.

Throughout the book, you'll hear from nearly seventy people from every continent who have clinically died and claim to have encountered God. I've chosen to weave some people's stories through several chapters, so you can experience the progression of their journeys as they discover the wonderous qualities of God and his thrilling world to come. But ultimately, this is not a book about NDEs; it's a book about God. The things you'll learn about God do not depend on NDE testimony; these global testimonies just add color to God's revealed character in Scripture.

I left my career in engineering to become a pastor largely because I wanted to help people discover the things I'm sharing in this book. I believe God is giving our global village evidence not only of his reality but also of the relentless and unconditional love he has for every single person on the planet. Though I write from a Christian perspective, as you'll soon see, I believe God cares about all people, regardless of religious background. We were all created to be his children. So I encourage you to keep an open mind and see what you discover for yourself.

Perhaps you are a Christian but still skeptical of NDEs, questioning if NDEs have anything legitimate to add to our understanding of God from Scripture. Let me say a few important things about this. First, I do not advocate forming your view of God (or the afterlife) solely from what NDErs say. If you read lots of NDE stories, you'll notice that each person *interprets* their experience within their own cultural understanding. While there are many varied interpretations of NDEs, what the majority of NDErs commonly *report* (as opposed to *interpret*) consistently aligns with what God has revealed throughout history, as I will show. The reason for so many varied interpretations is simple but requires an illustration to understand.[3]

Imagine your life is being lived in a two-dimensional, black-and-white painting hanging on the wall. Now imagine you "die" and your flat, two-dimensional form peels off the painting and floats out into a room of three dimensions and many colors. This "world" you could never see, limited as you were to two dimensions, was all around you the whole time. Now imagine being brought back to two-dimensional "life," pressed into the flat painting. How would you describe your three-dimensional experience and colors using only two-dimensional terms and black-and-white language? Or rather, how *could* you do it?

That's why NDErs struggle with language; they are forced to "sense-make" and somehow interpret this very sacred, mystical, extra-dimensional experience in limited, three-dimensional words. This is just like Ezekiel, Daniel, John, or others in Scripture who have written about their own heavenly experiences with descriptions that can sound strange.

Perhaps you're questioning the possibility of falsified NDE accounts. How do we know people aren't making up these near-death stories, either for money or to get attention? First, many of those whose stories I share are doctors, lawyers, CEOs, engineers, professors, and other established professionals who don't need to make up wild stories for money. In fact, most of them risk losing credibility when they choose to speak publicly about their NDE, yet they say nothing in life is more real or more important to them.

Second, these people come from all over the globe. In some cases, what they report not only goes against their religious culture, but actually puts them in danger. Some have lost family and friends or even survived deadly attacks, yet they say God sent them back to tell of their experience. What would motivate such sacrifice if they didn't believe it were true?

Third, even if one of these NDErs falsified their story, there are thousands of others who say similar things. Any one testimony could easily be replaced by many others. Plus, I have personally interviewed many of these people, and they are stable, credible, and respected. But also, what NDErs commonly report about their experiences with God is nothing new. They simply confirm in new ways who God is and what God has been doing throughout human history.

Having said that, I don't agree with every *interpretation* or conclusion of every NDEr, even though I do believe they had a real experience. I quote a few NDErs in this book whose interpretation or practices after their NDEs are ones I would not advocate or endorse. I quote them to show that what they report still aligns consistently with what God has revealed about his love and character. I'm trying to show the bigger story of God and how many of these NDE stories confirm what he's been revealing throughout history and in Scripture.

If you were to explore lots of NDE stories, you'd likely find varied interpretations of NDEs that might not align with the picture I'm giving here. Does that mean I'm being "interpretively selective"? Consider all the evidence I present, and then judge for yourself. But keep in mind, I'm not trying to answer every NDE question or address every issue.

My purpose for this book is to show the wonders of God: his epic story, his captivating character, and his love that is beyond our wildest dreams. My hope is that you'll realize that all the love you've ever wanted, ultimately, is found in relationship with God.

So, join me on this journey, and let's imagine the God of heaven.

PART I

GLOBAL EVIDENCE
OF GOD

I

THE GOD
OF ALL NATIONS

"CODE BLUE! CODE BLUE!" yelled the nurse over the intercom.

For an entire week, Santosh Acharjee had been fighting for his life. He realized he was dying. He had just given his wife, son, and daughter-in-law his final blessings when he went into cardiac arrest. The medical staff rushed into action to get his heart going again, but their efforts failed. Santosh clinically died.*

I always thought that once you die, your life is finished. That's it. But when I died, I discovered your life isn't over, there's another life after that. I realized, *I'm not dead; I can analyze, interpret.* I was curious and wondering as I saw a bright Light coming toward me. I could see my body lying on the hospital bed. This Light was so bright. I knew that this Light has

---

* Clinical death is a medical term typically referring to the cessation of blood flow and breathing in a patient, often caused by heart failure, resulting in no brain wave activity. Clinical death can be reversed by restarting the heart. However, without resuscitation, irreversible biological death follows.

superior authority—I had to obey that Light; no one had
to tell me, I just knew. When the Light came near me, He
engulfed me with His radiance, and all that I could see was
the Divine Light. I immediately fell in love with the Divine
Light. I knew the Light's purpose was not to harm me but
[to] protect me. I felt safe.[1]

Santosh had grown up in a conservative Hindu family in India.
His father was a revered scholar of Sanskrit and an honored Hindu
priest, which meant Hinduism was all Santosh had known from birth.
Santosh had become a well-respected manufacturing engineer, traveling
the world and living in India, Canada, Brazil, and the US while working. Life was great—until the day his heart went erratic, racing at over
two hundred beats per minute.

Doctors at the hospital initially thought Santosh was having a heart
attack, but it turned out to be gallstones that had ruptured with such
force that they perforated not only his gallbladder but also his pancreas.
Doctors gave Santosh the bad news that they couldn't operate when
his heart rate remained so high; all they could do was wait and hope it
would come down.

Day by day, things progressively got worse until the day Santosh's
heart stopped completely. Ultimately, doctors were able to stabilize
Santosh enough to put him in a medically induced coma, where he
remained on machines for three days and nights. Santosh clinically died,
yet he felt more alive than ever. He was traveling with a brilliant light
he knew was God.

I remember passing through some black holes, like big
round tunnels, at tremendous speed. Together, we traveled
for quite some time. . . . When the Light stopped, [He] was
still looking at me, and I was looking at Him, as well. I was
wondering, "Why did the Light stop moving? What do I
do now?" . . . I was seeing that the Light stopped inside a
large compound that was surrounded with very high and
extraordinarily beautiful walls.[2]

The Light was shining on this huge compound. A beautiful compound. And I could see everything far better than I can see normally in this world. My vision was unlimited—I could see from one end to the other end with no obstruction, and I could zoom in like a powerful camera can do. As I looked at this compound, I could see many, many beautiful homes—mansions—in it, surrounded by high, thick walls. Looking into the interior, I could see it was a square shape. And inside it, there were people. They were walking; some were floating in the air. It was like a city full of mansions, like a modern city you'd think of, but not [made] with the materials of this world—made of things we don't even know of here—gorgeous. I counted twelve gates all around [this city], but none of the gates were open for me. I wanted to go inside, but I could not go inside. I was just outside of the gate. I saw many angels there. I knew these angels were there to protect this beautiful compound, and I realized . . . I'm looking at the Kingdom of Heaven.[3]

Nothing in this world could ever come close to the beauty of this place. . . . The entire area inside the compound looked so peaceful and so calm that I instantly fell in love with this place. I kept thinking, "How do I get into this beautiful place? There has to be an Entrance somewhere. Where is the Entrance?"[4] . . .

Then the Lord spoke to me. He has a very deep, commanding voice, but, at the same time, I noticed His voice was also a loving one. . . . When the Lord spoke, I could understand what He said in any of the languages that I know (Bengali, English, Hindi, German, Portuguese, etc.). . . . He said to me in an authoritative, but loving, voice, "I'm sending you back to the earth. . . . Go back and complete your unfinished tasks. When you are back, I want you to love your family and love your children. Pay attention to your daughter. She needs your help."[5] . . .

We talked for a long time, I don't know how long it was. . . . I didn't know who He was except that He was God. I didn't have to ask or find out, I knew this was Lord of everything, Lord of all. To me, He was very kind, loving, and like a true friend with genuine concern for each and every one of us. . . .

When I came back, I was very troubled. Life got busy again . . . but it was bothering me, all the things I witnessed there. I was familiar with the Hindu scriptures, so I was wondering why I did not encounter any of the Hindu gods and goddesses and all these things we know. *Who was this I witnessed? He is not like them. Who was that?*[6]

It's intriguing that although the twelve gates Santosh witnessed in the heavenly compound were closed, he later discovered one "very narrow gate" that he said was open to him. Through it, he could see a way into the Kingdom of Heaven. As Santosh's story unfolds in the chapters ahead, we will explore more about what he experienced with God and what he discovered about the narrow gate. But first, who is this loving God of Light that Santosh and others from all over the world have encountered in their near-death experiences?

GLOBAL EVIDENCE

Since the age of modern medical resuscitation and access to digital communication, more and more reports have surfaced across the globe about people being brought back from clinical death. A Gallup poll found that eight million Americans have had a near-death experience (NDE).[7] A study presented in 2019 to the European Academy of Neurology found that about 5.5 percent of people across thirty-five countries reported having had a near-death experience, which involved a life-threatening situation.[8] Oftentimes, people have a cardiac arrest, no heartbeat, and no brain waves, and yet modern medicine (or miracle) brings them back after minutes to hours of no registered brain activity. They come back to testify about an experience they say was more real than anything they have ever experienced on earth. And the memory of this experience is not like other memories. As René from Australia says, "The memory of the NDE is more real than what I did yesterday."[9]

Each NDE account is unique to the individual, yet they all share striking similarities—core commonalities I have explored and written about extensively.[10] But by far, the most emphatic and consistent comment from the thousands of NDEs I have studied is that there is absolutely nothing on earth—no experience we could imagine—that compares to being in the presence of God!

Based on what NDErs report, the characteristics of this God are the same, no matter what nation, religion, or culture the individuals come from. Although NDErs may *interpret* the identity of this God from their own cultural and religious framework, the divine being they *describe* is consistent. For instance, regardless of where they're from, NDErs consistently talk about two key characteristics of this God: light and love.

God of Light

When people die clinically, many report experiencing a being of light they intuitively recognize as God. Hyperbole or piling on adjective after adjective seems to be the only way NDErs can convey, within the constraints of human language, the exhilarating light of God.

In Africa, Mario contracted *Plasmodium falciparum*, the most dangerous type of malaria-causing parasite with the highest mortality rate. His wife found him unconscious. When the doctor arrived, he discovered that Mario's heart had stopped.

> I lived the experience of my travel in this indescribable and wonderful LIGHT, where I have been enveloped with much love and peace, finding myself in a place where so much joy could be breathed, facing huge and wonderful flowers with intoxicating perfumes. There in that place, I met my parents who passed a few years ago. Only my mother talked . . . saying that it wasn't my hour yet. . . . My wonderful experience has erased any fear of death . . . [and] gives to me the certainty that God is waiting for us with joy.[11]

After attempting to restart his heart, the doctor took Mario to the hospital. Upon arrival, a neurologist evaluated him and initially declared him a closed case, yet he miraculously revived from clinical death.

God is the light that brings life. Yet, we live in a world that often breeds darkness and death. People do evil things, injustice lurks around every corner, people hurt us, and we hurt others even when trying to do our best. We have so many questions about life that seem to leave us in the dark: Who am I? Why am I here? Am I doing the right things? Why do I struggle so? Why does God, if there is a God, not seem to help? As we will learn, knowing God brings light into our darkness. And for Marsha, this truth was experienced in a very surprising, real way.

In America, a legally blind woman, Marsha, had an NDE. She had been born with ROP (retinopathy of prematurity). Though she could see some light from her left eye, Marsha needed a Seeing Eye dog. When the blind experience an NDE, they can see the same commonalities as the sighted. At age thirty-two, while in the hospital, Marsha lost consciousness with no pulse detected for thirty minutes. She found herself going up in a dark, black tunnel, and she heard music and bells, but said, "Not like bells here, it was different." A tiny white light far away grew brighter and bigger until it filled the whole end of the tunnel where she had stopped.

> First, all I see was the light and [then] I hear the voice. [And it says], "Come to the Light." I know I have to go. I know it was like God or something. It was like you see the face in the light, but you can't see it really. . . . And it's a different light. It's not like light on earth or sunlight. It's like white light but [more] like golden-white light. And it moves, it shimmers. It's not like any kind of light in the world. It's warm—like you were in the light. Not only [do] you see the light, but you become part of the light and the light goes around you. It's like God in the light. Nothing on earth is like that.[12]

Marsha saw angels who had bodies, but noticed, "You could see through them almost," which coincides with what some sighted NDErs also say. She saw her grandmother and aunt who had died years earlier. And to her surprise, she saw her friend Hank, who had also been blind, and died in 1982. Marsha noticed that although on earth, "[Hank] was blind, and he had amputated fingers and amputated legs . . . there in heaven, it was like his body was right [it was whole]."[13]

Even those who are blind on earth can clearly see in the light of God. This light brings hope into our darkness. As one NDEr from New Zealand discovered in God's presence, "He is light. . . . [His] love was healing my heart and I began to understand that there is incredible hope for humankind."[14] People all around the world need hope. I have traveled to thirty countries over the past thirty years, talking about real-world struggles with Buddhists in Mongolia, Muslims in Kazakhstan, and Hindus in India. I've listened to Norwegians, Australians, Africans, Koreans, Brazilians, and many others as they told me their struggles, failures, sins, and shame. We all struggle, we all fall, and we all need hope—everywhere!

Nan, a young woman of Middle Eastern descent, had lost all hope. When she tried to take her own life, she died, left her body, and found herself traveling while flanked by two women, one she identified as her guardian angel. She saw a pinpoint of light in the distance and realized they were moving very rapidly toward it. As they came closer to the light, the light grew larger and its white glow purer.

> I saw tens of thousands of beings dressed in white gowns all facing The Light and . . . in the service of The Light and apparently "singing" praises to The Light. The Light was filled with the most extraordinary, overwhelming, and indescribable feeling of LOVE. . . . The Light spoke in a man's voice, firm and direct, saying only, "Go back! You have a Great Deal to Learn."[15]

Many NDErs come back and seek to learn more about the God of Light, but others do not. God gives us the choice to seek him or ignore him. It's also important to note that just because an NDEr sees God does not mean that person knows God or is necessarily right with God. I believe these experiences simply offer the individual a peek into a greater reality, and they are a gift that allows all of us to learn more about who we are in relationship to God.

On every continent, NDErs say the light of God is alive and unlike any other light we know. It's a light that's palpable and experienced through multiple senses. It's a light that offers unconditional love and life and brings inexpressible hope and joy. As we will see, this God of Light is the love we all crave. In God's presence, we can all see more clearly who we are to God, how God feels about each one of us, and how that love can change us for the better.

God of Love

In London, Mary was pregnant but bleeding severely. As soon as she arrived at the emergency room, the staff came running to find Mary drenched with blood from the navel down and in extremely critical condition. Mary recalls hearing a *pop* and then all the pain suddenly stopped. She found herself up near the ceiling of the emergency room, looking down. She felt calm for the first time since learning of her pregnancy by a man who had deceived her. He had told her he loved her and wanted to marry her, yet the pregnancy revealed the truth. He had a wife and five children in another city, and he soon abandoned her. She pondered these things as she floated up by the ceiling, watching the doctors operating on her.

Mary heard a nurse, the only one in a blue smock, tell the doctors she had lost consciousness, yet she felt completely conscious and aware of every detail of what was happening in the operating room.

"I floated toward [a] tunnel and passed right through a ceiling fan and then the ceiling," Mary said. The tunnel was black and churning as Mary gained more and more speed, heading for a bright light. She felt the comforting presence of her deceased grandfather there with her, so she had no fear. As she came out of the end of the tunnel, she recalls,

> [I] was overwhelmed by a radiant white light that seemed to embody all the concepts of love. A love that was unconditional and like a mother has for a child. It was definitely a warm joyful presence . . . that radiated all the good and noble emotions known to man. I had given up the ways of the

Catholic church . . . but I knew in my heart that this was God. Words can't describe my awe in this presence.[16]

As time stood still, God showed Mary her life. She said he knew her every thought and feeling, and she never wanted to leave his presence. As he gave her a life review, Mary not only observed each moment; she experienced her life all over again, including the impact of every good or bad action. She actually *felt* how it made others feel, as if sharing some divine perspective on all the ripple effects and consequences of her actions.

It was a difficult time for me, but I was supported by [God's] unconditional love and weathered the painful parts. I was asked telepathically about whether I wanted to stay or return. . . . I fell to my knees in order to show my desire to stay with Him.[17]

Mary came back to earth after God showed her that her baby boy would live, and she needed to be there for him. She felt forgiven, washed clean, and unconditionally loved in God's presence. And Mary came back with dramatic evidence this experience was real. While she was floating up near the ceiling of the emergency room, Mary said she noticed a red label on the side of the blade of a ceiling fan facing the top of the ceiling.

After reviving in the recovery room, Mary kept asking medical personnel to listen to the amazing experience she had just had. Only one nurse listened, and only after Mary gave details of what she had observed during the operation, including what the nurse had said to the doctors while Mary was unconscious. Finally convinced, the nurse and an orderly got a tall ladder and checked for the red sticker Mary described in great detail on the hidden side of the ceiling fan. Mary said, "The nurse and an orderly saw the sticker, confirming all the details of its appearance as I described."[18]

As we imagine God's love accurately, it can change us from wanting to avoid God to longing to know God better. I believe God's love is the love we all crave. Howard Storm, a university professor and

NDEr I interviewed, described God's love this way: "Imagine all the love you've ever experienced—from parents, grandparents, lovers, spouses, children—and put all that love across your lifetime into a single moment. Then multiply by a thousand."[19] That's God's love for you!

HOPE FOR ALL PEOPLE

Never in history, until now, have we been able to hear from so many people around the world brought back from clinical death. I believe NDEs are God's gift to our globally connected world—widespread evidence of God's reality and his great love for people of all nations.

Already in this chapter, you've read about encounters with God described by Indian, African, North American, Middle Eastern, and European NDErs. As you will continue to discover in the pages that follow, people from diverse religious backgrounds and cultures encounter the same God of Light and Love in their NDEs. How do we explain such a diversity of humanity agreeing on the basic description of the God they encounter in clinical death? Could it be that God is reaching out to humanity in a profound way, offering hope to people of all nations?

Not only will you read stories of people from diverse cultures, but also from professors, psychologists, doctors, lawyers, CEOs—people who only lose professional credibility talking about wild stories of seeing God. People like Dr. Bell Chung.

A native of Hong Kong, Dr. Bell Chung earned his PhD in cognitive psychology and loved adventure travel. By the age of thirty, he had gone scuba diving, skiing, and mountain climbing in thirty countries. But the ultimate form of adventure and freedom for Dr. Chung was hang gliding—to fly as free as a bird.

While vacationing in New Zealand, he went hang gliding in the mountains one day. Just after liftoff, he noticed the glider was climbing too fast and at too steep an angle. Just as sharp as its ascent, the glider stalled and plummeted down like a broken kite, falling over one hundred meters.

Bang! As the glider hit the ground, it smashed into pieces. Dr. Chung found himself looking down on the wrecked body of the glider, glass and metal strewn across the ground.

"[I] saw a broken young man lying there dying," Dr. Chung said. "In horror, I realized this man looked just like me! That's my body!" Dr. Chung then noticed a warm, golden light that spoke to him.

"The darkness is over. Welcome to the brightness," the golden light said to me.

I found myself bathed in a sea of golden light, so peaceful and calm. I was fully embraced by a comforting love and gentleness. I also found my body dazzling, reflecting rays of golden light. The senses of warmth and love saturated me. . . .

"Would you like to go or to stay?". . .

Someone was speaking to me from the source of light. Our communication did not work through the voice, but the mind, like telepathy. I tried to look at the source of light but could hardly see anything or any person other than the halo of light. I had no idea who was speaking to me, but I knew that was the source of the greatest love. . . . Perhaps it's what we called God?

"To go or to stay?" I muttered. Does it mean I could choose between life and death?

"This is the last question of your life." He seemed to be able to comprehend my thoughts. . . .

"Before making your decision, you may wish to see your life in review." . . .

[I] found myself in a cinema, with thousands of screens around me. Playing on every screen were episodes of the different moments in my thirty years of life, from early childhood till the present. Some of which I remembered, some of which I had long forgotten. I was intrigued by this fascinating . . . panoramic picture of my entire life.[20]

Dr. Chung eventually returned. It took a rescue team thirty minutes to cut him out of the wreckage. After three days in a coma, he began the long road of recovery as a different man.

People of all nationalities, professions, and backgrounds encounter the same God of Light and Love in their NDEs. God is not experienced as an impersonal force, but as a personal God who knows each individual more intimately than they had ever imagined—recalling things about their lives even they had forgotten. They all come back knowing that God is love, and that love is what matters most to God.

LOVE HAS A HISTORY

As we will come to understand, our modern era of NDEs is not the first time this God of Light and Love has revealed himself. Near the beginning of written history, around four thousand years ago, and before any of the world's modern religions were formalized in a sacred text,[21] God claims he appeared with a plan to bless all the nations. "The LORD had said to Abram . . . 'I will make you into a great nation, and I will bless you . . . and all peoples on earth will be blessed through you'" (Genesis 12:1-3, NIV). We will explore how the same things NDErs say today align with God's heart revealed through history.

I am convinced God created all people in his image, and he is *for* all people of all nations. NDErs confirm God speaks to them in their native languages. This God sees all, knows all, wants to forgive all, and unconditionally loves each person uniquely. If you will keep an open mind and follow me on this journey of imagining God, I hope you'll see that a loving relationship, not religion, is actually what God wants with you and me.

As you read *Imagine the God of Heaven*, I hope you will begin to discover what I have found to be true. While I have never had a mystical spiritual experience such as those described by NDErs, I have clearly seen how this love from God is real and available to us ordinary, non-NDErs. God cares uniquely about each individual he created. I believe he wants us all to know and even experience his great love in a very personal way. Could you use more love in your life? Read on. I believe this book will help you discover the love you've always wanted.

SCIENCE, SKEPTICS, AND NDES

DR. RAJIV PARTI, CHIEF ANESTHESIOLOGIST of the Bakersfield Heart Hospital, had decided to attend this surgery personally due to the risky nature of the procedure. Hypothermic cardiopulmonary bypass and circulatory arrest is a procedure used only in extreme cases, often to repair deep brain aneurisms or an aortic tear that would otherwise kill the patient.

In the procedure, the patient's blood is replaced by a cool liquid that lowers the body's temperature to 50 degrees Fahrenheit (10 Celsius). No respirator is used to keep the patient breathing, so the lungs and brain receive no oxygen. The EKG machine, used to monitor heartbeat, shows a flat line, indicating that no blood is flowing to the brain. All organs stop functioning, and the patient's brain shows no waves on the EEG machine. By all measures, the patient is clinically dead. It's a very risky, no-other-options procedure.

The patient himself did not expect to survive. However, when he did survive, Dr. Parti entered the patient's room to rouse and congratulate him. The man looked up at him and smiled. Dr Parti shares what transpired.

"I was watching you guys in the operating room," the patient said. "I was out of my body, floating around by the ceiling."

That can't be true, Dr. Parti thought.

"Yeah," he said. "I saw you just standing at the head of the table, I saw the surgeon sewing the patch on my artery."[1]

The patient told Dr. Parti how many surgeons he'd seen. He described the nurses, the medical team's actions during the operation, and other details that could only have been observed from somewhere above them all.

Over the years, Dr. Parti had overseen hundreds of surgeries in which the patient's heart stopped or barely beat. He had heard cardiac arrest patients insist they'd seen friends who had died, a light at the end of a tunnel, or a being of light; but he wrote it all off as psychotic delusion. As he learned in medical school, if he couldn't see it on a monitor, hear it, or feel it, he should send it to the psych ward.

"Your heart was stopped," Dr. Parti argued. "Your brain didn't have any activity. You couldn't have seen anything. Your head was packed in ice." The patient, whom Parti referred to as "the frozen man," simply described more details from his operation, including tools doctors had used and what they'd said during the surgery. Finally Dr. Parti stopped him and gave him a shot of an antipsychotic drug.[2]

Rajiv Parti grew up in a Hindu family in India. He was taught to believe in the pantheon of Hindu gods and goddesses, but medical school training and his move from New Delhi to New York rooted out all belief of invisible gods or any afterlife. By his own admission, he worshiped at the altar of materialism.

But all that changed the day after Christmas, 2010. Dr. Parti's entire world turned inside out, changing most of his views about God, the afterlife, and this life. The troubling encounter with the frozen man came rushing back to Dr. Parti when, at the age of fifty-three, he found himself lying in the recovery room of the UCLA Medical Center, talking to an anesthesiologist about his own near-death experience. The anesthesiologist didn't believe Dr. Parti, or else he didn't care.[3]

"I saw you during my surgery," Dr. Parti said.

"Really," the anesthesiologist retorted skeptically, his smile fading.

"Yes. I left my body and watched you from the ceiling."

"Interesting," the doctor said as he fumbled through his papers, uninterested.

"No really," Dr. Parti insisted, explaining how he watched the surgeon cut him open and even heard the anesthesiologist tell a joke.

"Oh really. And what was the joke?"[4] Dr. Parti retold the crude joke about the smell after his intestines had been opened. The anesthesiologist blushed, mumbling that he must not have given him enough anesthesia. Dr. Parti reassured the anesthesiologist that he had given him plenty.

As Dr. Parti told him about visiting his mom and sister in India, then finding himself on the edge of hell, the doctor became noticeably uncomfortable. He said he would come back to hear more of Dr. Parti's story, but he never did. And the anesthesiologist wasn't the only one to dismiss Dr. Parti's experience that day.

When the surgeon came to visit, Dr. Parti recounted his out-of-body observations, his journey, and got all the way to the tunnel entrance before the surgeon reached for his phone and excused himself. When a resident physician came in, Dr. Parti peppered him with questions about healing of the soul. When Dr. Parti explained how two angels from the Bible took him to a being of light who discussed healing the soul, the resident quickly ended the conversation. Even though other doctors didn't believe him, Dr. Parti's own experience had transformed him from a skeptic to a believer of NDE accounts and of God.

SKEPTICAL ABOUT NDES

I first learned about NDEs in 1978, three years after Dr. Raymond Moody put out the first popular research of people who clinically died, were resuscitated, and returned to tell of a life to come. My dad was dying of cancer, and a friend had given him Moody's book, *Life after Life*. I was skeptical at first, yet also curious.

I was agnostic about God, Jesus, and the afterlife when I first read about NDEs. Yet, I wanted to understand how things worked and how they all fit together. My curious, analytical mind had led me to work in the field of engineering in Santa Barbara, California, in the eighties. It was a decade when more and more accounts of NDEs were going public, and Santa Barbara turned out to be an epicenter of research.

As I continued to encounter and study more NDEs, I had so many questions: What are these accounts? Are they actual scientific evidence for the soul and for God's existence? Or can NDEs be explained by natural means, like the effects of a dying brain or anoxia or drugs?

Over the past thirty-five years, I've interviewed countless individuals and studied thousands of NDE reports trying to answer these questions. I've since become convinced that NDEs are God's gift to our world—evidence of God's great love for all people. That same evidence has also convinced many skeptical doctors over the years. Among them are cardiologists, oncologists, and surgeons who started out as skeptics, just like Dr. Parti, but later changed their minds due to overwhelming evidence, despite the alternate theories.

ALTERNATE EXPLANATIONS FOR NDES

Over thirty alternate explanations for NDEs have been proposed over the years. Why so many? Oncologist Jeffrey Long, who went from NDE skeptic to researching over four thousand NDEs, has debated skeptics such as Michael Shermer about alternate explanations.[5] Dr. Long explains, "Skeptics themselves, as a group, can't come up with any consensus explanation of near-death experience. If skeptics had one or even a couple of explanations that made sense, you wouldn't need over thirty. . . . They absolutely have nothing that explains the totality of what we're observing in a near-death experience."[6]

Alternate explanations typically try to explain away one or two elements of an NDE, but they never take into account all common elements that together make a strong scientific case. Dr. Long contends, "NDEs provide such powerful scientific evidence that it is reasonable to accept the existence of an afterlife." He points out a basic scientific principle: What is real is consistently observed.[7] For that reason, rather than trying to explain what's missing in each of thirty different alternate explanations, a better approach is to focus on the evidence consistently observed by NDErs. A related scientific principle is that of

Occam's razor, which states, "Of two competing theories, the simpler explanation of an entity is to be preferred."[8] And the simplest explanation is almost universally given by NDErs themselves, who typically say, "There is a soul. I left my body, but I was still myself, fully alive in a world more real than anything I've experienced on earth."

TEN POINTS OF EVIDENCE FOR LIFE AFTER DEATH

There's an urban legend that says the government trains its agents to spot counterfeit bills by having them handle authentic bills. Once they know what real bills look and feel like, they can spot any fake bills because they're missing the evidential markings of the real thing. When it comes to NDEs, I take a similar approach. I want to help you see all the evidential marks* that any valid theory must explain. To do that and to better understand the scientific case for life after death, let's take a closer look at ten points of evidence.

1. Verifiable Observations

Like Dr. Parti, who heard the crude joke of the anesthesiologist, thousands of NDErs claim they left their bodies at the point of clinical death, yet their person or soul remained in the room observing their resuscitation. Dr. Long states, "About 45 percent of near-death experiencers report OBEs [out-of-body experiences] which involves them seeing and often hearing ongoing earthly events from a perspective that is apart, and usually above, their physical bodies."[9] Like Mary, who reported seeing the red sticker on the top side of the ceiling fan, many such observations have been documented and studied.

Verifiable observations convinced Dr. Michael Sabom, a cardiologist and a Christian, who told me in an interview that he initially set out to disprove NDEs. He had never heard his patients tell such wild tales. But after five years of asking questions and openly listening to heart attack survivors, he published a 1980 scientific study of NDEs in the *Journal of the American Medical Association*. Since then, over nine hundred

---

* Many of these evidential marks were first published by Dr. Jeffrey Long. See Jeffrey Long, MD, "Near-Death Experiences: Evidence for Their Reality," *Missouri Medicine* 111, no. 5 (September–October 2014): 372–380, accessed via NIH National Library of Medicine, https://www.ncbi.nlm.nih.gov/pmc/articles/PMC6172100.

scholarly articles on NDEs have been published in many respected, peer-reviewed journals.[10]

However, skeptics such as Dr. Michael Shermer claim NDErs are hallucinating the experience as the brain starts functioning again.[11] One of the things that convinced Dr. Sabom this could not be the case was how his patients "saw details of their resuscitation that they could not otherwise have seen."[12] Other skeptics such as Dr. Gerald Woerlee claim these NDErs are picking up audible clues that subconsciously form the experience.[13] In response, Sabom talks about the case of Pam Reynolds, which, for him, disproves that theory.

Dr. Sabom and Dr. Robert Spetzler, the neurosurgeon who operated on Pam's deep brain aneurism, both reported the case. Pam was a well-known singer and songwriter in the recording industry in the eighties and nineties. Her studio recorded music by everyone from Bruce Springsteen to Pearl Jam and REM. Pam was a Christian at the time of her NDE.

"I was in Virginia Beach . . . with my husband," Pam recalls. "We were promoting a new record. And I inexplicably forgot how to talk. I've got a big mouth. I never forget how to talk."[14] An MRI revealed an aneurysm, "a ticking time bomb," deep in her brain stem. Her only hope was a radical experimental surgery.

Like Dr. Parti's "frozen man," Pam's body was cooled to about 50 degrees Fahrenheit and her head was drained of blood. Her eyes were taped shut, she was put under deep anesthesia, and her brain stem activity was monitored with "100-decibel clicks emitted from small, molded speakers inserted into her ears."[15] Her entire body, except for the small area of the head they were operating on, was covered completely, so there should have been no possibility of hearing, seeing, or picking up clues about events in the room. Pam had no heartbeat and no brain wave activity.

Pam didn't recall the start of her surgery. "I remember the top of my head tingling and then I just sort of 'popped' out of the top of my head. And I was then looking down at the body."[16] It was an hour into the surgery, and she was looking down at her own body as if perched on her surgeon's shoulder.

> I remember the instrument in his hand looked like the
> handle of my electric toothbrush. I had assumed they were
> going to open the skull with a saw . . . but what I saw looked
> a lot more like a drill. . . . It even had little bits that were
> kept in this case, that looked like the case my father stored
> his socket wrenches in. . . . I remember distinctly hearing
> a female voice saying, "We have a problem, her arteries are
> too small."[17]

The female voice came from down by her legs, Pam says, which confused her because it was brain surgery. But it turns out they had to access the femoral arteries in the legs. Dr. Spetzler later confirmed it was the female cardiac surgeon, Dr. Milken, who had that exact conversation with him. Pam said she had never met her, nor did she know a female surgeon would be among the doctors in the operating room that day.

Spetzler emphasizes that it would have been impossible for a patient to see or hear anything at this point in the operation. Even if Pam had been conscious, the clicking modules in her ears would have prevented her from picking up conversations.[18]

In an MSNBC video, Dr. Spetzler shows the Midas Rex saw he used, which does look like an electric toothbrush with a long cord. He also shows the blades, kept in a case that was opened during the surgery. "It's pretty much what Pamela described in toothbrush form . . . and it's not something that is visible as you're coming into the operating room," Spetzler reflects, noting that the sterilized saw was not taken out until Pam was more than an hour into the deepest anesthetic state possible.[19]

After observing the operation, Pam says, she sensed a presence and then noticed a tiny point of light, which began drawing her to it. As she got closer, she recognized different people. "I distinctly heard my grandmother call me," Pam said, "and I immediately went to her."[20]

> I saw behind [my grandmother] uncles, aunts, cousins, a good
> friend of mine who was murdered young, a distant cousin I

didn't know had passed [but had]. . . . I wanted to go into the light . . . but they stopped me. They communicated that if I continued to go into the light, I would change and would not be able to get back into my body. . . . I know for a fact that God exists and permeates everything.[21]

Eventually, Pam says, she was told it was time to go back. As she returned to the operating room, she heard the surgeons playing "Hotel California" by the Eagles. She watched the doctors use the paddles to shock her, not once, but twice. When Pam revived, she reported back to the doctors what she had seen and heard—describing in minute detail the specialized instruments, the conversations, the song, and the two attempts to restart her heart. Doctors Sabom and Spetzler confirmed the accuracy of all the details, yet Pam had no brain waves, her eyes had been taped shut, and she had 100-decibel clicking in her ears.[22]

Pam's story is one of many accounts that demonstrate the accuracy of NDE observations. Dr. Pim van Lommel, a Dutch cardiologist, began studying NDEs in 1986 after reading Dr. George Ritchie's account of dying and meeting a God of Light he identified as Jesus. After studying thousands of NDE accounts, van Lommel notes, "In this experience people have veridical perceptions from a position outside and above their lifeless body. This out-of-body experience is scientifically important because doctors, nurses, and relatives can verify the reported perceptions."[23]

Multiple studies have quantified the accuracy of NDE observations. One of those was a prospective study conducted by Dr. Penny Sartori, who followed three hundred critical care patients in a Welsh hospital for a five-year period. Sartori reports that those who had near-death experiences were remarkably accurate in describing details of their own resuscitations. The control group that did not have NDEs was highly inaccurate and often could only guess at what occurred during their resuscitations.[24]

Dr. Janice Holden, a professor of psychology, studied ninety-three NDE patients who claimed to make verifiable observations. After investigating their claims in her retrospective study, here's what she found: 92 percent of these out-of-body perceptions were completely accurate, 6 percent contained some error, and less than 2 percent were completely erroneous.[25] Reflecting on the overwhelming accuracy of NDE observations, Dr. van Lommel notes, "This strongly suggests that [an NDE] cannot be an hallucination, i.e. experiencing a perception that has no basis in 'reality,' like in psychosis, neither can it be a delusion . . . nor an illusion." He adds, "Moreover, one needs a functioning brain to experience a hallucination, an illusion, or a delusion."[26]

The accuracy of these scientifically studied and verifiable observations provides strong evidence that grounds NDEs in reality. Alternate explanations do not account for the sheer volume or accuracy of real-world observations made by individuals during their NDEs.

2. Common Elements

Every NDE is unique, just as every individual life experience is unique. Yet, despite the uniqueness and cultural filters of each, NDE accounts from around the globe demonstrate a consistent order of common events. For instance, these include observing your resuscitation, traveling through a tunnel or pathway, and a life review in the presence of a God of Light and Love. Surveys in thirty-five countries indicate millions have had an NDE.[27] Combine this sample size of millions with the prevalence of consistent elements, and you have strong evidence of a real life to come. Remember the scientific principle: What is real is consistently observed.

To familiarize you with the way NDErs typically describe their experience, I've put together a composite story representing the elements many positive* NDEs have in common.

> I rose up out of my body and found myself up near the ceiling, watching the chaos below. I knew I was dead, and I watched as they tried to revive me. I was still myself and conscious. In fact, I felt even more alive—like I had fifty senses. Despite the chaos, I felt a profound peace. It was wonderful.

---

* I have not included hellish NDE experiences in this composite, although various studies show that 23 percent to as high as 50 percent of NDEs have negative or hellish experiences. I explore hellish NDEs more fully in my book *Imagine Heaven*, ch. 16.

I noticed a tunnel or pathway opening up above me, and I found myself traveling at great speed. I came out into a world of beauty, not unlike that of earth, yet so much more. The grass was greener, the flowers more vibrant, the mountains more majestic; and all of them were radiating vibrant new colors beyond earth's color spectrum. And the light was not like light on earth—it was palpable. The light conveyed life and love, and it didn't shine on things like on earth, but it radiated out of everything—out of the grass, the leaves, the birds, and even out of the people.

I looked and coming toward me was a welcoming committee of people I loved and knew—my grandmother and grandfather, friends and family members who had all died before me. They all looked in their prime, but fully recognizable. It was a glorious reunion as we hugged and kissed. Our communication was pure—like telepathy, but so much more. All thoughts, feelings, and understanding were passing perfectly between us. Nothing was rushed; there was no concept of time, or time worked differently.

Then I saw a light, brighter than the sun, but easy to look at. I knew this was God. He knew all my thoughts, all my good and bad deeds, and yet I felt an overwhelming, unconditional love and acceptance in his presence. On the other side, you understand things at light speed, and as fast as I could ask a question, my mind had the answer. In God's presence, I watched a 3D panoramic review of my life. I don't know how it was possible, but I reexperienced every scene. I not only experienced my own thoughts and feelings, but also how my actions affected other people. God was showing me what mattered most—how I loved and treated those around me.

There was a border or boundary I knew I could not cross and still return to earth. I desperately wanted to stay, but God told me it was not my time—I still had a purpose to fulfill on earth. When I returned, my life was changed.[28]

Based on Dr. Jeffrey Long's statistical study as well as my own research, I've summarized the consistent elements of NDEs and their prevalence in the list below.

Out-of-body/new-body experience 75 percent	Deceased family, friends, or angels 57 percent
Evidential observations 45 percent	Telepathic communication/ different hearing 45 percent
Heightened consciousness/senses 74 percent	God of Light and Love 48 percent
Peaceful, positive feelings 76 percent	Special knowledge 56 percent
Tunnel 34 percent	Life review 32 percent
Heavenly realms 52 percent	Border or boundary 31 percent
Increased visual perception 66 percent	Told to return or choice to return 59 percent
Light that is love 65 percent	Profound life change 73 percent[29]

Alternate theories need to explain why millions of people report so many similar elements. If NDEs are merely the activity of a dying brain, why are they not all precisely identical? Why is each experience unique, yet also consistent with the pattern of common elements?

No alternate theory has accounted for such a high degree of common claims, such as telepathic communication, light that is love, telescopic vision—things uncommon in our earthly lives. The combination of uniqueness and commonality in NDE accounts resembles the best kind of testimony in a court of law. If ten eyewitnesses all say exactly the same thing, it would appear to be collusion—that they talked and agreed on a story. But if ten eyewitnesses give unique but overlapping observations of an event, that's incredibly strong testimony. And that's what we see with NDErs.

3. Heightened Lucidity

In a study of 613 NDEs, approximately 74 percent indicated a heightened consciousness—more real and lucid than normal.[30] A woman whose severe sickness caused an NDE at age five said,

> THE MAN [her name for God] and I walked and talked together. . . . The colors were very vivid, not even as you can see colors in this world. . . . I don't know—I can't describe it, but they were very vivid, very bright.[31]

Years and even decades later, NDErs consistently say their experience was more vivid, more real than anything they have experienced on earth. And this sets NDEs apart from other kinds of altered experience. Dr. Jeffrey Long points out, "In any other altered type of human consciousness—dreams, hallucinations, psychotic events—you typically have confused sensorium. Experiences may skip around in dreams, you really have that hypo—or decreased—lucidity, and that's completely different in near-death experiences, which are hyper or increased lucid experiences. And near-death experiences flow, and they tend to be very logical and ordered."[32]

Alternate theories must explain how a dying brain, with no electrical activity, could produce heightened awareness, more vivid sights, and memories more "real" than what NDErs experience on earth. The simplest explanation: The soul lives on in a world of expanded dimensional experience.

4. Consistency—with or without Anesthesia

Many alternate theories posit that anesthesia or other drugs might be the cause of NDEs. Dr. Pim van Lommel and two other Dutch psychologists conducted a five-year prospective study in ten hospitals across Holland. They followed 344 patients who had heart attacks that resulted in a flat EEG. They reported their findings in Europe's most prestigious medical journal, the *Lancet,* and in the *Journal of Consciousness Studies*:

Between 1988 and 1992, 344 successive patients who had undergone a total of 509 successful resuscitations were included in the study. In other words, all the patients in our study had been clinically dead. Clinical death is defined as the period of unconsciousness caused by total lack of oxygen in the brain (anoxia) because of the arrest of circulation. . . .

Our study found that . . . 18 percent of the 344 patients reported an NDE. [33] . . . All the familiar elements of an NDE were reported in our study, with the exception of a frightening or negative NDE. . . .

We failed to identify any differences between the patients with a very long or a very brief cardiac arrest. The degree or gravity of the lack of oxygen in the brain (anoxia) appeared to be irrelevant. Likewise, it was established that medication played no role. . . .

We were particularly surprised to find no medical explanation for the occurrence of an NDE. . . . If there was a physiological explanation such as a lack of oxygen in the brain (anoxia) for the occurrence of this enhanced consciousness, one might have expected all patients in our study to have reported an NDE.[34]

So medication or lack of oxygen to the brain (sometimes referred to as fighter-pilot syndrome) does not explain an NDE. Drugs like DMT, LSD, or ayahuasca that supposedly reproduce a few NDE-like symptoms (tunnel vision, colors, connectedness, etc.) in no way make sense of the four points of evidence presented so far, much less explain the next point, which is how the blind can see.

5. The Blind Can See

Kenneth Ring, a former professor of psychology at the University of Connecticut, conducted a study on NDEs of blind people. Fourteen were congenitally blind, meaning they had been blind from birth and had no visual or light perception at all. Yet, in their NDE, Ring found not only could the blind see, but they described all the commonalities of sighted NDErs.

Ring describes an interview with Debbie, a forty-eight-year-old woman who lost her sight at birth. She was home recuperating from a severe burn injury when she felt like she was dying and fell unconscious on the bathroom floor. Debbie recalls: "I saw this beautiful light and it was different colors; it was, gee, what can I say? Colors I couldn't even begin to describe. It was fantastic."[35]

Looking down from above, Debbie could also see her body lying on the floor and her mother bending over her. Ring summarizes Debbie's description of what happened next:

> A being presents himself, comforts her, and helps her to cross over a bridge. She sees other people, including her deceased grandmother, who introduces herself to Debbie, and who shows her some of her friends and ancestors. She soon encounters another presence whom she understands is God and begins to plead to be able to stay. . . . [God] imparts a great deal of information to Debbie concerning future events, including the person she would marry and that she would have a beautiful baby girl (both of which have come true, Debbie said), and tells her that she will have to teach people when she returns to life.[36]

The following excerpts from Debbie's interview highlight the visual observations made while up above her body, watching her mom try to revive her and simultaneously seeing her deceased grandparents who had come to be with her. Remember, Debbie is blind.

Interviewer: What do you mean when you say you saw in stereo?

Debbie: Well, [I'd see] two different things at once. I'd see me lying on the floor, and then I'd see my [deceased] grandparents. [Then] I'd see my Ma bending over me, and my grandparents at the same time.

Interviewer: Was this the first time that you had visually seen your mother?

Debbie: Oh, yeah.

Interviewer: Could you describe your mother?

Debbie: Oh, gee, my Ma had gray hair, she was short . . . about just five feet. . . . And she was in her bathrobe. And I told her she was in her bathrobe, and she said, "That's right, I was."

Interviewer: Did you see the color of her bathrobe as well?

Debbie: I thought it was a dark color. . . . And I think she said, "Yeah, it was black."

Interviewer: Did you see yourself for the first time as well?

Debbie: I saw this thin girl, maybe brown hair with maybe a little bit of gray, you know, beginning [to gray] . . . and quite young. And no wrinkles or anything. And I knew it was me. . . . And, I had never seen my grandma, either as a young woman or an old woman. But she had brown hair and my Ma said, "Yeah, she had brown hair." And she was a young woman [in the NDE]. And I would guess her to be no more than thirty . . . nobody seemed old there [laughs].

Interviewer: Did you recognize anyone else?

Debbie: Oh, yeah. This girlfriend I had who died of nephritis, Darlene. I recognized her right away. . . . She said, "Hi, Debbie." I said, "Oh, Darlene." It was just like her voice. . . . She was thin. And when she was on earth, she wasn't thin. She had a thyroid problem. She had nephritis, which would swell her up. She had a lot of other problems and kids made fun of her when she was little; they called her "little fatty" and stuff like that.[37]

The fact that multiple blind people can see and report the same commonalities as sighted NDErs cannot be explained by the effects of a dying brain, drugs, chemicals, or any other alternate explanation proposed so far. The simpler explanation remains: There is life after this life.

6. Meeting Deceased People Not Previously Known

In recounting their NDEs, children sometimes describe meeting siblings who had died before they were born. Their parents had not told them about a miscarriage or a tragic death of a sibling, yet the parents verify what their children report about a deceased brother or sister they met during their NDE.

Adults also report similar encounters. Dr. Pim van Lommel published one woman's compelling story of meeting a relative she had not previously known:

> During my cardiac arrest I had an extensive experience . . . and later I saw, apart from my deceased grandmother, a man who had looked at me lovingly, but whom I did not know. More than ten years later, at my mother's deathbed, she confessed to me that I had been born out of an extramarital relationship . . . and my mother showed me his picture. The unknown man that I had seen more than ten years before during my NDE turned out to be my biological father.[38]

This is one example among many where a person meets someone in their NDE whom they had not previously known, or even known about. How could meeting a deceased, previously unknown sibling or relative be explained by purely brain-based alternate theories?

7. Knowledge beyond the Body

Dr. Rajiv Parti claimed that while his physical body was in Los Angeles, he traveled to New Delhi, India, and saw his mom and sister: "They were sitting in the lounge there and it was evening time. . . . My mom was wearing a green sari and a green sweater, and my sister was wearing blue jeans and a red sweater, which, after two or three days of me getting better, I called and verified."[39] Many NDErs make such claims of traveling while in their spiritual bodies, and when those claims can be verified, it provides even more evidence supporting the soul living on after death.

Tricia Barker had a head-on collision in her car as she was on her way to run a 10K race in Austin, Texas. Because she was a college student without insurance, it took seventeen hours to find a surgeon to operate on her. Having been in horrendous pain, she flatlined as soon as the anesthesiologist put the mask on her.

"At the time, I was agnostic," Tricia says, "and so I was so shocked the spirit goes on. I wanted to pop back in my body, wake up, and tell all my friends, 'Hey, we do go on!'" She saw her own body on the operating table, with her back opened up and blood everywhere. Then she noticed the flatlined monitor. Disturbed at seeing her mangled body, she didn't want to view the scene any longer. And with that thought, she was out in the hallway of the hospital. "I saw my stepfather, a health nut who would never touch sweets, getting a candy bar from a vending machine in the hallway of the hospital and eating it." After reviving, she told her stepfather what she'd witnessed. He was shocked but admitted his indulgence, explaining he was nervous about Tricia's surgery.[40]

Another NDEr described how she left her body, went into the hospital waiting room, and heard her brother-in-law say, "It looks like June is going to kick the bucket, so I better stay around and be a pallbearer."[41] Can you imagine how he felt when she later told him she was there listening? These cases create yet another source of powerful evidence that alternative explanations must address.

8. Memory Retention

Dr. van Lommel notes, "The prevailing [medical] paradigm holds that memories and consciousness are produced by large groups of neurons or neural networks."[42] He points out that ten to twenty seconds after a heart attack, brain waves cease, resulting in a flat EEG, an indication that there is no electrical activity. In his study, all 344 patients had no brain activity, yet 18 percent reported memories of an NDE.[43] The question, then, is this: If there is no soul that houses our consciousness, how are all the NDE memories retained in neural networks? In other words, when the "machine" stops and there is no electrical brain activity, where are these memories stored? No alternate explanations have answered this question.

Dr. Sam Parnia and Peter Fenwick conducted a British prospective study which included sixty-three patients who survived their cardiac arrest. They note, "Complex experiences as reported in the NDE should not arise or be retained in memory. Such patients would be expected to have no subjective experience."[44] Yet they do, and the memories are vivid and consistent.

9. Life Change

Numerous studies have followed the aftereffects of an NDE. If an NDE is not a real experience of a life to come, why would it change people's lives and perspectives so drastically? In the Dutch study of 344 cardiac arrest patients, the experiences of a control group who did not report NDEs were compared to those who did report NDEs. Researchers interviewed all 344 patients two years after their cardiac arrest and then again eight years later. Here is what they found:

> We were . . . surprised to find that the processes of transformation that had begun in people with NDE after two years had clearly intensified after eight years. . . . The people who had experienced an NDE during their cardiac arrest continued to be clearly different. In particular, they were less afraid of death and had a stronger belief in an afterlife. We saw in them a greater interest in spirituality and questions about the purpose of life, as well as a greater acceptance of and love for oneself and others. Likewise, they displayed a greater appreciation of ordinary things, whereas their interest in possessions and power had decreased. . . . It is quite remarkable to see a cardiac arrest lasting just a few minutes give rise to such a lifelong process of transformation.[45]

Cardiac arrest patients who do not have NDEs do not consistently experience the same long-term life transformations as those who do have NDEs. An alternate explanation would need to show why NDEs consistently cause dramatic spiritual life changes.

10. The Same God across Cultures

NDErs come from vastly different cultures, religious backgrounds, and belief systems, yet they encounter the same God of Light and Love. I believe this is profound evidence not only of a life to come, but also of God's reality and identity. No alternative theories account for this or explain how people who did not believe God existed encountered the same God as those who did.

Jang Jaswal did not believe in God, gods, or an afterlife. As a science-minded atheist and engineer, he spent much time and effort trying to convince his family, friends, and coworkers of the lunacy of their beliefs in God. Then Jang clinically died during a twelve-hour heart and kidney transplant. He found himself in a lush, green valley looking across at an extremely bright light. Telepathically, a superior intelligence communicated, "You think you're the center of the universe and are a very important person and you control everything. But you are not the center of everything. Let me show you the center of the universe."[46] Jang realized God was addressing his arrogance of dogmatically telling people there was no God.

> I saw earth spinning on its axis . . . and I saw whole galaxies
> going by. Then I realized how insignificant I am in the bigger
> picture of things. After that, the light started moving towards
> where I was. And pretty soon, the light was shining on top
> of me, like rays were falling on me. This light was the best
> experience I had ever had in my life. The light was of golden-
> white color. . . . This communication came to me, telling me
> that it's not your time, it's time for you to go back now. . . . It
> was so peaceful of an experience, so blissful. I never understood
> the meaning of bliss before—until I experienced this light.[47]

Jang came back seeking spiritual understanding and believing very differently than he had before his NDE. How would an alternate theory account for the NDEs of so many people of radically different religious and cultural beliefs, all describing the same God?

THE SIMPLE TRUTH

There will always be people who struggle to believe that God or an afterlife exists, but the evidence is there. New alternate theories will probably continue to be proposed. However, for any alternate theory to stand, it must coherently explain these ten points of evidence. Science looks for the simplest explanation of consistently observed data, and the simplest explanation is this: Every human being has a soul that lives on after death, in a world overseen by a God of Light and Love.

We now have forty years of impressive scientific research validating NDEs. But what does this mean for us today? If there is a God, has that God given evidence of his existence only through modern NDEs? Or are there clues in history that point to the same God? As compelling as NDE evidence can be, I've found God's history even more persuasive.

3

THE GOD OF LIGHT
IN HISTORY

"**THERE IS NO GOD. THERE IS NO HEAVEN.** There is no hell. When you die, you cease to exist. You are an accident of science. Your life has less significance than the tiniest microscopic speck of dust in this vast infinite universe. Jesus Christ was the greatest hoax ever perpetrated on mankind."

"These are my father's words," Heidi Barr recalls, "spoken day after day after day. You can imagine the impact they had upon the fragile psyches of young children. I am not exaggerating when I say *day after day*. I heard this mantra as long as I can remember."

Heidi grew up in a Jewish home in the small town of Council Bluffs, Iowa—Middle America. Her father was a well-known, respected lawyer in town. Having grown up during World War II with a brother in a German POW camp, Heidi's father was filled with hurt, hatred, and a fear of death that turned him to atheism. Although he tried his best to pass on his atheism and fear to his three daughters, he failed.

"My first memory is of God," Heidi recalls. "He was present at my bedside for as long as I can remember." Despite suffering her father's ongoing abuse that far exceeded his daily mantra, Heidi prayed to God every night.

> My mom didn't feel beautiful; she didn't feel valued, and that contributed . . . to my belief that I was unloved, except in the eyes of God. He loved me. I knew this even as a child. My *real Father* [in heaven] loved me. Knowing I had a real Father saved my life many times. Did God sit at my bedside, at the head of my bed? Yes, yes, he did. How do I know? I clearly remember *knowing* he was there. I had a powerful sense that he sat right next to me, listening to my childish hopes and fears, my dreams. He paid attention to my little complaints when some injustice had been done.[1]

And there were injustices—many evils were perpetrated against Heidi as she grew up, culminating at age twelve. She was sent to the local rabbi to prepare for her bat mitzvah—her coming-of-age instruction in the Hebrew Scriptures—but she was subjected to sexual abuse, which she tried to stop for a year. She tried to run. She begged her mom not to make her go. "I tried to tell her that the rabbi touched me, kissed me. . . . I didn't have the words to describe all the other things he did. Every time I tried to tell her, she said, 'How dare you! He's your rabbi. Don't talk about him like that. You do whatever he says.'"

Knowing Heidi's younger sister had also complained of the rabbi's inappropriate advances, her grandmother confronted Heidi's parents. Sadly, her father chose to protect the rabbi instead of his daughters. He used his power and influence in the Jewish community to have the rabbi transferred to another city, and to other unsuspecting victims.

As a sixteen-year-old, Heidi's one place of solace was riding her horse named Heather. Unable to afford a saddle, Heidi rode Heather bareback. Her two younger sisters had come along with her that day to play in the barn while Heidi rode. Heidi was riding on a narrow hillside trail near the barn when she heard the galloping of a runaway Arabian horse. She had previously noticed the horse leaving the barn with an inexperienced rider on its back. As the Arabian charged around the mountainous curve toward Heidi, Heidi's horse had nowhere to go. Her horse reared up and Heidi clung tightly to her mane. As the Arabian screamed past, Heather reared up a second time, only this time she flipped over backward. Heather's seven hundred pounds of flesh landed across Heidi's chest, crushing her.

I found myself up in the air, perhaps thirty or forty feet above the scene. I looked down upon my body and watched as Heather rolled over me. My lifeless body was tossed like a rag doll. I prayed, in that moment, that Heather wasn't injured. She righted herself and ran toward the barn. I was relieved to see that she seemed to be fine. I saw and heard my little sister scream and cover her eyes with her hands. I saw my middle sister, who had gone to the car, press her face against the car window.

I watched as the man on the Arabian ran into the barn. Heather followed. Chaos ensued. It was interesting that I could see everything happening inside the barn, as if the roof had somehow vanished into thin air. As I floated there, just watching. . . . I knew I was dead, but the fact didn't trouble me. My only concern was for my two sisters. I thought aloud, "I wish my sisters didn't have to see me die."

The moment I spoke, I noticed a light over my right shoulder. This light was a golden light, bathing everything before me in a golden hue, lighting up the entire scene. I knew it wasn't the sun. The sun was behind some clouds. And besides, the sun wouldn't have been shining from over my right shoulder. I turned to look, and I saw a man floating there with me, up in the air. I stared at his face. He smiled. I smiled. He moved forward until he floated right by my side.

I recognized him immediately. How could I not? This was the man, God, who had been at my bedside every single night. This was the man, God, in whom I'd confided before I fell asleep. This was the man, God, I'd done my best to ignore for four long years [since the rabbi's abuse started]. And here he was, grinning from ear to ear.

I don't remember my mouth moving, but I remember saying to him, "Hi! I know you!" There was no doubt in my mind, not one. This man was, without question, Jesus, or Yeshua. His was the name I'd never been allowed to utter in my home, at least not in a way that acknowledged him as anything other than a hoax. My heart overflowed with happiness at our reunion. What a joyous occasion! He grinned at me, every bit as happy as I was, happier, because he is all joy, and he is all happiness.

So much occurred at once. I wish I had the right words to explain my journey with Jesus, my experience with him. I don't. There aren't enough words to explain Jesus, God, or heaven. . . . Just as my dead body was immaterial, those things occurring below us became immaterial the instant I saw his face.

How we laughed together! We were thrilled to be reunited. I was once again the child I'd been when he would wrap me up in his light, soft as a cloud, and rock me to sleep. I felt exactly the same—safe and surrounded by his loving Presence. Jesus was all at once my Father, my brother, my best friend. I had known him my entire life. He was everything to me.

In that eternal moment, I didn't think of the bad things that had happened; they didn't matter in his Presence. My mind and my heart and my soul were focused on him and on how much he loved me. He loved me for no reason. I certainly didn't deserve his love. I hadn't prayed to Jesus. Ever. And I'd turned my back on God in my teenage hurt and confusion. . . . Yet, here he was! Just loving me.

Jesus offered me a life review. He held out his right hand and a three-dimensional movie (for lack of a better word) of my life began to play. Except, rather than the story of my life progressing from start to finish in chronological order, I saw my life all at once, from the moment of conception to the present day. He had been right beside me. . . . I saw him there [in my life review], exactly as I pictured him, sitting at the head of my bed, right beside my pillow, his head inclined toward me as he listened. And when he felt it was time for me to sleep, he, himself, surrounded me with his own light and rocked me.

It was during my life review that I saw him by my side, from the moment of my conception. He formed me in my mother's womb. I saw him there. "For it was you who formed my inward parts; you knit me together in my mother's womb" (Psalm 139:13, NRSVue). I didn't read that psalm until a few years after I'd died.[2]

Can you imagine God, the Creator of the universe, being as personally and tenderly invested in the highs and lows of your life story as he was with Heidi's? Heidi tangibly felt this reassurance from Jesus himself during her NDE, but this reality is no less true for us non-NDErs. God cares for all people he created no matter where we are from or what we've done. He calls us his beloved, and nothing can change the fact that we are treasured, valued, and of extreme importance to him. And even if he isn't important to us yet or we don't know his identity, he lovingly waits for us to seek his guidance and love.

Heidi grew up with an awareness that God was with her, despite her cultural and family upbringing. It is interesting to note that she recognized Jesus as God in her NDE, even though she was raised Jewish and heard his name used only in antagonistic and negative ways. Without a doubt, this would not have been how a young Jewish girl would naturally be inclined to interpret her NDE. However, this is what she says she experienced.

In some cases, NDErs do express their experience of God in terms consistent with their respective religious traditions. If some NDErs say they saw Allah, or one of the millions of Hindu gods, or just an unnamed source of light and love, does this mean that there are multiple divine beings that nevertheless reveal themselves in similar ways in NDEs? Are we just left with a diversity of interpretations, or has one God actually revealed himself before the age of modern NDEs? I have discovered that this same God of Light and Love *has* given verifiable evidence of himself in history. In fact, that is how I came to believe—not from NDEs, but from God's history. Follow me as I show you what I discovered. It's important because it can help us know God for who he really is and better understand the heart and character of this God NDErs encounter.

THE GOD OF LIGHT AND LOVE IN HISTORY

About the time human history began to be widely recorded, God claimed to do something to bless all people. Around 2000 BCE, God chose two people through whom he would create a "chosen nation." The word *chosen*, though, is sometimes misunderstood. *Chosen* does not mean "loved more" or "better than" but rather "set apart for a purpose." Abraham and Sarah, whose names were then Abram and Sarai, were chosen by God for a purpose: "The LORD [Yahweh] had said to Abram, 'Leave your native country . . . and go to the land that I will show you. I will make you into a great nation. I will bless you. . . . All the families on earth will be blessed through you'" (Genesis 12:1-3). God birthed a nation, the Jewish nation, for the sole purpose of blessing all people on earth.

God called Abraham and Sarah long before the sacred scriptures of our current world religions were written. God put this plan into motion close to 500 years before the Jewish religion began or the Hindu scriptures were codified; over 1,000 years before Zoroastrianism or Jainism had sacred writings; 1,500 years before Buddhism, Confucianism, or Taoism; 2,000 years before Jesus; and 2,600 years before Islam.[3] Here's why I think it's important to know this—because it clearly shows that God created people for *relationship*, not *religion*.

Religion is about humanity seeking God and about upholding moral law. It has its purpose, which is to keep evil at bay by providing moral and ethical boundaries. But within the walls of religion, people tend to develop an "us versus them" mentality, which designates "them" as an undesirable "other" or an outcast. This is the opposite of loving relationship and is counter to the purpose for which God created us all.

Yahweh [LORD in English translations] was the name God used with Abraham. God later declares that Yahweh is his eternal name, and he equates his name with the term translated, "I AM WHO I AM" (Exodus 3:14-15). God the Creator is *eternal*—he exists perpetually in the past, present, and future. Peter, one of Jesus' disciples, writes, "A day is like a thousand years to the Lord, and a thousand years is like a day" (2 Peter 3:8). Not surprisingly, this is exactly what NDErs consistently say about their experience of time in God's realm. God is not bound by time. God is eternal.

God is also *infinite*. He created time and space, so he exists outside the limits of our three-dimensional space. This means we can't physically go and "find" God. For us to know God, he must intersect our time and space. In the Bible, God claims he has done this to bless and love all people, from generations past to the generation in which we live today.

When God created the "chosen" Jewish nation, he did so to bless all people in two ways. First, he revealed his heart, his character, and his will through many Jewish prophets so that we can know and love him as he loves us. Second, he made the incredible and radical prophetic promise that he would send the Messiah, the Savior for all humanity, to bless all nations for all time. As you will see throughout this book, NDErs around the globe meet this same "I Am" that Jesus claimed to reveal (John 8:58).

THE "I AM" IN TEHRAN

I had recently met Saeed and wondered why he had invited his mother, Bibi Tahereh, to join us for lunch, since she spoke only Persian. Saeed grew up in Iran and had been part of Hezbollah, an Islamic political party, but had come to faith in Jesus through a vision and later led his sister to faith in Jesus.

"My mom is a Muslim of Muslims, related to the prophet Muhammad," Saeed told me. "In Tehran, as she walked the streets in her black burka, she was so esteemed she was practically worshiped."

"Is she still Muslim?" I asked.

"I'll let her tell you," he said.

With Saeed translating, Bibi began to tell me her fascinating story. She had helped build the mosque in their Tehran neighborhood, an esteemed gated community, where she lived next door to a prominent government official. When her two adult children became followers of Jesus, Bibi was so distraught with heart-crushing guilt and anxiety, it literally killed her as she lay in bed one night.

"That night I was so hopeless," Bibi explained, "feeling I was not a good servant to Allah, that I had failed, and my children had gone astray. The pain was so great that sometime in the night, I had a heart attack. My heart stopped. I saw my spirit leave my body, and I found myself in another world."

Bibi knew she was dead and fearfully waited for the Imam Ali to come to judge her, as Shiite Muslims believe happens after death. She saw a vision of her burial and a large stone hitting her head, which in Shiite tradition meant she would be condemned as a horrible sinner. She waited in fear, but Imam Ali didn't come.

Instead, Bibi saw a giant man in a majestic white robe approach her. "He was so tall and his robe very long," Bibi recalls. "I was trembling and shaking. There was a presence of power and strength about him, and I could look at his face, but I didn't recognize the face at the time." The man spoke thought-to-thought to Bibi and said in Persian, "I AM HE WHO IS." "When the man said, 'I AM HE WHO IS,' my soul fell back into my body, and I woke up alive again, but with a peace I had never experienced before."[4]

After her NDE, Bibi no longer worried about her children's beliefs, and she no longer cared so much about what people thought about her. Instead, she felt a new joy and freedom. But inside, she desperately wanted to know who this God was, the one who left her with so much peace and called himself "I Am." Bibi spent the next year praying, seeking, and asking God to reveal himself to her. That next New Year's Eve, as her adult children prayed for her, Bibi had a vision.

I again could see the man in the white robe. The first time [in the NDE], he looked huge, with a white robe [and] without a discernible face. The second time, he was our size and had a human face, like a glorious king with a scepter in his hands. I grabbed his robe, and he was so close I could touch his face. The second I touched his face, I knew this was Jesus. Jesus was the face of the unknown God. He said, "It's not the time. You still have an unfinished job. One day, I will come back for you, but I have a mission for you."[5]

Several years later, Bibi and Saeed had to flee Iran because their neighbor, the government official, wanted them dead for talking about Jesus. But why would a Muslim meet the "I Am" in her NDE and then identify him with Jesus? And why would Heidi, a Jewish girl, know with certainty that Jesus had been present with her all her life? As you will see in the pages that follow, there are Hindus, Muslims, Buddhists, Jews, Christians, and even atheists who, when they have an NDE, somehow know that Jesus and the God of Light and Love are connected. And I will show you how God's self-revelation in history makes the same connection.

THE GOD OF LIGHT IN A BUSH

Interestingly, about five hundred years after Abraham, Moses claimed a direct revelation from the God of Light in what appeared to him as a burning bush. Moses saw a brilliant light on Mount Sinai and said to himself, "Why isn't that bush burning up? I must go see it" (Exodus 3:3). According to the Hebrew Scriptures, this God of Light told Moses he had heard the cries of the Jewish people in slavery, he cared about the injustices they'd suffered, and he was sending Moses to deliver them.

When God revealed himself to Moses, the Hebrew Scriptures indicate it happened at an actual location (Mount Sinai) and a specific time in history (during the reign of Rameses II in Egypt, around 1446 BCE).[6] This is significant because again and again, the Hebrew Scriptures claim God intersected actual human history to relate to us. When Moses asked this God of Light for his name, God replied, "I Am Who I Am. Say this to the people of Israel: I Am has sent me to you. . . . Yahweh, the God of your ancestors—the God of Abraham, the God of Isaac, and the God of Jacob—has sent me to you" (Exodus 3:14-15).

The God of Moses revealed that he is the self-existent one, the uncreated Creator, the "I Am"—infinite and eternal. He appeared to Moses and the Israelites as a brilliant light or eternal fire who guided them through the desert and communicated his heart and will. God spoke face-to-face with Moses: "When there is a prophet among you, I, the Lord, reveal myself to them in visions, I speak to them in dreams. But this is not true of my servant Moses. . . . With him I speak face to face, clearly and not in riddles; he sees the form of the LORD" (Numbers 12:6-8, NIV).

When Moses came back from speaking with God and receiving the Ten Commandments, "the skin of his face shone, and [people] were afraid to approach him" because the light of God radiated from him (Exodus 34:30, NASB). And as we will see, this same God of Light told Moses that *love* was his motive for creation. The first four commandments tell us how we can love God, and the next six spell out how to love our neighbors as much as ourselves. This, too, correlates with what NDErs around the globe say about having a life review in God's presence—God is love, and what matters most to him is how we love each other. But how can we be sure this is truly God?

HOW WE CAN KNOW

Before the world's religions were codified, the God of Light revealed to Moses how we can know if God is truly communicating to humanity through a prophet:

> "Any prophet who falsely claims to speak in my name . . . must die." But you may wonder, "How will we know whether or not a prophecy is from the LORD?" If the prophet speaks in the LORD's name but his prediction does not happen or come true, you will know that the LORD did not give that message.
>
> DEUTERONOMY 18:20-22

God created a test for the Jewish prophets to root out deception and false claims about God. True prophets who spoke from God would be able to tell what the future held, and those words must come to pass 100 percent of the time to prove that the prophet was speaking on God's behalf.

God did this because false claims and false guidance abounds. God wants to be our guide because he truly cares for the well-being of each person. So God repeats what he told Moses through the prophet Isaiah. False guides and false gods cannot perfectly predict the future: "'Present your case,' says the LORD . . . 'declare to us the things to come, *tell us what the future holds, so we may know that you are gods'*" (Isaiah

41:21-23, NIV, emphasis added). God answers his sarcastic challenge with certainty: Only he knows the future because he alone is God.

> Who foretold this long ago, who declared it from the distant past? Was it not I, the LORD [Yahweh]? And there is no God apart from me, a righteous God and a Savior; there is none but me. Turn to me and be saved, all you ends of the earth.
>
> ISAIAH 45:21-22, NIV

God intersected history telling us his heart and his will, wanting people of all cultures to know they are special to him. He cares about each individual, and he wants to love and guide every willing person. But we must desire God's love and guidance—we have to seek God and want to know him for who he truly is.

WHAT ABOUT OTHER "GODS"?

Some readers may be thinking, *If you're claiming this God of Light NDErs see is the God of the Bible, what about those of other religions who see their god or goddess in an NDE?* I don't deny that some NDErs claim to see their god or goddess, but let me give you a sample of what they often report compared to their *interpretations* of what they report. This is a critical distinction to make.

Arvind, a Hindu from India, had a cardiac arrest and was taken to the hospital. He writes,

> I was given electric shocks. I started drifting upward. From a height, I could see my own body with many doctors and medical personnel working on my body. . . . Then I saw a huge light in the center of the hall, and I started drifting towards it. There was a huge light coming in from that huge hole. . . . I firmly believe in our Goddess, Mother Kaalika. I could feel that she was there on the other side of that beam of bright light. . . . That was the last thing I remember from the out-of-world experience.[7]

Arvind reported this brilliant light he knew to be divine, and he interpreted the light to be the goddess Kaalika. But consider how the goddess Kaalika, or Kali, is typically described. "Kali is most often characterized as black or blue, partially or completely naked, with a long lolling tongue [and] multiple arms."[8] What Arvind *reports* seeing resembles nothing like a black or blue, four-armed woman with her tongue hanging out, yet what he *describes* is consistent with the God of Light. This is commonly what I find. An NDEr may *interpret* what they saw as a certain goddess or god, but their *description* often matches the God of Light and Love described in the Hebrew Scriptures.

Fifteen-year-old Neha and her family were visiting a wildlife refuge in South Africa when the ranger unlocked and entered the lion enclosure and persuaded Neha to join him. Here's how Neha describes what happened next.

> After walking five steps into the cage, a lioness jumped up and attacked me. As I blacked out, the lioness took three bites to my head. . . . then I lost all consciousness. While I was in this unconscious state, I went through the most amazing, beautiful, blissful experience. . . . I went to this amazing, beautiful place: Some call it heaven; some call it God. . . . The glow looked like the sun, fire, light, morning. This glow guided me to my safety. . . . God definitely exists. . . . I saw 'god' through a sixth sense as a beautiful glow.[9]

Neha later interprets this God of glowing "sun, fire, light" as the goddess Durga. "I felt the presence of Durga Maa," she says. "Goddess Durga is the mother of the universe and believed to be the power behind the work of creation." Then she says, "I felt a distant presence of Jesus Christ. I came back understanding Christianity, which previously I did not."[10]

Neha interprets her experience through the lens of her religion, yet her description aligns more with the God of Light than it does with Durga. Durga is described as a beautiful woman "riding a lion and with eight or ten arms, each holding the special weapon of one of the gods."[11]

That's not who Neha describes. She also receives a new understanding about Jesus. Why Jesus if she had no previous knowledge of Jesus?

Again, why would people from other faiths, who have no expectation of Jesus, encounter him in their NDEs? As we will explore more deeply, Jesus claimed to be the Messiah that the Jewish prophets foretold. Jesus said, "I am the light of the world. Whoever follows me will never walk in darkness, but will have the light of life" (John 8:12, NIV).

This same God of Light also gave an unmistakable sign to *our generation,* which we will discuss next. For me, this sign shows verifiable evidence that the God of Light NDErs experience cares deeply for every individual he created, and he has been relentlessly at work throughout human history to bless the people of all nations.

HISTORY FORETOLD

It's important to understand God's claim in Scripture: He created the Jewish people to protect and preserve his self-revelation through the Hebrew prophets. God put in place many of the cultural laws and ordinances we read in the Old Testament as a protective shield. He did this to keep the Jewish people faithfully communicating with him and living by his words—for their benefit and for our benefit as well.

Throughout the Hebrew Scriptures, the Jewish prophets often use the phrase, "The Lord said." It was their way of claiming their prophecies were not their own words, but words inspired by God himself.[12] Dr. Mortimer Adler, editor of the *Encyclopedia Britannica* and an agnostic philosopher at the time, wrote a book called *Truth in Religion.* In his research, he found that no other sacred scriptures *even claim* that God himself spoke directly to real people within human history.[13]

Over five hundred times in the Bible, this God of Light speaks concerning all the nations.[14] This same God revealed himself to over forty biblical authors during a 1,500-year period. The Bible is a compilation of sixty-six books written across generations by these Hebrew prophets and by followers of Jesus. But more significantly for us, it contains close to 2,500 individual predictions from God, many that can be verified today.

Astrophysicist Hugh Ross became convinced by the same historical evidence that convinced me. He says of the two thousand predictions already fulfilled, "The odds for all these prophecies having been fulfilled by chance without error is less than one in 10^{2000} (that is 1 with 2,000 zeros written after it)!"[15] We'll explore some of the more evidential historical prophecies as we go along, but the one of greatest global magnitude is the sign God gave to our generation. The fulfillment of this prophecy confirms God's words to Abraham to bless all nations through the Jewish nation.*

In the passage below, which records what God said through Isaiah around 700 BCE, God foretells a time after the Messiah comes. The Jewish people would be scattered to all the nations, and then God would bring the people back to Jerusalem as a sign that he is the true God. Isaiah refers to the Messiah as the "Root of Jesse" because other prophets said the Messiah would come from the line of King David, whose father was Jesse.

> In that day the Root of Jesse [the Messiah] will stand as a
> banner [a sign] for the peoples; the nations will rally to him,
> and his resting place will be glorious. In that day the Lord
> will reach out his hand a second time to reclaim the surviving
> remnant of his people [Israel]. . . . He will raise a banner
> [a sign] for the nations and gather the exiles of Israel; he will
> assemble the scattered people of Judah [the Jewish people]
> from the four quarters of the earth.
>
> ISAIAH 11:10-12, NIV

A CLEAR SIGN FROM GOD

This prophecy of Isaiah says God will give a sign for all nations. In the days after the Messiah comes, when the nations rally to him, the Jewish people will be scattered to the north, south, east, and west—the "four quarters of the earth." The Jewish people had been exiled the first time to Babylon and then returned from exile in 444 BCE. Here, God tells

---

*It's important to note that this does not mean everything the Jewish people or the nation of Israel has done is God's will. God can use people for good even if they do harmful things (see Ezekiel 36:22).

Isaiah they will be scattered a *second time* to all the nations. This happened in actual history forty years after Jesus was crucified.[16] In 70 CE, history records that the Roman general Titus marched on Jerusalem, leveled the city and the Temple, and just as Isaiah foretold, the Jewish people were scattered a *second time* to all the nations—for 1,900 years! This is real, verifiable history.

God told Isaiah around 700 BCE that he would regather the scattered Jewish people from all the nations as a sign to all people. The prophets Isaiah, Jeremiah, Ezekiel, and even Jesus[17] foretold the miraculous event that happened in 1948—the regathering and birth of a nation in one day. God said to Isaiah:

> "Who ever heard of such a thing? Has a nation ever been
> born in a single day? Has a country ever come forth in a mere
> moment? But by the time Jerusalem's birth pains begin, her
> children will be born. Would I ever bring this nation to the
> point of birth and then not deliver it?" asks the LORD. . . .
> "I will gather all nations and peoples together, and they will
> see my glory. I will perform a sign among them. . . . They
> will bring the remnant of your people back from every
> nation. They will bring them to my holy mountain in
> Jerusalem."
> ISAIAH 66:8-9,18-20

Not only would the Jews be scattered a second time, but they would also return from all the nations to become a new nation "in a single day." On May 15, 1948, the *New York Times* reported: "The Jewish state, the world's newest sovereignty, to be known as the State of Israel, came into being in Palestine at midnight."[18]

When we're searching for God, we might say, "God, give me a sign if you're real." But are we even looking for the signs he's already clearly given? Never in the history of the world has a nation been born overnight. How did the Jewish nation remain "a people" while scattered across the globe, with no king, no government, no common language, no land for nearly 1,900 years (from 70 CE to 1948)? Then, suddenly,

Russian Jews, Ethiopian Jews, European Jews, Australian Jews, American Jews, and others from all over the world, speaking different languages, came back as one "chosen" people to form a new nation—born overnight! How else can you explain that? God foretold it as a historical sign to all nations—God is real!

God revealed himself in history and through Scripture because he wants us to know him, love him, and follow him. Others may say, "Follow me and life will be good," but only God knows us intimately and truly cares about our best interests. Having a way to verify God's identity is very important because deception is rampant in this world, and deception and evil are just as real on the other side.

God has intersected history, more than once as we will see, and he has given verifiable evidence to his identity. He is the God of Light and Love who invaded human history with a plan to bless all people of all nations. He is the God both NDErs and Scripture say loves us more than we can imagine—but let's *try* to imagine truly unconditional love!

PART 2

GOD'S LOVE STORY

4

THE UNCONDITIONAL
LOVE OF GOD

IT WAS AN OCTOBER DAY IN 1984 and Dr. Ron Smothermon had just finished his last lecture of the week in Bristol, England. He found it so satisfying to use his medical training in psychiatry and neurology to heal families. After he had written a trilogy of books, his week-long seminars had been in demand around the world. Now he was headed back to San Francisco where he lived and worked in private practice. Ron believed in Jesus, and he taught families in crisis how to access the love of God. But at times, he struggled with not feeling or experiencing this magnificent love himself. But that would soon change.

After a grueling eleven-hour flight from Heathrow to San Francisco, Ron was picked up by his assistant, Pamela. She drove him to his home, where his friend Amin* had been house-sitting for the week. Amin had recently been evicted from his own house and would have immediately

---

* Amin is a pseudonym.

been homeless if Ron hadn't mercifully invited Amin to house-sit while he was in England that week. Little did Ron know that a psychotic timebomb was about to go off.

"How are you, Amin?" Ron asked. "You don't look well." Amin was sitting on the stairs in the entryway of the house. Ron could see from the deranged look in his eyes and the sweat beading on his forehead that something was off with the muscular twenty-eight-year-old. As Ron reached out his hand to check him for a fever, Amin let out a bloodcurdling scream and struck Ron on the side of the head with the edge of a steel tennis racket he had been holding. The blow knocked Ron to the ground.

Ron got up, yelling, "Amin, what are you doing?" He was knocked to the ground again. Amin had suffered a psychotic break. Ron didn't realize Amin had a ten-inch knife in his other hand, and he was stabbing Ron each time he knocked him down. Pamela ran for help. When Ron got up again, he saw blood on the walls and the knife in Amin's hand and finally realized it was his own blood. Amin screamed, "I am going to kill you!" Ron grabbed Amin's shoulders, looked into vacant, evil eyes, and pleaded, "Amin, don't kill a man." Amin stabbed Ron thirteen times in the chest, neck, and back. Ron watched as Amin drew back his arm, aiming the fourteenth blow for the heart to finish him off.

And time stopped.

I notice over [Amin's] left shoulder a hallway appeared. It is made of something that appears to be solid light. Strangely, I am calm and not attached to the outcome of this insane event. *That looks like infinity,* I thought, as I neared death. The light explodes into being, blocking my view of Amin and the hallway—brighter than the sun, yet not hurting my eyes. It is not an ordinary light; it is a living being, a *who*, not a *what*. If this person of light came down that hallway, he must have traveled at warp speed. The light itself is a person, exactly my height. Instantly, the qualities of this person are written across my awareness—not in one-two-three fashion, but imprinted instantly into myself, my heart, my consciousness. . . . I am stamped with the knowledge of the nature of God. I do not have to wonder about the identity of this light. There is no room for doubt. This is God.

How will I even describe this to you? I never really understood that "glory of God" thing before I witnessed it. God is truly glorious, magnificent, awesome, without equal. His glory is a light but made of infinite love. God's light appears like a sudden, silent, atomic bomb blast of white light, full of his power. Imagine being five feet away from the source of a nuclear explosion. But his light is more than light—it is overwhelming, a literal tsunami of infinite, unconditional love. All it touches transforms into perfect peace, and [it] blows away into irrelevancy any consideration about what is happening, replacing it with ineffable ecstasy, irresistible joy, love beyond comprehension—all in a singular package. A nuclear bomb blows life away. God's love blows death away.[1]

"Looking back, I don't think time stopped," Ron explained to me as he described this event. "I think time accelerated to the speed of light with the presence of God." Ron had no concerns at all about the attack as God's love exploded within him.

With Amin still poised to strike a fourteenth blow, Ron had a direct encounter with God's nature. "All his qualities are contained in his love, *for love is his overarching nature,*" Ron recalled. Along with the bomb blast of love, Ron described nine qualities of God that were immediately imprinted on his soul: God is infinite love, infinite knowledge, infinite power, authority, humor, kindness, joy, purity, and humility. "Wrap these qualities in his light, and you have the glory of God. God is holy," Ron said.

And his love is not an enhanced version of human love. . . . It is a love beyond our experience, simply overpowering. . . . It fills you with his essence, and you know him intimately. . . . When your time comes, and it will, it is you and God, and no one else, swimming in an ocean of love. It is hard to describe what happens—you become his love, and you are together in his light. . . . Confronting God's love person-to-person inspires an intense desire to make his love known to every life form in the universe.[2]

Perhaps that's why Ron responded as he did when God asked him, "Will you come now or later?" Ron was shocked to have a choice. Even more shocking was his first concern if he chose to stay with God: *"What will happen to Amin's well-being? What would having murdered a man do to his life and those who love him?"* Ron wondered in the same picosecond, *"Why am I concerned about this man who is trying to murder me?* But I could not turn it off. I thought about my three-year-old son, who needed me . . . and how my murder would affect him and others." Ron gave God his answer, thought-to-thought, in a single word: *Later.*

Clink, clink. "I look down at the floor and I see two pieces of what was once a solid piece of steel. The knife blade had been cleanly sliced into two pieces. I realized later that whatever sliced through hardened steel like butter must have produced heat that forced Amin to drop the handle of the knife." The police arrived and subdued Amin, and an ambulance took Ron to the hospital.

Ron recalled, "The doctors could not understand how the knife had made a trek through my left supraclavicular fossa, brachial plexus of nerves, by my throat, past my cervical vertebrae missing the nerves, without hitting the carotid artery, jugular vein, or vital nerve, and exiting the back of my neck." And that was just one of the thirteen knife wounds Ron miraculously survived. Amin spent thirteen years in prison. A decade later, a news show picked up the story and recreated it, but nothing could recreate the explosion of God's infinite love that Ron experienced that day.[3]

GOD *IS* LOVE

"God is love," Jesus' youngest disciple John declared (1 John 4:8). Jesus said that God's love is a love that changes us, "But I say, love your enemies! Pray for those who persecute you! In that way, you will be acting as true children of your Father in heaven" (Matthew 5:44-45). This is love of another kind, another order of love, a love that extends to enemies (even murderers), as Ron discovered while bathed in God's love.

But it's hard for us to grasp what the words *God is love* truly mean, and how that truth can shape who we become. I believe NDEs are God's gift to fill in with color the black-and-white words written in Scripture. Scripture reveals God's character and helps us understand God's love; NDEs can help us imagine what all of that means as we try to relate to God today. The apostle Paul, who wrote many of the New Testament books, may have had an NDE. When Paul went to the Roman colony of Lystra, the crowd turned on him: "They stoned Paul and dragged him out of town, thinking he was dead. But as the believers gathered around him, he got up" (Acts 14:19-20). Paul later wrote:

> I was caught up to the third heaven fourteen years ago. Whether I was in my body or out of my body, I don't know— only God knows. . . . But I do know that I was caught up to paradise and heard things so astounding that they cannot be expressed in words, things no human is allowed to tell.
> 2 CORINTHIANS 12:2-4

Paul says what NDErs commonly report—that they are not allowed to either retain or retell all the knowledge they received. Paul also described the inexpressibly great love of God he wanted everyone to experience:

> I pray that from [God's] glorious, unlimited resources he will empower you with inner strength through his Spirit. Then Christ will make his home in your hearts as you trust in him. Your roots will grow down into God's love and keep you strong. And may you have the power to understand, as all God's people should, how wide, how long, how high, and how deep his love is. May you experience the love of Christ, though it is too great to understand fully.
> EPHESIANS 3:16-19

The deeper our understanding of God's unfathomable love, the greater our trust; the greater our trust, the more we will experience the powerful reality of this transforming love and life today. And it starts with understanding the greatest love story ever told.

THE GREATEST LOVE STORY EVER TOLD

The Bible is a love story from start to finish, though it can be easy to miss this metanarrative given all the accounts the Bible also includes of humanity's cruelties, betrayals, wars, and brutally honest history. We have to remember that the Bible is written in sixty-six books and contains thousands of years of human history, which means it covers a lot of ups and downs in God's relationship with human beings.

The story starts with God creating people for his love. Relationship has always been God's motive, but maintaining loving relationship seems to complicate God's life just as it does ours. So in God's love story, inscribed across biblical history, we find rejected love, broken promises, betrayal, and divorce, as well as sacrificial love, loyalty, forgiveness, and reconciliation. The culmination of the whole story is a great wedding, as we will see.

It's a strange, mysterious, but powerfully wonderful love story. God's grand story shines light on many questions we all inevitably have that leave us in the dark, like why God sometimes seems so reluctant to intervene. The more we understand the uniting thread of God's love story, God's motives, and God's loving character, the more we will trust him. As we trace God's love story in the chapters that follow, you will see how NDEs today confirm the story God has been telling from the dawn of creation.

God's love story starts with God—the Person. And God is *personal.* God is not a force, nor is God "the universe." As Ron told me, "The universe is nothing compared to God."[4] NDErs do not describe some impersonal feeling, but the love of a Person, even when their personal views, faith traditions, or cultures should have led them to expect an impersonal force or nothing at all beyond this life. Just ask Chen.

Chen joined the Chinese communist party in college, as all good Chinese students did. She did not believe in God, yet she confesses,

"I [had] an NDE and it has changed me completely." When Chen clinically died from an allergic reaction to penicillin, she found herself leaving her body.

> I dropped into a dark tunnel, rushing with an incredible speed. I was extremely frightened because I didn't know what happened to me. . . . I couldn't imagine why I did not lose my consciousness and why I still exist[ed]. However, my fear gradually disappeared. I felt myself floating somewhere and it was comfortable. An indescribable "stream of consciousness" was accompanying me. He gave me the answer to my every question, and he comforted my frightened heart. I didn't know how to describe him. He had no shape or voice, but he was bright and broad-minded, warm, and gentle. He could answer every question. He surrounded me and guided me. He communicated with me through telepathy. . . . I was no longer in the tunnel, but I was in the bright warm world. I felt a complete relief from pain and suffering. I felt the existence of everlasting harmony and happiness.[5]

Chen experienced this very personal God she hadn't expected. Although she refers to God as "a stream of consciousness," she also uses the personal pronoun *he* to describe his personal nature. God has consistently revealed himself in intimate and personal ways throughout history.

God has characteristics we associate with personality, such as intellect (Jeremiah 29:11) and will (Matthew 6:10). He is described as having senses, such as seeing (2 Chronicles 16:9) and hearing (Genesis 16:11). He experiences emotions, including grief (Isaiah 63:10), regret (Genesis 6:6), anger (Deuteronomy 31:29), jealousy (Exodus 34:14), and compassion (Joel 2:13). He is creative (Psalm 148:4-5), humble (Matthew 11:29), and loyal (Isaiah 44:21-22).

Theologians often call these characteristics *anthropomorphic*, which Webster's dictionary defines as "ascribing human characteristics to non-human things."[6] But saying this can almost *depersonalize* God. Yes, God transcends our human characteristics, but we are created by God and in the image of God, so all our human characteristics are derived from something greater than us, not less than us. God is not *less* personal; he is actually *more* personal than we are. And NDErs who encounter God confirm this.

Dean Braxton, a youth probation supervisor, became septic during a routine kidney stone procedure that led to an hour and forty-five minutes of clinical death. He found himself in a heavenly field of gorgeous grass and flowers on the edge of a forest. After walking through the forest, which he described as being more like "gliding," he discovered that God's love is intimately personal.

> As I went through the forest, it seemed like everything in the forest was saying to me, "He's going to see the King." When I got on the other side of the forest, that's when I saw Jesus Christ. He was really bright, brighter than any light I've ever seen, even the sun. He was glowing. It was a bright white light. He was standing in a field, and before him [were many beings]. I don't know if it was thousands or millions. Some were angels, and some were people that had been on this planet Earth. He was addressing them, like a big crowd before him. I came up on the side of him.
>
> I looked at his feet, and when I looked at his feet I saw the holes—not in the feet but the ankles, in the talocrural joint. All I could think of was, *You did this for me.* I dropped to my knees saying, "Thank you, thank you, thank you." I remember thinking to myself, *His feet love me.* It was like I was literally receiving the fullness of the love of God through the feet of Jesus.
>
> Then I started looking up and every portion of him was loving me. His entire being loved me. What got me was he only loved me. I knew he loved the others, but it seemed like he only loved me. When I finally looked at him, his eyes met my eyes. I remember looking into his eyes, thinking, *He loves me so much, by the time I'm thinking of him loving me, it's old*

news because he even loves me more! I used to think he just loves you, and that was it, but it's a growing love every moment, uniquely for you.[7]

When God's love story began, God created us saying, "Let us make human beings in our image, to be like *us*" (Genesis 1:26, emphasis added). The use of the word *us* may seem like a strange choice because God revealed that there is only one God (Deuteronomy 6:4). Yet, from the beginning, God refers to himself in the plural—for a reason, which we will later explore.

God also revealed that his image is reflected in both male and female: "In the image of God he created them; male and female he created them. Then God blessed them and said, 'Be fruitful and multiply. Fill the earth and govern it'" (Genesis 1:27-28). God created humanity in plurality—male and female—for relationship with God because God is a relationship of love. God is neither male nor female, but male and female together reflect the image of God (Genesis 5:1-2), especially when united as one (Genesis 2:24).

You and I were created for a unique relationship with God. A relationship of love, unity, and cocreating with God. Unlike any other species, human beings have the capacity to create, care for, and develop God's creation in loving partnership with God. The only problem is that human love can't be guaranteed—it's risky.

RISKY BUSINESS

In his book *Disappointment with God*, author Philip Yancey describes God as a *creator* who made choices—and every artist knows that each creative choice comes with self-imposed limits. For example, if you choose to draw with a graphite pencil, you limit yourself to a black-and-white sketch, not color. Michelangelo created the images on the ceiling of the Sistine Chapel using paint on plaster. It was a self-limiting choice that could never produce the three-dimensional reality he achieved with his bronze or marble sculptures. When artists choose a medium, they choose to limit themselves, and no artist escapes this. Not even God.

When God created everything out of nothing, every creative choice also came with self-imposed limits. God created humans to reflect his image, as in a mirror. Human beings could love, imagine, cocreate, and be united to God and each other, but this choice required one divine self-limitation—giving human beings free will. Yancey writes, "Of all God's creatures, [human beings] had a moral capacity to rebel against their creator. The sculptures could spit at the sculptor; the characters in the play could rewrite the lines."[8] When God chose the medium of free will, he also chose the limitations that came with it. Why? Because of love. Love must be free to choose. Think about it.

Let's say you fall in love with someone and deeply desire them to reciprocate your love. If you were wealthy, you might shower your beloved with gifts and give them whatever they wanted. But it's risky because they might love the gifts but never love you. You might try to manipulate them with promises of a wonderful future, and they may love the idea of a blessed future but still not love you. In desperation, you could even try to coerce them into love by threatening them or demanding they love you, but we all know that would not be love, even if they pretended to love you out of fear. Love can't be bought, manipulated, or coerced—it must be freely given. And therein lies God's risky business. No amount of good gifts, promises of a bright future, or even God's infinite power can make us love God.

Genesis tells us that everything God created is good, yet that same creation allowed for human beings to choose the knowledge of both good and evil. Evil is the absence of God and his loving ways. When we choose "my way" against God's way, evil enters the world. In his mercy, God limited the life span of the human experience so we would not experience evil forever.

We live in the knowledge of good (all of God's good gifts, such as joy, peace, compassion, empathy, beauty, and love) intermixed with the knowledge of evil (the absence of God's will and ways as seen in disease, decay, lies, hatred, apathy, and abuse). We live between a muted taste of heaven and a merciful taste of hell—for a time. Missing from planet Earth, by God's self-limiting choice, is the unlimited reign of God's loving will and ways. For a time, God stays partially hidden, allowing people to do very unloving acts, but overcoming evil through willing people who freely choose to love and obey him. And despite all our evils and abuses, God's love will heal and restore all that was lost.

A LOVE THAT HEALS OUR WOUNDS

As the ambulance rushed Sarah from the car accident to the hospital, her whole life began to play backward. Time seemed to stop as she relived her short fourteen years. She questioned God about why she would die after such a hard life. "I don't have even one happy memory," Sarah recalls. "I was abused, unloved, and unwanted. It was a really crappy childhood."

Once in the hospital and still rapidly losing blood, Sarah had an NDE. She found herself up by the ceiling, but she felt peaceful and calm. She saw a light in the distance, then realized the light was quickly approaching her. As an abused child, she was scared she might be hit in the face, and so she spun around and cowered in fear. When nothing bad happened, she turned slowly to see what she described as a magical, color-filled light, sparkling like brilliant diamonds, shining with gold and pink and other beautiful tones. She was mesmerized by the light because it was alive and calling her inside it.

> I put my hand in first and it felt so incredible. One's mind can't express in words the feelings of immense LOVE. . . .
> I became ONE with the light. I was held immediately so close and tight. It felt like someone was hugging me. . . . I allowed my walls to come down for the first time. . . . I danced in the light and spun around. I was so happy to have felt good for the first time in my life.[9]

Sarah then found herself transported to a beautiful world of light—everything alive, everything glowing with light, even the plants and flowers. She felt amazed by the pristine beauty surrounding her. She walked down a path, gazing at the beauty everywhere, but then she came to a crossroads. Up ahead, she could see two women walking toward her. Afraid she would get in trouble for being there, she hid behind a tree. To her surprise and delight, she actually went into the tree instead!

After she hid for a while, she was surprised to hear a light-hearted male voice ask her if she was planning to hide in the tree forever! She giggled and replied she didn't think she was allowed to go anywhere else.

The voice reassured her, "This is your HOME and you can go anywhere you wish."

"Really?" she asked.

"Yes!" the voice replied.

Sarah felt so excited by this she started to do gymnastics down the path. She wasn't a gymnast but had always loved gymnastics. Somehow in this new world of wonder, she discovered she could tumble down the path like an Olympian.

Then she stopped and began thinking of all she had endured in her life up to that point. She recalled all the questions that were on constant replay in her thoughts: *Why wouldn't God protect me from being abused? Didn't I love him enough, that he might help me like the people in the Bible?*[10] She started to hear answers back to her thoughts. The voice, tender and soothing, was offering her healing replies. Feeling reassured, Sarah asked more questions.

"Why won't God protect me?"

The voice replied, "He will."

"Why won't God stick up for me?"

The voice explained, in a comforting way, that all these things were only temporary. With each reply, this abused young teenager felt the crippling, crushing weight she had carried release from her spirit. In this loving presence, Sarah realized she felt safe for the first time in her life. She opened up to him about the things she had been accused of that she had not done, and the pain she felt when nobody believed her.

"I believe you," he said.

She began going through the rest of her thoughts in the freedom of his comfort and safety.

"I wish I were beautiful."

"You are," he said reassuringly.

With each answer, Sarah felt joy filling her spirit until she thought she would burst.

"I wish I was perfect."

As someone who had suffered abuse for not measuring up, Sarah always thought perfection was the only way to be accepted and loved. She feared God would be mad at her, too, because she wasn't perfect.

She heard, "You are. . . . There is nothing you could do that could ever change the way God feels about you. . . . God loves [you]."

"He does?" she asked, astonished.

"Yes, he does," the voice said gently.

"I wish I was special, like the people in the Bible."

"You are."

"Really? I am?" Sarah couldn't imagine holding so much value to anyone, and each reassuring reply was healing her wounded soul.

"Yes, you are," he said.

Sarah shared that every molecule in her body was "bursting with LOVE and BLISS" from the overwhelming joy she was feeling. Then she suddenly exclaimed, "I just want to be with God. I just want to be with you!" As she turned around, what she saw took her breath away:

> There before me was the most BEAUTIFUL man I have ever seen in my whole life! . . . His eyes were wide with excitement and overflowing with LOVE and JOY. . . . There is no living person to ever exist that could match the BEAUTY of Jesus Christ. He was perfect in every sense of the word. He ran to me, and me to him. He embraced me and held me so close.[11]

Sarah's NDE reminds us that God's love for us is real, even when we don't feel it in our broken, hurtful world. We often assume that if God truly loves us, he will stop people from doing harmful things. God promises in Scripture that he will—all of this is temporary. He will stop the evil, but not yet, because of the law of love.

THE LAW OF LOVE

God's story consistently tells of the greatest love we could imagine. And yet, it is also a story in which people ignore God and follow their own ways instead. God pursues us in his love, but we turn from God, thinking, *I know best. I'm right. My will be done.* And we easily believe lies about God and ourselves because of the evils around us. The book of Genesis reads like the story of a parent with unruly children who grow up to become rebellious, dangerously out-of-control teens. Because of this, God lays down the law.

When God gave Moses and the Israelites the Ten Commandments around 1500 BCE, he appeared to the Israelites as a brilliant burning light. Moses reminds them, "At the mountain [Sinai] the LORD spoke to you face to face from the heart of the fire. I stood as an intermediary between you and the LORD, for you were afraid of the fire and did not want to approach the mountain" (Deuteronomy 5:4-5). Through Moses, God reiterates that he does not force his ways on people. We must choose to walk with him in loving trust. And loving trust is what God wants most:

> Hear, O Israel: The LORD our God, the LORD is one. Love the LORD your God with all your heart and with all your soul and with all your strength. These commandments that I give you today are to be on your hearts. Impress them on your children. Talk about them.
> DEUTERONOMY 6:4-7, NIV

This became the *Shema*, the creed of the Jewish people: Love God. The first four of the Ten Commandments are all about what it means to love God, and the next six are about loving people. This is the law of love. As we will see, these same basic commands (or moral laws) are found in all the world religions. But don't miss this: Before any current world religion was formalized, God revealed his love for humankind and his desire for us to freely love him back.

The story of God's love recorded in the Bible is also the story of a fallen humanity, which is why parts of it can be confusing. The Bible records an unflinching record of the brutal realities of human behavior when we turn from God's loving ways and go our own ways. This is why it's good to remember that *descriptions* of events in the Bible do not necessarily equal *prescriptions* for God's ideals.

God warned people about the consequences of a world created with the medium of free will. God says that our choices matter: "I have set before you life and death, blessings and curses. Now choose life, so that you and your children may live and that you may love the LORD your God, listen to his voice, and hold fast to him. For the LORD is your life" (Deuteronomy 30:19-20, NIV). This God of Light and Love is life—he desires to give you and me life, love, and blessings as we listen to his voice and follow his will and ways. But we have to be willing. Willingness is how we offer love back to God.

There is nothing we have to offer God except what he's given us—free will. God can lead us to love others with a God-sized kind of love, but only if we are willing. NDErs who have life reviews in God's presence consistently say, "Little acts of loving-kindness matter to God." God told Moses, "Do not seek revenge or bear a grudge . . . but love your neighbor as yourself. I am the LORD" (Leviticus 19:18, NIV).

Jesus took it even further, saying when we stand before God, he will say, "I was hungry, and you fed me. I was thirsty, and you gave me a drink. I was a stranger, and you invited me into your home. I was naked, and you gave me clothing. I was sick, and you cared for me. I was in prison, and you visited me" (Matthew 25:34-36).

And even though we may not think we did these things for God, he will say, "I tell you the truth, when you did it to one of the least of these my brothers and sisters, you were doing it to me!" (Matthew 25:40). This is the law of love. Loving others *is* loving God, something many NDErs come to understand, especially when their experience includes a life review.

Erica McKenzie grew up being bullied. It started in kindergarten when her teacher picked on her for being left-handed. From first to third grade, her peers teased her for attending special education classes to help her with dyslexia. However, the brunt of the bullying focused on her appearance. She followed Jesus from an early age, but in her teen years, she struggled with an eating disorder that later led to an addiction to diet pills.

After years of battle, her heart began to crash one day when she was alone in a hotel. As a registered nurse, she knew death was lurking. Crying out for God's mercy and forgiveness, Erica ran out into the street, forcing a car to slam on the brakes, almost hitting her. Suddenly, Erica heard in her mind, *"Get in the car, now!"* She also heard the name *"Rodolfo,"* followed by a message she felt compelled to relay to the driver. God in his mercy was guiding her.

Erica pleaded for help, saying, "Rodolfo, . . . God knows you are a Christian man; he sees your heart and he has heard all of your prayers . . . for your family in Mexico, one of which is suffering with cancer." The driver was indeed named Rodolfo, and his eyes filled with tears, stunned by what Erica had said. How could this woman know his name or anything about his family? In shock, Rodolfo quickly drove Erica to his church, where the pastor called 911 and prayed for her just as her heart stopped.

> I went up and up, and I knew I was going to Heaven. It seemed as if I rose infinitely past the stars and farther into the all-encompassing light until I had finally reached the end of the tunnel. Once there, the most all-encompassing feeling of love overwhelmed me. My human words cannot accurately describe the enormity of the feeling that filled each cell in my body with more love than imaginable. This love was so tangible I could touch it. While I could not see a physical image, I distinguished this brilliant Presence as the voice I had heard all my life. It was the voice that told me to run [for help that night], it was the voice that knew Rodolfo's name. . . . It was God. This Presence was so powerful and intense.[12]

In God's presence, Erica saw a review of her life in two parts. First, she saw the memories of those things that gave her joy and are considered important to humanity. Then God gave her a second life review as she wore what she called "God-glasses" to see from God's perspective what matters most.

> I saw myself helping an elderly person with their groceries, comforting a friend in need, saying something kind when others were mean, standing up for the unwanted, advocating

for those who couldn't find their voice, and being a patient listener to those who desperately needed to be heard. It was giving the homeless money when I didn't have money to give and putting others, often complete strangers, first over my own needs because my heart told me it was the right thing to do. It was having a huge heart for all animals, giving love to them, rescuing and caring for them in times of need. . . . I felt the immediate effect of my words, thoughts, and actions on others. A great majority of these things I did not remember I had done because they were mostly things I did when no one was looking. But God was looking. I understood in that moment that these things were displays of love, kindness, and compassion. They were the only things that mattered in God's eyes. They all required love. Love was the answer to everything![13]

God is love, and God loves all of us—every single person! Even the smallest ways we show love to others, expecting nothing in return, turn out to be some of the greatest ways we can love God. And this requires faith.

WHY FAITH MATTERS

Just as love matters to God, so does faith. Why? Because faith is the primary way we use our free will to love God. Scripture says, "It is impossible to please God without faith. Anyone who wants to come to him must believe that God exists and that he rewards those who sincerely seek him" (Hebrews 11:6). Throughout history, God reiterates that faith is what he wants.

Scripture says Abraham, who lived around 2000 BCE, "believed the Lord, and the Lord counted him as righteous *because of his faith*" (Genesis 15:6, emphasis added). The prophet Habakkuk around 600 BCE declares, "Look at the proud! They trust in themselves. . . . But the righteous will live by their *faithfulness to God*" (Habakkuk 2:4, emphasis added). In the first century CE, the apostle Paul says, "So we are made right with God *through faith* and not by obeying the law" (Romans 3:28, emphasis added).

But why faith? What is faith? Faith is not believing something without evidence, as people sometimes think. Faith involves trust, and that's what makes people right with God—they trust God. Faith and trust matter to God because they are foundational for love. You can't have a relationship without trust. Think about the faith required with a spouse. It's faith that keeps me and my wife, Kathy, married. We believe, trust, and have faith *in* each other and are faithful *to* each other. God wants us to have faith because God wants a relationship. And putting our trust in God is how we love him. Loving God happens only by faith.

The more you realize that God is the source of all love and that the love you've always longed for is ultimately found in God, the more you will want to seek God and trust him in faith. Nothing pleases God more. No other love compares to the love you are destined to experience when you trust in God.

Ron Smothermon uses the analogy of an ocean to describe the difference between human love and God's love.

Perhaps you have someone who loves you or whom you love. It may be the most magnificent love you've ever experienced. . . . You're waist-deep in the ocean and the waves are gentle. That would be human love. Now imagine a wall of seawater the height of a skyscraper appears. That's God's love. It is the love of which you've never dared to dream, and it is two-way. I love him so intensely because he loves me more than I could ever love.[14]

How do you imagine God? I hope you see there's never been anyone who has loved you more or could love you more than God does. As you grow in a trusting relationship with God, he can help you love others better. You can trust him because, as we will see, no one gets you better than he does.

THE PASSIONATE
COMPASSION OF GOD

SANTOSH, WHOM YOU MET IN CHAPTER 1, stood on a very high platform gazing over the most beautiful city he had ever seen. A massive walled city, like one of our modern cities, yet constructed of otherworldly materials. Surprised by his new telescopic vision, he could see for miles across a beautiful landscape inside the walls. It was a world bustling with life, angels, and people going about their business. He noticed how happy and peaceful all the people looked, and he felt he belonged there. He had never imagined such a gorgeous place existed.

Of course, Santosh never imagined life after death existed either, until he heard the nurse yell, "Code blue!" as his heart beat its last beat. He was shocked to find himself fully alive, the same analytical engineer he'd aways been, now looking down on his lifeless body. And then a brilliant light of divine love had come.

"I instantly fell in love with this Divine Light," Santosh says. The

Light took him to an amazing place that gave him a lofty vantage point to gaze on the city.

> I was following the Light and when He stopped, He stopped like the sun over this beautiful compound. I'm trying to figure out, what is this place? I could see the entire place is a square shape, same distance, mansion after mansion, just beautiful. Surrounding the city was a very high and very thick wall. A gorgeous wall. When I saw this compound, I fell in love with this place. I knew my purpose was to enter there. So, I was desperately trying to see if there was an entranceway. I could zoom in on anything a great distance away. As I looked around it, I saw these twelve beautiful gates, three on each wall. At each corner, thousands of miles apart, stood a magnificent, larger gate, with two additional gates spaced equal distances along each wall. It was like the entrance of ancient cities, but so much more spectacular. The gates were closed to me, they were not open. I became sad because I knew this was the ultimate goal of life—to enter that compound. Then I saw angels around the gates, and I knew they were protecting those gates. That's when I knew this was the Kingdom of Heaven.[1]
>
> Nothing in this world could ever come close to the beauty of this place. . . . The entire area inside the compound looked so peaceful and so calm that I instantly fell in love with this place. I kept thinking, "How do I get into this beautiful place? There has to be an Entrance somewhere. Where is the Entrance?"[2]
>
> I was standing on what seemed like a great platform, thousands of feet long, very high up, and overlooking this beautiful place. I had the thought, "Why am I standing up here on this platform that has no railings; what if I fall off? Where would I fall to?" And I looked to my left, and, down below, what I saw was a deep dungeon, [a] dark world that I would fall into—there was no light there. The place I was going to fall was a burning lake of fire.

I was very sad because I so wanted to enter this beautiful compound, but it was closed to me, and my only option seemed to be the darkness below. It was an abyss—I could tell there's no way out once I fall into it. At that moment, I sincerely wished I had an alternative. I looked to the center of this platform, and I saw that there were three steps, each seven feet high, like an altar, and on the top was a huge throne. And on this throne, it looked like somebody was sitting there.

When I looked, I saw the Lord Almighty. I didn't know who He was except that He was God. I didn't have to ask or find out; I knew this was Lord of everything, Lord of all. I looked at this face only once, but I could not look a second time because shame and guilt overcame me. I had committed so many sins and when I looked at Him, every sin I had ever committed was flashed before my eyes. I could not look at His face, and kept repeating, "Lord, please forgive me. Lord, please forgive me. I committed so many wrongdoings in my life; please forgive me." I was begging for His mercy, looking at His feet, and I was shaking. I knew this would be my end unless He had mercy, and I knew His mercy was all I had or it was that abyss. . . .

Then the Lord spoke to me in a deep authoritative voice, yet it had so much love and compassion. . . . He said, "I'm sending you back to the earth, but when I send you back, I want you to love your family and love your children." I was afraid, and I was thinking of the worst, but when He spoke, I could hear the tenderness, the mercy, and compassion in His voice.

When I was looking at His feet, on his left side [my right] I saw that there was a very narrow door, like a narrow gate, and that was the only gate open to me—that narrow gate. All others were closed, but this narrow door was open, and through it I could see [into] the Kingdom of Heaven. When the Lord appeared like this, He was a giant—He was a giant maybe seventy feet tall (but thirty-five to forty feet or so seated above me), so I could not go through that gate unless He said I could.

The Lord was going to send me back, so I got some courage and said, "Lord, when I go back, please tell me, which temple, which mosque, which church or synagogue do I go to?" That was all I knew—which religion do I choose; where do you want me to go? And the Lord did not respond. And I kept pleading, "Lord please tell me where I should join because when I go back, I'm going to be committing the same things over and over. But next time when you see me, I want to go through this narrow door here."

"I want an honest relationship," was His reply. "I want to see how true, how sincere, how honest you are with me, not just once a week, but every day, 365 days a year. How honest are you—that's the relationship I want."

I sincerely didn't understand, so I said, "Lord, I'm a simple man, please tell me what I must do so that next time you see me, I can walk through that door. Please give me some instructions."[3]

God had given Santosh a vision of the narrow gate open to him, but now he also gave a directive and five instructions:

[The] first directive was, "Love your family and love your children." That was mandatory; "You must love your family and love your children."

Then the first instruction was, "Always tell the truth." Always tell the truth has two meanings for me. First, don't lie. But second, tell the truth about what you are witnessing here in front, God's reality and the narrow door, and what you are seeing on your left, this abyss of darkness and lake of fire. And I knew he wanted me to share the truth with anyone about what he was showing me.

[The] second instruction was, "The wages of sin is death; from this day forward commit no more sins."

[In the] third instruction He said, "Surrender yourself completely—I should underline completely—in your daily life."

[The] fourth instruction [was], "Walk with Me." I did not understand what that meant, "Walk with me." I came from a different background; it made no sense. . . .

And the fifth instruction, "Always be kind to the poor; be generous to the poor. They need your help.". . . [And people] can be physically poor, spiritually poor, emotionally poor, as well as financially poor.

We talked for a long [time]; I don't know how long it was. . . . He asked me to write two books.* I said, "Lord, I've never written a book in my life." He said, "Don't worry, you *will* write two books."[4]

The Lord said, "Do not be afraid. I will be with you, and I will guide you." By then, I noticed that I was not feeling afraid of God anymore. To me, He was very kind, loving, and like a true friend with genuine concern for each and every one of us. I asked God a few more questions. He answered all of them.[5]

God sent Santosh back. The doctors were all amazed at how Santosh miraculously recovered from multiple terminal complications. But life as Santosh knew it had been upended.

I must admit to you that I was quite confused after my return from the Encounter with the Lord. Even though I wrote the two books as per His Instructions, I was continuously searching for the Truth. What are the meanings of all the things that I witnessed? How can I find their true answers? Where can I get them? I was desperately searching for their meanings. . . . I kept on praying and meditating upon the Lord daily. I also wondered often what was the reason for His grace upon me?

---

* Santosh did go on to write two books: *Code Blue 99: A Miraculous True Story!* and *The Light, The Truth, and The Way.* He then wrote a third book, which is a compilation of and reflection on the first two books, titled *My Encounter with Jesus at Heaven's Gates.*

I did not do anything special to deserve His Mercy. Yet, I felt all along that He loved me. He showed His Compassion to me. . . . Relentlessly, I prayed for His Guidance and asked Him to show me the Truth and the Way. And He did! He answered all my prayers. Thankfully, I found the Light that I was looking for, and, gradually, I found the meaning of everything that I witnessed and much more. Through His Grace, I found my true identity in Him.[6]

Santosh met a God he was not expecting, and in God's presence, with all his sins and failures exposed, he found love, care, mercy, and genuine compassion. I find that God does not often reveal his identity during an NDE, except with hints or clues, reminiscent of how Jesus taught in parables. He wants to know if we will seek to know him. The promise of Scripture is, "If you search for [God] with all your heart and soul, you will find him. . . . You will finally return to the LORD your God and listen to what he tells you. For the LORD your God is a merciful God" (Deuteronomy 4:29-31). Santosh had to seek before he discovered the meaning of all he saw and heard, but eventually he discovered this God of compassion has also revealed himself in history.

THE COMPASSIONATE GOD

People around the world who have NDEs describe this same God of Light, who is personal, relational, merciful, kind, and compassionate. When the God of Light revealed his identity to Moses, he declared himself to be, "Yahweh! The LORD! The God of compassion and mercy! . . . Filled with unfailing love and faithfulness" (Exodus 34:6).

Orthopaedic surgeon Dr. Mary Neal had an NDE when she was pinned in a kayak under a waterfall for thirty minutes. She was held by Jesus. When I asked her what he looked like, she said, "He looked like bottomless kindness and compassion." "How can anyone look like compassion?" I asked. "I know it doesn't make sense here on earth," she said, "but that's how he looked to me, like bottomless kindness and compassion."[7]

You were created for loving relationship with a God who has bottomless kindness and compassion *for you*. Bathed in God's love, all our loves deepen—his love becomes our love, and his compassion becomes our compassion. In fact, when you stop and think about it, all our human love and compassion is borrowed from God.

When my kids were little, I often went to their rooms to pray for them late at night as they were sleeping. As I watched their sweet little faces and their peaceful breathing, I thanked God for them. And as I thanked God, I felt overwhelmed with love for them. I remember one night, as I felt my heart would burst from the love and gratitude I had for my kids, I sensed God whispering to me, "I love you more!" The thought caught me off guard. I knew this was not something I was telling myself. I believed it was from God.

As the apostle John wrote, "We love each other because [God] loved us first" (1 John 4:19). All our loves are borrowed love. If you've ever felt love—pure, intense, self-sacrificing love, for another person or from another person—it came from God first. The same with compassion. The apostle Paul writes, "[God is] the Father of compassion and the God of all comfort, who comforts us in all our troubles, so that we can comfort those in any trouble with the comfort we ourselves receive from God" (2 Corinthians 1:3-4, NIV).

We are channels, or conduits, of God's loving compassion—and we can choose to either allow or block the flow of his love and compassion through us to others. We are not the source of our own love or compassion. In fact, everything good in life, all that we love, comes from our Maker and flows from him. So all of the love, all the compassion, all the kindness you feel on earth is an experience of God. This means that, ultimately, *God is what you and I desire most*. King David understood this: "Whom have I in heaven but you? I desire you more than anything on earth" (Psalm 73:25).

There is no one who loves you more, understands you better, or believes in you more than God. That's why the Bible uses every relational metaphor to describe the incredible love, compassion, and understanding God has toward you. Three of the most prominent metaphors the Bible uses for God are *parent, friend,* and *lover*. As you see how intimately God understands you and the compassion he feels for you, imagine how this could change the way you relate to him.

A Compassionate Parent

We mostly think of God from our own perspective. Why does God allow this to happen to *me*? Why doesn't God answer *my* prayer? Yet, throughout the pages of Scripture, God shows us how he feels relating to us. He reveals his parental care and compassion, as well as his parental heartbreak. When God speaks of Israel as his child, he's also speaking of each person he created to be his child (Romans 9:6-8). To the prophet Hosea, God says,

> When Israel was a child, I loved him, and I called my son out of Egypt. But the more I called to him, the farther he moved from me. . . . I myself taught Israel how to walk, leading him along by the hand. But he doesn't know or even care that it was I who took care of him. . . . I myself stooped to feed him.
>
> HOSEA 11:1-4

God likens himself to a doting parent. In vulnerability, God also wore his parental heart on his sleeve when he spoke of his desires to the prophet Jeremiah:

> I thought to myself, "I would love to treat you as my own children!" I wanted nothing more than to give you this beautiful land—the finest possession in the world. I looked forward to your calling me "Father," and I wanted you never to turn from me.
>
> JEREMIAH 3:19

God has the heart of a caring and compassionate parent. He wants to teach, develop, protect, and pour out good gifts on his children. And the Bible uses the metaphors of both father and mother to convey God's parental love and compassion for us.

THE COMPASSION OF A FATHER

Jesus explained that "God is Spirit" (John 4:24). God transcends gender. However, Jesus also called God "Father" and told us he is good—he's a *good* father. If your father turned away from God's model of fatherhood, it may be difficult for you to view God as "Father." But God's fatherhood can heal those wounds. Jesus taught, "If [your children] ask for a fish, do you give them a snake? Of course not! So if you sinful people know how to give good gifts to your children, how much more will your heavenly Father give good gifts to those who ask him" (Matthew 7:10-11).

Kaline Fernandes, a civil engineer in Brazil,* experienced God's fatherly love when she died of acute appendicitis. She felt perfect peace in her NDE and didn't want to go back to her life on earth. She describes arriving in a clear, nondescript room and hearing a male voice speak to her telepathically. "I knew it was a voice superior to me, like a parent. The voice of a person I had to respect. I had to obey. . . . [He told me] he gave life, and he also took it away, and he decided . . . it was not my time." She knew instinctively this was God.

> The place brought me a lot of peace, but I was interested in him, not the place. He was what I wanted. . . . I wanted to stay, and I wanted to see; I wanted to know who was talking to me . . . that he understood my anxiety to see him. He understood that on earth I didn't feel peace.
>
> I was feeling many afflictions [and] I was having a lot of trouble . . . but [He] wouldn't allow me to die yet. . . . [He said,] "You're not in your body anymore, but you need to go back. I know you don't want to, but did you see that it's you there [on the operating table]?"[8]

Kaline said, "I'm very stubborn." She did not want to leave. He explained again, "It's your mother and your daughter; they need you still." He felt like a father, even though I did not see him. He was like a gentle, kind father, who, after reasoning with his daughter, finally demanded, "Okay, if you're not going willingly, you're going pushed."[9]

---

* This interview was in Portuguese so some of the tone may be lost in translation.

Kaline said, "It was . . . both hands, pushing my [spirit] back to my body onto the operating table." And she was back in her physical body, hearing the anesthesiologist say, "Kaline, come back." Still, Kaline resisted, "Why did you make me come back? I didn't want to go back." God said to her, "Look, at the most critical moment I stayed with you; when you didn't understand I explained to you. Now you are where you are supposed to be [in your body]."[10] Kaline experienced the kind, gentle, yet firm love of a Father who promised to be with her.

THE MOTHERLY HEART OF GOD

The Bible also reveals God's nature to be like that of a mother who would never abandon her child, no matter what. When his people said, "The LORD has deserted us; the Lord has forgotten us," God responded through the prophet Isaiah: "Never! Can a mother forget her nursing child? Can she feel no love for the child she has borne? But even if that were possible, I would not forget you! See, I have written your name on the palms of my hands" (Isaiah 49:14-16). Everything about you is precious to God, your identity is permanently tattooed on his hands. You are God's beloved, one-of-a-kind child.

God has a mother's nurturing, protective instinct for you and me. The prophet Isaiah wrote, "For this is what the LORD says: . . . 'As a mother comforts her child, so will I comfort you'" (Isaiah 66:12-13, NIV). Jesus used another maternal image to describe his love and compassion when he said of those who had rejected him, "How often I have wanted to gather your children together as a hen protects her chicks beneath her wings, but you wouldn't let me" (Luke 13:34). And many NDErs experience this same maternal compassion of God.

Micki had suffered many heartaches in life and thought her marriage was ending. She despaired, thinking no one really cared for her—until she had an NDE. As she floated over the top of her bed, looking down on her lifeless body, she knew she was dead. She found herself being pulled through a tunnel until she was standing in front of a beautiful wrought iron Victorian gate, covered in brilliant-colored flowers, six times larger than she'd ever seen. Just before she placed her hand on the gate to enter in, she heard a voice speak to her in her mind and she turned to look to her left:

There stood Jesus Christ. I could see his nail prints in his hands and feet. . . . I ran to him and wrapped my arms around his feet, kissing his feet, and telling him how much I loved him. His arms came down and he held my head close to him as I cried hard.[11]

Micki was moved to tears of love and joy in the presence of Jesus. After being immersed in his physical embrace, Micki saw a brilliant light shining down from a throne high above her, and she knew this was God. God also responded with a tender, maternal love when he said her time had not yet come and she had to go back.

God then spoke mentally to me and told me how much he loved me. . . . [I] fell to my knees, begging him not to send me back. . . . I suddenly felt God's arms come down . . . and he lifted me off my feet and cradled me as a mother cradles her baby against her breast. He rocked me and held me in his arms.[12]

The Lord gently put Micki back on her feet and told her she had to go back because children were going to be born to her. The doctors had told her she could never have children. When she opened her eyes, her husband was on his knees praying to God to bring her back to him. Micki's marriage healed, and she did have children just as God had promised.

If it seems hard to believe that God would care for you as tenderly as God cared for Micki, ask yourself why. Why might you imagine God's compassion to be any less tender, nurturing, or comforting than that of a loving mother? God is a compassionate parent, but he also tells us he's an understanding friend.

A Compassionate Friend

We all long for a best friend, someone who knows everything about us—the good and the bad—and still stands with us in loving solidarity. What's truly amazing is that God wants to be that kind of trusted best friend to each of us, if we will let him. No one knows us better. No one can be trusted more. We can come to him with all our burdens and worries, any time of day or night because he says, "I am the one who answers your prayers and cares for you" (Hosea 14:8). That's the kind of honest, intimate, twenty-four seven, 365-days-a-year relationship God wants with us. King David expressed his amazement at this aspect of God when he wrote:

> O LORD, you have examined my heart and know everything about me. You know when I sit down or stand up. You know my thoughts even when I'm far away. . . . You know everything I do. You know what I am going to say even before I say it, LORD. You go before me and follow me. You place your hand of blessing on my head. . . . You saw me before I was born. Every day of my life was recorded in your book. Every moment was laid out before a single day had passed.
>
> PSALM 139:1-5, 16

God revealed this same intimate knowledge to the prophet Jeremiah: "I knew you before I formed you in your mother's womb. Before you were born I set you apart . . . . I, the LORD, search all hearts and examine secret motives (Jeremiah 1:5; 17:10). God knows everything—even our motives—which sometimes we don't even understand ourselves.

Jesus promised that God knows and cares about us: "Not one [sparrow] will fall to the ground outside your Father's care. And even the very hairs of your head are all numbered. So don't be afraid; you are worth more than many sparrows" (Matthew 10:29-31, NIV). God knows you better than you know yourself (unless you know how many hairs you have—or had!), and God values you more than you can imagine.

God understands us fully, and he is merciful and compassionate, even to those who don't yet know him. In her NDE, Deborah discovered she had a best friend she had never known.

Now I learned [this being of light] knew me. It knew me in all I was, in all my life, in all my truth. I could not hide anything from it. I had no desire to hide anything. I felt no fear or shame that it "saw" all of me. Then it dawned on me. I got the first hint of truly understanding the meaning of the word *grace*.

That being knew all of everything I ever was and loved me. Not just loved me but everything that defined me as myself, unique from any other bit of creation, was wonderful to [this being]. . . . It didn't want to love me like a pet or a possession; it wanted to love WITH me, like a friend. . . . I was desired as a personal, loving friend. To love like that, I had to really know it, all of it. That is what it showed me. . . . I loved it, but it had loved me first.[13]

Deborah was sent back, but she now realized the great worth she had to this compassionate best friend. It changed her view of herself. Years later, her husband encouraged her to read the Bible, where she discovered her friend's identity. She wrote her story, saying, "I am doing this for the man who brought me back to Jesus."[14]

We can't hide, and we don't need to hide, because God is the best friend we could ever imagine. And to experience the joy of that friendship, God invites us to freely share with him all of who we are and to choose to be his friend by getting to know him better.

God called Abraham his friend, but it wasn't because Abraham never sinned. In fact, he struggled and failed many times. And yet, God refers to him as "Abraham my friend" (Isaiah 41:8). Why would God call Abraham a friend? Because Abraham trusted God in faith.

The apostle James writes, "'Abraham believed God, and God counted him as righteous because of his faith.' He was even called the friend of God" (James 2:23). That's how we become friends with God—we walk with God daily, trusting him in faith. And when we fail, we fail forward with God, and God helps us grow into the people we were intended to be.

Moses is another person the Bible characterizes as a friend of God: "The Lord would speak to Moses face to face, as one speaks to a friend"

(Exodus 33:11). Jesus also told his disciples: "You are my friends if you do what I command. I no longer call you servants, because a servant does not know his master's business. Instead, I have called you friends, for everything that I learned from my Father I have made known to you" (John 15:14-15, NIV).

Friendship with God, walking with him by faith, is how we grow up into spiritually mature adults. We become people who do right things not out of religious obligation—to prove we are good—but out of the desire to love and please God. Because God loves us more than the most caring parent, more than a best friend, and even more than a lover or spouse.

A Compassionate Lover

Maybe the most surprising analogy of how God feels about us is that of a lover to the beloved. The union God desires with you is greater than any earthly oneness, surpassing the depth of relational ecstasy even of the most intimate marriage. Hard to believe? Feel strange to think about? NDErs confirm it. Remember—all we experience on earth is a reflection of God's eternal reality—this life is just a temporary shadow of a greater reality God intends for us to enjoy with him and with each other forever!

God called the prophet Hosea to enact a dramatic and prophetic show-and-tell of God's crazy love for us, even when we are unfaithful to him. He instructed Hosea to take Gomer as his wife, and when she cheated on him again and again, God told him to forgive her and take her back. Then he elucidated his ultimate desire for our faithfulness: "'When that day comes,' says the LORD, 'you will call me "my husband" instead of "my master." . . . I will make you my wife forever, showing you righteousness and justice, unfailing love and compassion. I will be faithful to you and make you mine, and you will finally know me as the LORD'" (Hosea 2:16, 19-20).

God reiterated this same desire years later when he said to Isaiah, "As a young man marries a young woman, so will your Builder marry you; as a bridegroom rejoices over his bride, so will your God rejoice over you" (Isaiah 62:5, NIV). And NDEs tell us this is more than metaphor.

After Bibi Tahereh had her heart attack in Tehran, she constantly longed for the God of love she had met. In her NDE, he told her, "I AM HE WHO IS." When she encountered the same God again in a vision, she knew he was Jesus. He picked her up and she touched his face. "I started kissing his face, and I felt complete. He put me down, and I kept asking him not to put me down; he is everything I've ever wanted."[15] He smiled at her and encouraged her. "You're so persistent," he laughed as he picked her up in his arms again. Suddenly, off they flew.

> There was so much glory coming from his face, it was like a river. I felt like he was like a lover; I just wanted to be with him forever. He was holding me, and it was like I was in him—it was so deep. It was like [we were] united, one—he was in me, and I was in him. It was what I was searching for my entire life. I thought doing good religious work in Islam would get me there, but it never happened. But I found all I was looking for in him.[16]

And it's not just women, but men, too, who experience this ecstatic oneness with God, who is neither male nor female but more than both. Wayne Fowler is an aerospace engineer and lawyer in Australia who had a horribly painful heart attack. When I interviewed Wayne about his NDE, he described his encounter with God with great emotion, recalling what he experienced when he emerged from a tunnel.

> Into his presence, brighter than ten thousand suns—and I'm transfixed! It is awesomely beautiful. And I can see down into this light. At the center is the form of a man, arms outstretched towards me, like to welcome me and to hug me. At that moment, I entered, I merged with the light, and the light merged with me. Like when Jesus said, I am in you, and you in me [John 17:21]. I was like a glass container being filled up, filled up, filled up with him. And I was experiencing the most ecstatic love. It was bliss beyond belief, rapture beyond reason, ecstasy beyond explanation—love times a billion—but

our word *love* fails so badly. Imagine every loving relationship combined all together, then blow them up billions of times all of that.

I'm feeling more and more until I thought, *I'm going to explode*, and when I had that thought, it started to subside slightly. And I realized, he heard my thoughts, and I said, *"No!* Don't stop; give me all you've got!" And I heard him chuckle. He thought that was funny, and he began to increase the outpouring of his love. And I know who this is—this is Jesus, the one I gave my life to the week before this [NDE] happened.[17]

God loves us passionately—more than the most passionate couple loves each other. But if God loves us so passionately—as a parent, a friend, and a lover—we have to wonder, why does he often seem to hide? Why does he ask us to seek him so diligently and then show up in ways that seem obscure or mysterious? As I've wrestled with these questions, I've concluded that our relationship with God while we're on earth is something like an engaged couple living in separate cities—we long for the day we will be united as one, but that day is yet to come. God wants to know, "Will your heart grow cold or stay faithful? Will you read the messages I send, or get busy and forget about me?" But he also promises, if you seek him with all your heart, you will find him (Jeremiah 29:13).

SEEK AND YOU WILL FIND HIM

Santosh kept praying and searching for God with all his heart, trying to find answers to his questions: Who is this God of loving compassion? What does the mystery of the narrow gate mean? Why was the narrow door the only door he could go through to enter the Kingdom of Heaven? After two years of praying and seeking, he finally found what he was looking for.

When Santosh's daughter was invited to sing in an Easter choir at her friend's church, Santosh and his wife attended the service. "I immediately felt His presence, the presence of the very same Mighty Giant of Pure Light," Santosh recalls. "That day, the pastor was preaching a sermon as if he was talking to me. The sermon was on the narrow gate. He explained Jesus' words: 'Everyone who seeks, finds. And to everyone who knocks, the door will be opened.' Jesus said, 'You can enter God's Kingdom only through the narrow gate. The highway to hell is broad, and its gate is wide for the many who choose that way'" (Matthew 7:8, 13). Santosh was riveted as the pastor explained how Jesus is the gate and calls us his sheep:

> I tell you the truth, I am the gate for the sheep. All who came before me were thieves and robbers. But the true sheep did not listen to them. Yes, I am the gate. Those who come in through me will be saved. They will come and go freely and will find good pastures. The thief's purpose is to steal and kill and destroy. My purpose is to give them a rich and satisfying life. I am the good shepherd. The good shepherd sacrifices his life for the sheep.
>
> JOHN 10:7-11

"I went back and read about it in the Bible," Santosh says. "I came back week after week, learning. And I started reading the Bible. I realized that [He] was none other than Jesus Christ [whom] I met in Heaven. Jesus is the one we can meet in the human form of God. And I realized God *is* love—that's what I experienced, and it's what I read in the Bible."[18]

Santosh gave his life to Jesus. He also discovered that the heavenly compound and even the lake of fire he'd seen in his NDE were also described by John, one of Jesus' disciples, who was taken to see the same city of God. John was brought up on a "great, high mountain" overlooking the city (Revelation 21:10), yet he could read the names on the gates, apparently with telescopic vision, just like Santosh experienced. John describes the same square, walled city, which Santosh knew was home.

> The city wall was broad and high, with twelve gates guarded by twelve angels. And the names of the twelve tribes of Israel were

written on the gates. There were three gates on each side—east, north, south, and west. The wall of the city had twelve foundation stones, and on them were written the names of the twelve apostles of the Lamb [Jesus]. The angel who talked to me held in his hand a gold measuring stick to measure the city, its gates, and its wall. When he measured it, he found it was a square, as wide as it was long. In fact, its length and width and height were each 1,400 miles. Then he measured the walls and found them to be 216 feet thick.[19]

REVELATION 21:12-17

John also wrote, "I heard a loud shout from the throne, saying, 'Look, God's home is now among his people! He will live with them, and they will be his people. God himself will be with them. . . . For the time has come for the wedding feast of the Lamb [Jesus], and his bride has prepared herself" (Revelation 21:3, 19:7).

The Bible is the ultimate love story—from the Genesis Creation of new love to humanity's unfaithfulness and betrayal; from God pursuing us and sacrificing himself to win back his beloved; to the final eternal wedding when God unites forever with those who love him. In the meantime, God has compassion on you and me. He gets you, he knows you, he understands how difficult this life can be, and he wants to help you through it. Do you imagine God that way? He wants to lead you to a fulfilling life of purpose and joy. But in order for that to even be possible, the passionate love of God and the justice of God had to meet. That was a day long foretold in history.

6

THE HIDDEN JUSTICE
OF GOD

SEVEN-YEAR-OLD MELANIE LOVED being in her babysitter's home, just down the street from her house in Calgary, Alberta. When her babysitter's family moved, Melanie felt terribly sad, since she loved the family like her own. Losing her babysitter left Melanie lonely—and vulnerable. After she noticed activity going on over at the babysitter's former house, precocious little Melanie marched right over and knocked on the door. When a man named Rodger* opened the door, she said, "Hi, I'm Melanie. What's your name?" Rodger invited her in and explained he had just moved from New Zealand.

Melanie recalls, "I continued to visit Rodger and the men who lived with him. Rodger gave me lots of attention. He was fun, and he wrestled and tickled me, and I really liked him. I trusted him." Innocent seven-year-old Melanie could not have known this taxi driver from New Zealand was actually a pedophile, grooming her.

---

* Rodger is a pseudonym.

One day I remember he made me toast with jam, and he made a great deal of it. I remember he said you had to put the jam right to the edges. The jam must have been drugged, because the next thing I remember, I was up in his room with another man. I was wearing a pretty dress. I remember saying, "Oh, this dress is so pretty. Can I take it home to show my parents?"

"No!" they both exclaimed emphatically. It was a negligee, but I didn't know that. They were both kneeling in front of me.[1]

The abuse that followed was a horror that brought Melanie to the edge of death. Mercifully, God took her out of her body and comforted her. "What I remember was being up above in the dark," Melanie recalls, "looking down at two men discussing whether I would live or die." As Melanie's spirit floated up above the scene, she suddenly realized Jesus was standing beside her.

I really knew nothing about Jesus except what my babysitter told me. My parents had not taken me to church. But I intuitively knew exactly who this was: This was Jesus, and in his presence, I felt safe and loved. I had been scared in the dark, hearing the men talk about whether I should live or die, but now with Jesus I felt safe. He said to me, "Don't worry. You're going to be okay." And it felt like he infused me with a peace or protection of his love, because I went right back to being that happy little girl.

Sadly, what happened is I was brutally raped. Before I left, Rodger told me, "If you say anything to your mommy or daddy about today, your daddy is going to kill me, and then he will go to jail, and you'll never see your daddy again." I never told my dad.[2]

Several days after this horrific event, a friend invited Melanie to her church. In Sunday school, they explained that Jesus came and died in order to forgive us all and guide us through life. "If any of you want to let Jesus in your heart, raise your hand," the teacher said. Melanie jumped up, hand in the air. Jesus was wonderful—she knew him—the one who loved her most; of course she wanted him in her life.

A nice couple started taking Melanie to church with them for the next seven years. During that time, Melanie heard a verse that struck her, and she memorized it, "Even though I walk through the valley of the shadow of death, I will fear no evil, for you are with me" (Psalm 23:4 ESV). When she got older, she tried to press charges to protect other children, but international law did not allow it. God had protected her mind and soul as a child, but the trauma had to be dealt with as Melanie became a young adult.

> I battled sexual compulsions constantly growing up, but I didn't know why. It started the day of the rape, along with horrible thoughts that would invade my mind. I was in therapy in my twenties, and I had been praying for God to heal me, when one night I had a vivid dream. God spoke to me in the dream. Jesus said, "Come with me." First, he brought me into the house where the abuse happened. As we were passing in the hallway, there was a man in a chair with drug paraphernalia on the armchair, and he was high. Looking forward on my left was the entrance to a bedroom, and there was a bright light shining out of it. Jesus said, "Yes, you were hurt in there, but you will never remember! *I covered you.*" Then in the vivid dream, God showed me that in the spiritual realm, the men who raped me were held hostage by a powerful demon and just as much victims of evil as I had been, and he wanted all of us set free.[3]

After years of spiritual growth, professional therapy, and healing, Melanie finally felt free. Decades after the incident, she came across Rodger's email. Although reaching out to an abuser can be dangerous and is not advisable without counsel from a professional, Melanie wanted justice. She wanted God's justice—that Rodger would be set free of the evil that harmed her as a child.

I told him how Jesus had died to pay for our sins—to forgive us all for our wrongs. I told Rodger that Jesus loves him, and that he will heal Rodger and set him free, just like he had done for me. A few years later, Rodger [emailed and] thanked me and told me he had accepted Christ as his Savior and was now following Jesus. He asked me if I would I forgive him for hurting me. I said, "Of course."[4]

Melanie's forgiveness offered to her perpetrator can only be explained as supernatural, not what people naturally do nor would be expected to do. When Melanie first told me the story, I felt intense emotion, thinking how I might feel if what happened to her had happened to my own daughter. I would want justice *my way*. She believes God wanted her to forgive, for her own sake, but also for God's justice to be done—for evil to be conquered in Rodger's life. Although Rodger would have a long way to go to become the man God intended him to be, that's how God's hidden justice works—overcoming evil from the inside out.

GOD'S LOVE IS JUST

Try to imagine just for a moment that you are God and love is the motive for everything you do. You passionately love every single person—more than any human parent, friend, or lover ever could. You would do anything to love, comfort, guide, and protect each person. Your goal is to create a loving family forever. But there is more to the story. As God, you are not only love, but also *justice* and *righteousness*. Your ways are right and just and good—they are truth, and the way reality works. Which means you can't turn a blind eye to sin and evil.

Remember God's self-declaration to Moses?

Yahweh! The LORD! The God of compassion and mercy! . . . Filled with unfailing love and faithfulness. I lavish unfailing love to a thousand generations. I forgive iniquity, rebellion, and sin. But I do not excuse the guilty.

EXODUS 34:6-7

Because he is a God of *justice*, God cannot excuse, ignore, or "wink" at sin or evil.

We demand justice be done whenever we are wronged or when we hear of horrific abuse, such as what happened to Melanie. Our innate desire for justice comes from God. Can you imagine the evil God sees daily across the globe? The prophet Hosea captured a snapshot of that when he wrote, "Hear the word of the LORD, you Israelites, . . . 'There is no faithfulness, no love, no acknowledgment of God in the land. There is only cursing, lying and murder, stealing and adultery; they break all bounds, and bloodshed follows bloodshed'" (Hosea 4:1-2, NIV). God has witnessed and continues to witness every single act of evil ever committed. It angers God, and his love demands justice.

When we witness or experience a wrong, we often accuse God of not bringing justice swiftly enough. But we also need to consider what God's swift justice might mean for *us*. What if God brought instant justice, not just to those who we think deserve it, but to every single root of evil, no matter how small, including our own. Who could survive God's justice? The apostle James writes, "Wherever there is jealousy and selfish ambition, there you will find disorder and evil of every kind" (James 3:16). Selfish ambition, self-will, doing it "my way," is the root of all evil—and we're all guilty of it.

If you have ever wondered how God feels about all the evils humans do to each other, read the Old Testament prophets. Over and over, God pleads and warns, "O people . . . change your hearts before the LORD, or my anger will burn like an unquenchable fire because of all your sins" (Jeremiah 4:4). God doesn't pull punches when it comes to evil. But it's God's love that motivates his passion for justice. King David declares, "Your righteousness is like the mighty mountains, your justice like the ocean depths. You care for people and animals alike, O LORD" (Psalm 36:6). God's anger is a temporary response when the people he passionately cares for abuse and harm themselves and one another and his creation.

When Dr. Ron Smothermon had an explosive download of God's attributes during his NDE, he "knew [God] was the righteous judge—pure, correct, and humble. . . . Like if you were accused of something, you would want this judge because he would be perfect and right, and you'd be happy to be judged by him. In his presence everything is clear—it's so clear."[5] Many other NDErs report similar things, saying essentially, "There's no hiding from the truth—it's all right there in the open, no debating."

GOD IS GOOD

Let's go back to imagining that you are God for a moment. Because you are just, all wrongs must be made right. You're not like humans who live in the gray twilight of both good and evil; you are wholly *good*. "Only God is truly good," Jesus declared (Mark 10:18). You are the source of all good. The only thing that exists apart from you *is* evil. And hell is the place where you choose to stay out. Hell is where you give free-willed creatures what they demand when they don't want your love or leadership. Can you imagine how God feels?

It breaks God's heart to be separated from those he loves, but the just payment for rejecting God is giving people what they want— separation from God. And separation from God is death—not just physical death, but spiritual death—the "second death" described in Revelation 21:8. The apostle Paul put it simply, "For the wages of sin is death" (Romans 6:23), which is to be separated from God's love, light, and life. That's why God warns, pleads, and even begs us to admit our rebellion and just come home.

> "My faithless people, come home to me again, for I am
> merciful. I will not be angry with you forever. Only
> acknowledge your guilt. Admit that you rebelled against the
> LORD your God and committed adultery against him. . . .
> Confess that you refused to listen to my voice. I, the LORD,
> have spoken!
>   Return home, you wayward children," says the LORD. . . .
>   "But you have been unfaithful to me, you people of Israel!
> You have been like a faithless wife who leaves her husband. . . ."

For they have chosen crooked paths and have forgotten the
LORD their God.

"My wayward children," says the LORD, "come back to me,
and I will heal your wayward hearts."

JEREMIAH 3:12-14, 20-22

When we reject his love and guidance, God feels the intense heartache of a betrayed spouse or a parent with self-destructive teenagers.
During her NDE, Erica, the nurse who was introduced in chapter 4,
was shown God's intense sadness over any person who rejects him.

> Until now, I'd only felt the most overwhelming, unconditional
> love in the presence of God. Yet, now I was overcome by some-
> thing else, a deep, aching sadness. The only thing on earth I
> could compare it to would be the death of a child. . . . I was
> feeling the death of a child multiplied millions of times over.
> It was then that I realized it was coming from God. I just had
> to know why He felt such deep sadness and pain. As soon as
> the thought entered my mind, He asked me who in my family
> believed in Him. . . . I thought about everyone in my family who
> believed in God and, strangely, I felt such relief that they did.[6]

Erica suddenly realized that God's great sadness came from losing his
children—those who had rejected his love on earth. After showing her
a vision of the earth consumed in flames with millions of souls shooting like stars from earth to heaven, he let her see the source of his grief.

> I could see millions of people left behind. Frantic, I turned
> back to God for an answer.
> "It's free will, Erica."
> "Free will?" I asked.
> "With the gift of life, I give you free will."
> "But why can't You save them? Don't You love them too?"
> "I love all of My children," God said. "But I can't make
> them love Me back."[7]

After getting a distant view of the Kingdom of Heaven in God's presence, Erica found herself on the edge of hell. According to one study, hellish NDEs are reported by 23 percent of NDErs.[8] A more recent study across thirty-five countries found hellish NDEs are even more prevalent.[9] We cannot take the heavenly NDEs without also making sense of the hellish ones.*

It's important to note that at times God seems to give NDErs a glimpse of hell's reality, but that does not mean hell is their eternal destination. In the same way, God also gives some people who have rejected him a view of himself and heaven, possibly in the hope they will choose to love and follow him, but not all do.[10] Given this, NDEs appear to be for our instruction as well. God told Santosh he must tell others the truth about *all* he saw—heaven and hell. I've also noticed that many NDErs who cry out for God to save them at the last second first glimpse hell before God rescues them. Maybe this happens so they understand God's grace, or maybe so they can return to teach us that life apart from God *is* hell.

This is uncommon, but Erica also experienced a glimpse of hell after her wonderful experience with God.

> One moment I stood with God and the next . . . the absence
> of His unconditional love was obvious. This was Hell. . . .
> They were criticizing and judging each other. There were angry
> and jealous conversations, full of gossip and spitefulness. These
> conversations were the exact opposite of the unconditional
> love and acceptance that emanated from God. Along with the
> conversations came . . . the most extreme emotions of sadness,
> anger, hatred, loneliness, jealousy, self-loathing, unworthiness,
> and everything you can imagine that was negative. . . . I can't
> even find a human word to explain the degree of sheer terror
> I felt.[11]

As a Christian, Erica was in terror, hurt and confused as to why God would have her experience this hellish place of darkness and evil,

---

* To learn more about hellish NDEs, see *Imagine Heaven*, ch. 16, "What about Hell?"

with people devoid of God's light, love, and life—all of them victims or victimizers of one another. God then gave her a download of understanding. He wanted her to warn people and let them know what Jesus meant when he said, "It is not my heavenly Father's will that even one of these little ones should perish" (Matthew 18:14).

> God wanted me to see and understand the magnitude of what He was trying to explain in Heaven. . . . I received the knowledge that God did not put those people there. They put themselves there by choosing separation from God and His love. With the gift of free will, they chose separation from Him. After the unconditional love I felt from God, why would anyone want to be separate from it? . . . Once again, I felt the depth of God's sadness knowing He had to allow those souls to disconnect from Him.[12]

Free will is necessary for love, and rejecting God's love and guidance has real ramifications, because justice must be served. As Oxford professor C. S. Lewis wrote, "A man can't be *taken* to hell, or *sent* to hell: you can only get there on your own steam."[13] Hell is justice for the free-willed creature who demands God "stay out." As Lewis also stated, "The doors of hell are locked on the *inside*."[14] But God is good and God is love, so there exists in God a very real tension. His justice must allow the horrific consequences of rejecting God,[15] yet he loves us so passionately, he would do anything to have us with him eternally.

THE MORAL LAW

We get a snapshot of the tension that exists between God's love and his justice when God says to Moses, "I will certainly hide my face in that day because of all their wickedness" (Deuteronomy 31:18, NIV). This does not mean God turns a blind eye to evil, but he hides in the sense that he does allow the consequences of our choices against him to play out. He allows them to affect everything about life on earth in the hope that we will discover what's missing—God!

When commercial airline pilot Captain Dale Black died in a plane crash, he experienced the opposite of what feels "normal" to our world. He notes how much sin affects everything on earth—a stark contrast to heaven, where God's will perfectly rules.

> There was no strife, no competition, no sarcasm, no betrayal, no deception, no lies, no murders, no unfaithfulness, no disloyalty, nothing contrary to the light and life and love. . . . The absence of sin was something you could feel. . . . There was no need to hide, because there was nothing to hide from. It was all out in the open. . . . I had been in heaven for some time before I recognized sin's absence. Now I contemplated the one thing that *dominated everything* on earth.[16]

While God stays hidden in the sense that he allows sin's consequences to affect everything, he is also present and active behind the scenes, sustaining all things (Hebrews 1:3, NIV). He is the source of all good gifts (Acts 14:16-17). God is also present on earth (unlike in hell), lovingly holding back evil's full expression through moral law intended to protect us. While moral law can't change human hearts or make us want to do good, it can protect us and others from runaway evil—that's God's mercy.

When people say, "All religions basically say the same thing," they are usually referring to principles of moral law that all religions have in common. The apostle Paul affirmed this when he wrote, "Even Gentiles, who do not have God's written law, show that they know his law when they instinctively obey it, even without having heard it. They demonstrate that God's law is written in their hearts, for their own conscience and thoughts either accuse them or tell them they are doing right" (Romans 2:14-15). So it's no wonder this common moral law from God comes out in most all our religious writings.

C. S. Lewis was a literary scholar. He quotes numerous historical sources showing the common moral laws found in almost every ancient culture and world religion, which can be summarized as follows:

Don't do harm to another human by what you do or say (the Golden Rule).
Honor your father and mother.
Be kind toward brothers and sisters, children, and the elderly.
Do not have sex with another's spouse.
Be honest in all your dealings (don't steal).
Do not lie.
Care for those weaker or less fortunate.
Dying to self is the path to life.[17]

In just about every culture and religion since the beginning of recorded history, these principles reflect a commonly accepted moral law. So, it's reasonable to assume that human beings have always known or at least had some sense of right and wrong. But how well have we kept the moral law? Is the history of humanity a peaceful and loving one? No! Watch the news.

The history of humanity indicates we don't always honor parents, we fail to be kind to siblings and the elderly, we're sexually unfaithful, we are dishonest, untruthful, greedy, and only a few of us are involved with the less fortunate because we get so consumed with ourselves.

So, what do the world's religions teach us? We all know the right things to do—we always have—and yet, the history of humanity shows that we fall short of what we know to be right. The apostle Paul put it simply, "For everyone has sinned; we all fall short of God's glorious standard" (Romans 3:23). Whether we are Christians, Jews, Buddhists, Muslims, Hindus, Sikhs, atheists, or something else, we all have a sin problem. And we all desperately need God's help.

After discovering the truth of the narrow door, Santosh pondered all he had experienced in his NDE and the moral law he had learned growing up Hindu.

The Hindu heritage has a beautiful culture and tradition that goes back to the roots of the Indus Valley civilization tracing back to 4,000 BC. Growing up in that ancient but rich culture, I remember learning many values, not only from my parents, but also from neighbors. . . . Values such as honor your father and your mother; respect the elderly; respect your teachers; do not steal; do not tell lies against anyone; do not commit murders; do not commit adultery; do not be greedy to own other people's belongings. Those days I didn't have the slightest clue that these values, which I learned, were almost very identical to the Laws in the Ten Commandments, which God established through Moses. . . .

I found that my background was creating some confusion as well as dilemma for me. . . . As a Hindu, I grew up with the concept of the Heaven and the Hell. Also, I had the concept of the angels. But who is this Divine Giant Lord of Pure Light, whom I encountered? He is unlike any of the Hindu gods or goddesses that I have been familiar with. His face was brighter than the sun I know. His body was radiating with pure Light. His eyes were like blazing fire. I looked at His face once; then I had no courage to look at His face again. I was continuously looking at His feet and pleading for His Mercy. His feet were of shiny brass or bronze color.* Who is this Lord? I did not know Him; yet He knew me so well; He knew everything about me. . . .

Hindus also believe that God is all powerful and omnipresent, but He is beyond us to know Him personally. He is separate from His creation. Only He exists forever. Everything else is *Maya* or illusion. . . . Only through the repeated reincarnations, is it possible to achieve the ultimate liberations of the trapped souls to be united with the Great Soul. . . . The Hindu faith teaches that the Creator of the universe or Brahma is impersonal. Nobody gets to know Him personally. But, the Divine Giant of Pure Light, whom I encountered, I knew instantaneously that He was the Supreme Lord, the Creator of the universe. He was very personal to

---

* Santosh identically described the God seen by Daniel in Daniel 10:4-6 and by John in Revelation 1:12-15.

me. He knew everything about me. He knew all the things that I had done, both good and bad, even though I myself had forgotten some of them, but He didn't.

Another thing that created a dilemma for me was that He didn't send me to another cycle of reincarnation. When I was standing there before Him, I had only two options, either plunge on my left to the deep dungeon dark world with burning flames or be qualified to go through the very narrow door on his left that I witnessed. There were no other choices for me. . . . Often, I wonder, why did He have such mercy upon me? Why did He give me a second chance? I was not a sinless person. I committed many sins in my life. Since the wages of sin is death, I definitely deserved to be dead.[18]

Just as Santosh realized, the moral law we all share reveals only our failures, yet he encountered a God of mercy who offered grace rather than condemnation. Why?

RESOLVING THE TENSION

From the beginning, God told us how he would resolve the tension between his justice and his love. God's justice cannot tolerate evil and sin, but his parental love would do anything to save the children he created. God had given the moral law, but the law was limited—it could restrain evil (with painful consequences), but it could not change the human heart. The core problem of humanity was disconnecting from God, the Source. Without being reconciled to the source of love, light, and life, we could not become who God created us to be, because he created us for relationship with himself!

So, God decided to do what the law could not do—God himself would enter into humanity as our Messiah, our Savior. He would pay the price his justice demands to freely offer forgiveness and restoration to all willing people. God foretold this nearly seven hundred years before Jesus appeared, so we could know it's not just myth or fairytale. God revealed himself in a form we could relate to—God became one of us.

In the future [God] will honor Galilee. . . . The people walking
in darkness have seen a great light. . . . For to us a child is
born, to us a son is given, and the government will be on his
shoulders. And he will be called Wonderful Counselor, Mighty
God, Everlasting Father, Prince of Peace. Of the greatness of
his government and peace there will be no end. He will reign
on David's throne and over his kingdom, establishing and
upholding it with justice and righteousness from that time on
and forever. The zeal of the LORD Almighty will accomplish
this.

ISAIAH 9:1-2, 6-7, NIV

Again, Isaiah originally wrote this seven hundred years before Jesus
came, saying that the mighty God would be born a child, a son in the lineage of King David. He would live in Galilee and bring peace and justice
to humanity forever. Jesus was, in fact, born in the line of King David, and
he taught, healed, and performed most of his miracles in Galilee. Many
historical facts about Jesus have been verified even outside the Bible.* Of
course, skeptics may claim these prophecies about Jesus the Messiah were
added after Jesus came, but we have proof that was not the case.

BEDOUIN PROOF

In 1947, the year before Israel became a nation overnight (foretold by
Isaiah), three Bedouin shepherd boys were chasing a lost goat in the
mountains around the Dead Sea, thirteen miles east of Jerusalem. One
boy climbed up to a cave high in the desert mountain and threw a rock
inside, hoping to scare his goat out of hiding. He heard the rock crash
into something breakable. Fearful, but also curious if he might have
found a hidden treasure, the boy squeezed through a tiny opening and
lowered himself into a dark cave. Inside, he found *biblical* treasure!

The Qumran cave was filled with pottery, and well preserved inside
the sealed clay jars were 2,200-year-old parchment scrolls. He grabbed
three of the scrolls, scrambled down the mountain, and took the scrolls

---

* See Gary R. Habermas, *The Historical Jesus: Ancient Evidence for the Life of Christ* (Joplin, MO: College Press,
1996).

to Jerusalem to see if he could sell them to an antiquities dealer. In the ensuing years, archaeologists discovered a total of eleven caves containing around nine hundred texts. Preserved in what came to be called the Dead Sea Scrolls were copies of thirty-eight of the thirty-nine books of the Old Testament, most predating Jesus by hundreds of years. One scroll the Bedouin boy grabbed turned out to be a complete copy of the book of Isaiah. You can read the English translation of the Hebrew text online.[19] It reads almost identically to contemporary English translations of Isaiah based on other texts, even after two thousand years!

Scientists have radiocarbon dated the Isaiah scroll to between 335 BCE and 107 BCE. Paleographers dated this scroll at between 125 BCE and 100 BCE.[20] The Israel Museum, where the Great Isaiah Scroll resides, indicates the scroll was written around 100 BCE, at least 130 years before Jesus was crucified.[21]

Prior to this significant discovery, skeptics would claim the prophecies of Jesus were not written beforehand but edited into later copies by those who lived after Jesus. The Dead Sea Scrolls proved that theory false. Consider the English translation of the Isaiah Dead Sea Scroll, handwritten one hundred to three hundred years before Jesus was born, and what it clearly foretold. Isaiah said, first the Messiah would suffer for all our sins to bring justice God's way. The crucifixion of Jesus was given in detail *before* it happened:

> See, my servant [the Messiah] will prosper, and he will be
> exalted and lifted up, and will be very high. Just as many were
> astonished at you—so was he marred in his appearance, more
> than any human, and his form beyond that of the sons of
> humans—so will he startle many nations. Kings will shut their
> mouths at him. . . .
> Who has believed our message? And to whom has the arm
> of the LORD [Yahweh] been revealed? For he grew up before
> him like a tender plant. . . . He was despised and rejected by
> others, and a man of sorrows, and familiar with suffering.
> ISAIAH 52:13-15, 53:1-3, DEAD SEA SCROLL VERSION[22]

Notice several things Isaiah says: The Messiah would come as a suffering servant for all nations. He would not reveal all of God's majesty but would be like God's arm reaching into humanity. He would grow up among us as inconspicuously as a tiny plant. God's plan from the beginning has been to bless all nations—*all willing people* from every tribe, language, and ethnicity—through his Messiah. But he asks, "Who has believed our message? To whom has the LORD revealed his powerful arm?" (Isaiah 53:1). Isaiah also said that his appearance would be horribly marred and disfigured. Mel Gibson's movie *The Passion of the Christ* is rated "R" for sequences of graphic violence. It is truly hard to watch the torture that Jesus endured. But according to Isaiah, "so was *he marred* in his appearance, more than any human" (emphasis added). It was not only foretold, but accurate. He suffered and died for us all.

IMAM MEETS JESUS

Swidiq Kanana[23] grew up the son of a Muslim sheik in Rwanda. His mother considered herself a "witch" who could manipulate the supernatural world by the power of the African goddess Biheko. Swidiq became an Imam in his twenties, a leader in the mosque, and a gifted apologist for Islam. He would debate Christians openly in a forum called *muhadhara* (or "open air"). "[My] self-confidence and ability to project power . . . also served in defeating Christians in *muhadhara*," Swidiq recalls. "I loved the feeling of making a Christian look silly or confused or afraid."[24]

But all that changed when Swidiq had a mental breakdown. His mom took him to a witch doctor. Nothing helped. His father took him to a neuropsychiatric hospital in the capital city of Kigali. Diagnosed with a psychotic break, he was kept sedated in a mental hospital for months. The Muslim leaders came to do an exorcism. Nothing healed his mind. Almost a year after his mind snapped, his mother, desperate to help her son, reached out to the Christians at the Anglican church. The priest and church fasted and prayed for Swidiq, and on the seventh day, his mind was cured. "The conclusion was painfully obvious and also very confusing," Swidiq admits. "Were I to tell truly what I knew, that Jesus brings the power of God . . . I would run the risk of being silenced—physically and forever."[25]

After seven months of agonizing over wanting to know more about Jesus, yet afraid to, something happened. "I felt a tearing inside my abdomen. It seemed as if my organs were being pulled apart."[26] Swidiq was taken to the hospital in Gisenyi, and after extensive testing, the doctor gave the devastating news: Swidiq had an aggressive blood cancer; palliative care was all they could do.

> On the evening of February 27, about 8:00 p.m., I became terribly alert. A horrible sensation like nothing I had known was washing over me. . . . And then I went. I was gone from my body. Dying itself was not nearly so bad as the process leading up to it. It was very . . . seamless. Immediately, I seemed to fall down into an enclosed room. It was a room with no doors, but large windows lined one wall. As I looked, one of the windows opened by itself. From outside, from wherever or whatever was outside, four horrific figures stepped one at a time onto the sill and jumped down into the room. They were in the shape of men, each one wearing a long, black robe.[27]

Leading up to this hellish NDE, Swidiq's mother had been praying to Jesus. Jesus helped her son once; could he help him even facing death?

> The demon carrying the bucket and the one with the scythe set down their tools and attacked me, forcing me to the ground . . . the spirit with the axe stood over me, with one foot on my stomach . . . he lifted the axe high over his head. As I winced, the evil spirits suddenly stopped, and all looked towards the windows. Someone else had entered. Though I could not immediately see him come, I felt him enter just as they did. As I turned my head, I saw sandaled feet and a white robe. In the presence of this man, I completely forgot about the others, who fell back dismayed and then seemed to evaporate. I was captivated by him, totally uninterested in anything else but the sight of this person.

The one now standing in the room, wearing a long white

robe, looked just like the Jesus of *The Passion of the Christ*, the film by Mel Gibson. I had once gotten a deal for three American films dubbed in Kinyarwanda, and the first one in the lineup had been *The Passion*. Although I was a Muslim and had no interest in seeing the Jesus story, I had gone ahead to get my full money's worth. And now he stood there, looking at me. His face was serious and intent on me—the kind of expression that holds absolute authority—but the flicker of a smile or perhaps delight played across all his features. He stood a moment just looking at me. Whether it was just an instant or a long time, I don't really know. . . . At some point, he lifted his hands slightly, with palms up, revealing holes in each hand. Then he raised his right hand and gestured towards me. With lifted hand at last he spoke, clear and firm, "I died for man. And you are among those I died for. Do not deny it again. You must tell others. Reveal it." I am telling you in English, but Jesus spoke Kinyarwanda. Then he disappeared.[28]

Swidiq returned to his body. He pulled a sheet off his face, climbed off the table, then realized he was standing there wearing nothing but a loin cloth. He had been dead for over twelve hours, and a large gathering of Muslims was about to lay him in the grave. Swidiq recalls, "I began shouting, 'Jesus is here! Jesus is here! . . . He brought me back! It was Jesus who got me and brought me back!'" That was too much for this crowd of terrified Muslims. They began running hysterically in all directions.[29]

Swidiq became a follower of Jesus, and eventually an Anglican priest, which almost cost him his life many times. The passion of Jesus' love meeting the passion of God's justice changed him forever. Jesus truly came as the blessing for all nations.

THE SOLUTION

The problem with the world is we all think more about ourselves than we do about God or other people. We hide from God in fear and justify doing what we want until our consciences become hardened. This leads to all the world's worst problems. But what God did through his

Messiah is provide a solution to the world's core problem—he brought justice and restoration by bringing all willing people back to God. The Dead Sea Scrolls' version of Isaiah 53 says:

> Surely he has borne our sufferings, and carried our sorrows. . . .
> he was wounded for our transgressions, and he was crushed for
> our iniquities, and the punishment that made us whole was upon
> him, and by his bruises we are healed. All we like sheep have
> gone astray; we have turned, each of us, to his own way; and the
> LORD has laid on him the iniquity of us all. He was oppressed
> and he was afflicted, yet he did not open his mouth; like a lamb
> that is led to the slaughter. . . . From detention and judgment he
> was taken away—and who can even think about his descendants?
> For he was cut off from the land of the living. . . . Then they
> made his grave with the wicked, and with rich people his
> tomb. . . . Although you make his soul an offering for sin, and he
> will see his offspring [spiritual children], and he will prolong his
> days [resurrection], and the will of the LORD will triumph in his
> hand. Out of the suffering of his soul he will see light.
> ISAIAH 53:4-8, 10-11, DEAD SEA SCROLL VERSION[30]

Before Jesus was born, God foretold how his love and justice would meet. Jesus would die for our sins, but he would conquer sin and death by his resurrection.[31] And through him, we, too, can overcome evil and death. We ask, "Does God care? Does God understand? Why doesn't God do something about all the evils, all the sorrow, all the brokenness?" He says, "I did! I entered into your poverty. I experienced your pain. I felt your rejection. I bore your sorrow. I took on the condemnation for all your wrongs. I paid the price of justice to purchase your peace with God, and by my wounds you can be healed."

This is God's solution to overcoming evil. Instead of destroying every little root and seed of evil in his outward justice, and thereby destroying all the people he loves, he pays for justice himself. He patiently overcomes evil in sometimes hidden ways, one willing heart at a time.

Is your heart willing? That is all God requires to forgive and forever reconcile you to himself, the source of light and love. Then, as you are willing, he can lead you to forgive others and to become a wounded healer, even as Melanie did for Rodger, setting others free by the power of God's love.

One day, ultimate justice will come. Light and darkness will no longer coexist like on earth. Those who love the light will go to the light. Those who love the dark will go to the dark. In the meantime, God is working through you and me to bring light into this dark world.

THE UNWAVERING
FORGIVENESS OF GOD

DR. RAJIV PARTI WAS A CHIEF ANESTHESIOLOGIST and pain management specialist, a science-minded doctor himself, yet no doctors were willing to listen to his near-death experience. When we left off with his story in chapter 2, he was in a hospital recovery room following his own NDE that changed his mind about life after death. But it all began the night his wife rushed him to UCLA Medical Center.

Lying in the back seat of the car, Rajiv was bombarded with thoughts of how unlucky his life had become—he was prone to infection, diagnosed with cancer, and now experiencing depression. He hated to admit it, but he realized that he had become addicted to pain pills.[1] Regret overcame him as he thought of how materialistic, demanding, unloving, egotistical, and angry he'd become. His pride had caused him to deny the seriousness of his medical condition, and now he was at rock bottom, almost.

At the hospital, Rajiv was wheeled into emergency surgery for an infection spreading throughout his body cavity. Twelve minutes into surgery, Rajiv's consciousness began to rise out of his body, and he watched the glossy surface of the ER ceiling approaching. He observed the surgery and heard the crude joke the anesthesiologist told. He was somehow able to also observe his mother and sister having a conversation in India, halfway around the world, as if he could travel at the speed of thought. Then things changed.

> From there my consciousness traveled to different realms. The first realm it traveled to was a very hellish realm. It was pitch dark, there were thunderstorms, lightening, and very dark entities with crooked teeth running about.[2] . . .
>
> I could hear other souls crying and wailing. I was taken there kicking, too. I didn't want to be there, and it was smelling of burnt meat. And then I was wondering, *Why am I here, what have I done?*[3]

What imprinted in Rajiv's mind was *Naraka,* the Hindi word for hell. He thought, *What is my karma?*[4] He heard a voice inside,

> "You have lived a very loveless life." I had been mean. I wanted to get ahead in life no matter what it cost me. If I had to step on others' toes, I did not mind doing that. And I was not good to my patients. . . . A seventy-year-old lady came to my office for arthritis medicine. She wanted to talk to me because her husband was dying of lung cancer. . . . [But] I just wrote the prescription in two minutes and walked away. I treated her like a disease . . . not as a human being.[5]

Rajiv felt shame as he thought about these things and how verbally abusive he had become to his son. "There appeared to be no way out, but I prayed for one anyway. 'My God, give me another chance.'. . . I was praying and had repentance, and who showed up was my father."[6] As soon as Rajiv cried out for God to save him, his deceased father approached him. Rajiv's father had been very abusive toward him, and Rajiv had begun to treat his son the same way. Rajiv's father had been sent as a messenger, clearly knowing Rajiv was going back to earth: "Don't pass the anger to your sons," he said.[7] His father led him away from hell to a tunnel, through which he traveled to another realm of great light and beauty.

> [Once] outside the tunnel, it was very bright, and I was greeted by two very robust young men with wings behind them. Without talking to me, but telepathically, they told me they were my guardian angels. Their names were Michael and Raphael. . . . Being a Hindu, I least expected them to show up.[8]

Rajiv found himself lifted by them and guided forward toward a "Light Being." As they flew together over a serene landscape, the angel Michael told him, "If we let you go, you wouldn't know how to move forward."[9]

> They guided me towards a place where it was very beautiful. Meadows of roses of different colors, there was a mountain stream there, . . . a gentle breeze blowing. It had even a sweet smell. . . . And from there I was in the presence of a Light Being. It was like one thousand suns at the same time, but . . . it was not hurting my eyes.[10]

The closer they flew to the being of light, Rajiv noticed the angels became more and more translucent until they nearly disappeared. Once in the presence of the divine light, Rajiv was bathed in love.

> I knew I was loved and that [the Light Being] knew more about me than I about it. I was wrapped in its total knowledge. . . . It began gently whispering in my ear. And as the words started, pure love—I don't know what else to call it—pervaded everything.[11]

"You need to look at your life one more time," the being of light told him. The divine being wanted Rajiv to understand the changes he would need to make. With that, Rajiv experienced a painful life review covering things he was not proud of. Rajiv felt undone, full of shame in the presence of this loving being, and he feared he might be sent back to hell. "I had no idea what to expect. But rather than receiving something bad, I felt a deep sense of love coming from the Being of Light, the kind of love I should have exhibited with my son."[12]

God told him it was not his time, and he was sending him back to his life on earth. Relieved, Rajiv felt an overwhelming sense of gratitude for God's love and mercy.

> The Being clearly understood all, especially that none of us is perfect. It gave me another chance. . . . In retrospect, I think the Being of Light might have been Jesus. . . . If it wasn't Jesus, it was some other Being that loves us, understands our weaknesses, and helps us develop new intentions.[13]

Dr. Parti revived, and he told his wife about the NDE. When he told her that two Christian angels[14] escorted him to God's light, she stopped him. "She was surprised and she asked me, 'How come you didn't see any Hindu gods?' You know we have so many gods and goddesses. But I really had no explanation."[15]

God seemed to give him the answer later that year. Rajiv had been meeting with his dying friend, Naresh, helping Naresh understand the forgiveness and love of the God he'd experienced in his NDE. The very night Naresh died, Rajiv was home sleeping, when the room suddenly filled with light. As if seeing into the heavenly dimension, Rajiv saw Naresh standing before a portal opening above him. He witnessed the same brilliant light that looked like a thousand suns—this time coming to get Naresh. Rajiv recalls,

> I felt the presence of the Being of Light, the same Being I had encountered during my NDE. This time, however, a Being emerged from the Light, a tall man with a pale-brown complexion and a beard, wearing a majestic white gown. Most memorable were his deep blue eyes. He was

radiating unconditional love. "Who are you?" I asked the
Being. "I am Jesus, your savior," he responded.[16]

Rajiv bowed in Indian custom and said, "Namaste," while touching
Jesus' feet. "[Jesus] told me it was not my time to leave earth and that I
had to go back and spread his message of universal love."[17]

THE MESSAGE OF JESUS

What is the message of Jesus? NDErs may have differing interpretations about that, but Jesus clearly told us his main message, called the
gospel (which means "good news"). The gospel is how he demonstrated
his universal love for all. When he appeared to his followers after his
resurrection, he said:

> It was written long ago that the Messiah would suffer and die
> and rise from the dead on the third day. It was also written that
> *this message* would be proclaimed in the authority of his name
> to all the nations, beginning in Jerusalem: "There is forgiveness
> of sins for all who repent."
>
> LUKE 24:46-47, EMPHASIS ADDED

The word *repent* simply means to turn back to God. That's the message, his good news for all people. Forgiveness is available for all who
turn back to God. God wants us to live engulfed in his grace—his
unconditional love, forgiveness, and acceptance, as his beloved sons
and daughters, secure forever. He wants us to walk in daily relationship
with him.

I have seen NDErs come back with a different message as they try to
interpret their experience. It's important to remember that NDErs are
just people, and they can be swayed and led astray as all of us can. That's
why we need to understand Jesus' message that God foretold through
the prophets. If NDErs come back and report messages that contradict
the message of Jesus while he was on earth, follow Jesus' words recorded
in Scripture, not an NDEr's interpretation of his message.[18]

Without understanding the message of what God did for us through

Jesus, we tend to live either under the weight of judgment and shame (knowing we sin and fall short but feeling responsible to try harder in our own power), or we harden our hearts and run from God. So, God made another way forward.

Some Christians may wonder why God would reveal himself in a near-death experience to those who don't believe in him. They forget God's heart longs for *every person* from every nation and every language to come home—we are all created by him and for him. And remember, there are no lengths to which he will not go to get us back. He took extreme measures to rescue evil Nineveh, as we read in the book of Jonah. He revealed himself in a brilliant light to Paul, then called Saul, as he was on his way to arrest and murder followers of Jesus. And the Old Testament prophets foretold the ultimate extreme measure God would take.

Around 1000 BCE, King David prophetically described the coming Crucifixion through the Messiah's eyes.

My God, my God, why have you abandoned me? . . . My life
is poured out like water, and all my bones are out of joint.
My heart is like wax, melting within me. My strength has
dried up like sunbaked clay. My tongue sticks to the roof of
my mouth. You have laid me in the dust and left me for dead.
My enemies surround me like a pack of dogs; an evil gang
closes in on me. They have pierced my hands and feet. I can
count all my bones. My enemies stare at me and gloat. They
divide my garments among themselves and throw dice for my
clothing. . . . The whole earth will acknowledge the LORD and
return to him. All the families of the nations will bow down
before him.

PSALM 22:1, 14-18, 27

Now fast-forward over one thousand years to Jesus in the garden of Gethsemane on the night before his Crucifixion. He would have read this prophecy in the Hebrew Bible many times at this point in his life. He knew the depth of suffering he would soon endure. In fact, he cried out some of these very words the next day as he willingly offered his life on the cross. And he chose to go through with it because he saw you, he saw me, forgiven and set free.

Jesus came and died just as David had foreseen more than one thousand years prior. David describes aspects of Roman crucifixion over five hundred years before the Roman civilization began, including bones out of joint from hanging and being pierced through his hands and feet. The apostle Matthew writes that during the Crucifixion, "At noon, darkness fell across the whole land until three o'clock. At about three o'clock, Jesus called out with a loud voice, *'Eli, Eli, lema sabachthani?'* which means 'My God, my God, why have you abandoned me?' . . . Then Jesus shouted out again, and he released his spirit" (Matthew 27:45-46, 50). Jesus cried words written by David in Psalm 22 as he felt all the suffering, abuse, addiction, rage, betrayals, and murders of every generation. Jesus willingly allowed the worst of human evil to nail him to a cross, while praying, "Father, forgive them, for they don't know what they are doing" (Luke 23:34). It was the darkest day in history.

Two ancient Greco-Roman historians commented in their records on the mysterious darkness Matthew describes. It covered the Mediterranean region. One called it a solar eclipse, though an eclipse could not have been the cause of this darkness.[19] Jesus was crucified at Passover, which occurs during a full moon, and a solar eclipse cannot occur during the phase of a full moon. Mysteriously, something else blocked the sun that day. In 800 BCE, God foretold through the prophet Amos, "'In that day,' declares the Sovereign LORD, 'I will make the sun go down at noon and darken the earth in broad daylight. . . . I will make that time like mourning for an only son'" (Amos 8:9-10, NIV).

At that moment of darkness, Jesus took on himself all the sins, all the hatred, all the evils, all the rebellion and pride, guilt and shame of humanity, and felt separation from God the Father for the first time. His human heart collapsed under the weight of it all. Psalm 22 foretold it, "My heart is like wax, melting within me." Jesus died of heart failure.

We know this because of what the apostle John says happened next. The Roman soldiers did not break Jesus' legs, as was common practice to hasten death. Instead, "One of the soldiers . . . pierced his side with a spear, and immediately *blood and water* flowed out" (John 19:34, emphasis added). Dr. Alexander Metherell explains that when a heart attack occurs, clear pericardial fluid builds up around the heart, which would appear as "water" flowing out with blood.[20] Lacking modern medical knowledge, there's no way King David and the apostle John could have known the significance of their words, written more than one thousand years apart and unrecognizable until our medical age! Jesus died of heart failure when he took on the sins of us all.

Paul explained what God accomplished for us that day: "God made you alive with Christ, for he forgave all our sins. He canceled the record of the charges against us and took it away by nailing it to the cross" (Colossians 2:13-14). That's the message of Jesus. For all who want forgiveness and freedom from the burden of guilt, he says, "You're forgiven. I'm not against you, I'm for you!"

I'M FOR YOU

For forty years, Father Cedric Pisegna has lived a life of service to humanity as a Passionist Catholic priest. "Passionist" is a reference to the passion or suffering of Christ, and Passionist priests focus on proclaiming God's love revealed in the Cross of Christ. Growing up, Cedric didn't get anything out of the Catholic church and turned away from God and his faith. Like many of us, he lived with a vague sense of God. "To some degree I had that harsh image of God ingrained in me," Cedric confesses. "I wasn't really sure if God was true or if I could know him."

At twenty, living a life of partying and dating women, Cedric got his girlfriend pregnant, and they chose to abort the baby. Guilt overwhelmed him. He knew he had separated himself from God. A year after the abortion, he sought forgiveness and searched for God. One night as he drifted off to sleep, Cedric claims he had an NDE. [21] He left his body and moved upward toward a tunnel.

> The interesting thing about this is that I didn't want to go through the tunnel! I thought, *Oh, no,* because I knew I

was not ready to come before God. This portal to eternity
is a place that transcends time. It was so different that it
somehow made time, as we know it, stand still. Before I
knew it, I was at the end of the tunnel. Suddenly, I found
myself in the presence of God, standing before the Throne.
The only way to describe it was a living luminescent light
that embraced me.[22]

God's love for me was intensely personal. I sensed that I
was known and loved even before I was born into this world.
His love was unconditional. God's care and affection for me
were not conditioned on my goodness; rather, there was such
powerful, pulsating goodness radiating from God that it was
overwhelming. . . . God's love is an energetic passion. God's
love is affectionate. It is very intimate and personal. I realized
that not only did God love me; he was in love with *me*! What
I mean is that he knew me through and through and still had
his heart set upon me. . . . As God communicated with me
telepathically . . . I remember being amazed at how vulnerable
and intimate God wanted to be. I remember thinking, *He
loves me so much it is scary.* Scary is a strange adjective to use
about love, I know, but I was overwhelmed with the intensity
and intimacy of God's love. God is obsessed with us! Agape
love was displayed through Jesus in his willingness to be
tortured on the Cross. True love is sacrificial and willing
to suffer. This love is inexhaustible, indefatigable, and so
penetrating. . . . There was a wonderful oneness with God.
I had a deep personal union of which marriage is but a
symbol.[23]

As I stood close to the Glorious person of God, I had an
awakening to the Holy Spirit at the Throne of God, and I
knew it was Jesus who took me to the Throne. I was bathed
in the pleasurable electricity/glory of God. Jesus had his arm
around my neck and said telepathically, "I will protect you."
The fact that he would put his arm around a twenty-year-
old's shoulder who had had an abortion, and he would treat

me like an intimate friend, melted my heart. He's a friend of the outcast, the marginalized, the poor. It was [due to] Jesus, because of his passion, that I was summoned to the Throne of God, because of my humble seeking prayer. I sensed Jesus' radiant smile. I was beaming, and Jesus was radiant. Jesus taught about the joy in heaven when someone lost is found, and I can tell you from experience, there is ethereal jubilation.[24]

As I stood before God, I experienced a life review. . . . In a flash, my life was simply laid bare. There was no hiding, no pretending, and no putting on. There were no excuses to make. . . . I drank, smoked marijuana, dated and partied with girls. I didn't pray or attend Mass and didn't give to anyone but myself. . . . My life revolved around me. I was all about me. I was very selfish, narcissistic, and stingy. Sad to say, I did nothing for people and loved things to find happiness. . . . All the while, I deluded myself thinking, *I don't hurt anyone. I'm a good person.*

As I stood before love itself, I realized to my shame that I wasn't even close to being a loving person. The opposite of love is not hate. The opposite of love is selfishness. Love is generous and cares. Selfishness is stingy and cares only for itself. . . . I understood that the purpose of my life was to journey from selfishness to selflessness.

The first words I heard from God was a comforting "I will protect you." The second and final message I remember in his presence was challenging. God told me, "You must justify your soul." . . . In justification, we are declared right before God and made upright. In Jesus, we have been vindicated and declared innocent and forgiven by his blood. In addition, in Jesus we become the very righteousness of God (2 Corinthians 5:21). . . . Through his grace, I was forgiven and declared upright before him by the blood of Jesus. Legally, I am innocent and upright. It all happened through the blood of the Cross. However, experientially, because I was so selfish and lacking in virtue, God was telling me that I needed to change. . . .

But when I encountered God's love, I came to know in the depths of my being that God had been for me, not against me! Throughout my life, I haven't been able to manage my behavior as I want. In spite of my powerlessness, I have found that God actually helps me rather than condemns me. . . . If I stumble along the way, it is God himself who picks me up. If I fail, it is God who forgives me. When I am weak, it is God who gives me strength. "If God is for us, who can be against us?" (Romans 8:31). As I left God's presence, I promised: "Now that I know, I will be my best!" [25]

Cedric came back knowing he was forgiven, and it was God's love that compelled him. It was not guilt but love that led him into the priesthood. The summons to God's throne was actually a call to the priesthood. Cedric's life mission has been to teach people about God's overwhelmingly passionate love and forgiveness poured out for all on the Cross.

NO CONDEMNATION

God's not mad at you. The gospel message is that forgiveness is available for all people, of all times, everywhere, for anything. It's ridiculously good news. What God did through Jesus, he did for all nations. God wants all people to know that he does not stand ready to judge us or condemn us for our wrongs; he stands ready to forgive and take us back into loving relationship! But not *against our will*—it's only if we're willing. He did this because being reconciled to God and reconnected to the source of love and truth conquers sin and evil. The apostle Paul explains how this happens:

So now there is *no condemnation* for those who belong to Christ Jesus. And because you belong to him, the power of the life-giving Spirit has freed you from the power of sin that leads to death [spiritual death]. The law of Moses [religious moral law] was unable to save us because of the weakness of our sinful nature. So God did what the law could not do.

ROMANS 8:1-3, EMPHASIS ADDED

The moral law can't save you, but God can! The law can't change the human heart, but connection to God, the source of love, can. And as we will see, that connection enables us to overcome temptation and evil, walking confidently and daily in loving relationship to God.

If you feel condemned, guilt-ridden, shameful, or fearful, God wants to set you free from all of that. Jesus said, "You are truly my disciples [followers] if you remain faithful to my teachings. And you will know the truth, and the truth will set you free. . . . So if the Son sets you free, you are truly free" (John 8:31-32, 36).

None of us is perfect, and none of us can save ourselves by trying to live a sinless life. No Jew or Christian has ever perfectly kept the law of Moses; no Hindu has perfect karma; no Muslim perfectly keeps the five pillars of Islam; no Buddhist perfectly adheres to the Eightfold Path; and even agnostics and atheists fail to live up to their own moral standards. We all fail. Ever secretly vowed, "I'll *never* . . ." but you did? That's because there's a limit to what moral laws can do. They can't save us from ourselves, but they can be a tutor, teaching us our need for Jesus. The apostle Paul put it this way: "The Law has become our guardian [literally "child teacher"] *to lead us* to Christ, so that we may be justified by faith" (Galatians 3:24, NASB). Honesty about our sins and failures helps us see our need for the forgiveness God offers through Christ.

NO FEAR OF JUDGMENT

God knows all our secrets, all our hidden motives, all our good and bad deeds, thoughts, attitudes—all of it. Theologians call this his *omniscience*. The life review many NDErs experience confirms this attribute of God. Heidi, the teenage girl who was crushed by her horse, got a peek into God's omniscience as she floated in midair with Jesus.

As I floated, a three-dimensional vision of my life began to unfold before me. I could see and feel the events of my life from my own perspective, but at the same time I could also feel the impact I had on others. If I hurt someone, I hurt myself. If I was kind to someone, I felt their happiness as my own. The vision itself was neutral, as was my companion [Jesus]. I realized I wasn't being judged; I was the judge. I judged my own life. Any wrongs I'd done to others, I did to myself. Any pain I'd caused anyone, no matter how slight, I felt it. It was a life-altering experience. At the same time, it seemed as if the universe lay exposed before me. I had no more questions. All those nagging questions like, Why am I here? What is the meaning of life? . . . Everything made sense.[26]

Everything makes sense in God's presence because he is all-knowing. NDErs get a taste of what the apostle Paul meant when he said, "All that I know now is partial and incomplete, but then I will know everything completely, just as God now knows me completely" (1 Corinthians 13:12). NDErs confirm God's omniscience as they get a life review. Things they've forgotten, God knows. They see from God's perspective. This thought might scare you unless you know the heart and grace of God—he is *for* you!

During their life review, when NDErs feel judgment, it is from judging themselves with unvarnished truth. God is unconditionally loving them and teaching the importance of love through review of their actions. Some NDErs have mistakenly concluded there is no judgment after death because God is not judging but loving. Jesus told us, "There is no judgment against anyone who believes in him. But anyone who does not believe in him [who rejects him] has already been judged" (John 3:18). Our own consciences judge us even now. That's what I think Jesus means. Without God's grace, our guilty consciences cause us to run and hide from God. But that keeps us disconnected from the Source who can help us grow.

Jesus also said, "You must give an account on judgment day for every idle word you speak. The words you say will either acquit you or condemn you" (Matthew 12:36-37). This is exactly what the life review confirms—all the words, thoughts, actions of our earthly lives judge us accurately.

However, this life review NDErs experience is not the Judgment Day—that event comes at the end of human history (Revelation 20:1-12). The life review is a reminder for today of what matters most to God—how we love God and treat each other. Professor Howard Storm told me that during his life review with Jesus, he felt God's forgiveness and unconditional love, even though his actions caused God deep pain:

> As my life progressed, my adolescence into adulthood, I saw myself turning completely away from God, church, all that, and becoming a person who decided that life was all about "the biggest, baddest bear in the woods wins." And now I began to experience Jesus' and the angels' literal pain. Emotional pain with watching the sins in my life . . . and here's the nicest, kindest, most loving being I've ever met who, I realized, is my Lord, my Savior, even my Creator—holding me and supporting me, trying to give me more understanding of my life. And it was figuratively—not literally—like I was stabbing him in the heart as we're watching this stuff. And the last thing I want to do is to hurt him, and I don't want to hurt him to this day.[27]

Howard was motivated to turn away from sinful behaviors, not out of fear of condemnation, but out of his desire to no longer hurt the one who loves him most. Jesus came to remove all fear of judgment. "There is no judgment against anyone who believes in him" (John 3:18). Judgment is not something you need to fear, unless in your pride you say, "I don't need God's help. I don't need Jesus to pay for my wrongs. I'm good." Reject God's free gift and on that day, your own words will judge you, just as NDErs attest.

THE GOD OF GRACE

Jesus revealed a God of *grace*. The reason NDErs do not feel judged by God is because of God's grace. Grace is unearned, undeserved favor for those who deserve judgment. In that sense, grace is also scandalous—it trips us up because it's human nature to want to *prove* we are "good." Grace is why God does not immediately execute justice each time we do wrong. We all need grace.

God has made relationship with himself and entrance to heaven so simple that anyone, anywhere, can call on his name and be saved—set right with God. Jesus told us he made that possible: "I am the way and the truth and the life. No one comes to the Father except through me. If you really know me, you will know my Father as well" (John 14:6-7, NIV). Jesus is the means by which God can still be just, yet also forgive and restore all who call to him. The apostle Paul wrote, "Everyone who calls on the name of the LORD will be saved" (Romans 10:13). The only thing that can keep us out of heaven is our pride.

But what about those who have never heard the name of Jesus? Ultimately, Scripture does not tell us. What we do know is that God looks at the heart, he is just, and Scripture tells us it is by faith, not by deeds, that a person is saved—it's a gift of God (Ephesians 2:8-10). Salvation is found in no one but Jesus, as Acts 4:12 declares. Yet, according to Hebrews 11, many people who never knew the name of Jesus will be in heaven because of Jesus—among them Abraham, Moses, and Rahab—people of faith who lived before Jesus. God somehow applied Jesus' payment (which was then still to come) based on their faith in the light and knowledge they did have. Maybe God still does the same for those who have never heard his name today. (For more on this, see "What about Those Who Have Never Heard?" in the appendix.)

Jesus indicated we may all be surprised by who is or is not in heaven: "Many Gentiles will come from all over the world—from east and west—and sit down with Abraham, Isaac, and Jacob at the feast in the Kingdom of Heaven. But many Israelites—those for whom the Kingdom was prepared—will be thrown into outer darkness" (Matthew

8:11–12). It's not for us to judge who will or will not be saved by God's amazing grace.

Dean Braxton was a Christian when he had his NDE due to sepsis (chapter 4). He was shocked to see his aunt in heaven. "With my belief system, I had her in hell. I'll be honest with you. There she was in heaven. I came to understand it wasn't up to me. It's up to Jesus. Sometimes we may make a judgment over a person, but that's between them and God. He knows. Then I came to understand it didn't matter if I knew. It mattered if he knew."[28]

Scripture states, "The eyes of the LORD search the whole earth in order to strengthen those whose hearts are fully committed to him" (2 Chronicles 16:9). And God promises, "If you look for me whole-heartedly, you will find me" (Jeremiah 29:13). God wants all people to hear and know about his love and forgiveness offered through Jesus. He does not want us to live condemned by our sin, in fear of death or judgment. Instead, he wants us to live in the confidence of knowing we are in right relationship with God, now and forever.

Here's God's grace explained:

> This is how God loved the world: He gave his one and only
> Son, so that everyone who believes in him will not perish but
> have eternal life. God sent his Son into the world not to judge
> the world, but to save the world through him. There is no
> judgment against anyone who believes in him.
> JOHN 3:16-18

That's grace. And that's all God needs—a heart turned to him in trust. Remember, God's not mad at you. Have you turned to God in trust? Do you want to be assured you are right with God forever? Tell him right now, "God, I want your love and forgiveness. I want what Jesus did to count for me. Come and lead my life to be what you intended." It's a gift—it's that simple. But it is not a cheap gift—it cost Jesus his very life blood!

SECURE IN GOD'S LOVE

There are commonalities in the life reviews many NDErs experience, yet each is also unique. In Alexa's life review, she saw how condemning accusations can't stand against the truth of God's grace. She also realized her actions matter to God—that grace is for growth today, not complacency until heaven. Alexa went into labor with her second child, but after the baby was delivered, Alexa looked down and saw she was bleeding profusely.

> I felt the Life force oozing out of me. I said a quick prayer inside myself: *"Oh Jesus, I hope you're everything I've been worshiping all these years! Please take care of my new little son; please take care of my beautiful daughter. I love them so much. God, I give You my Soul."*
>
> And I was suddenly above my body! It seemed the most natural thing in the world! I had hands, feet, and everything was as normal; I was me in some sort of soft gown. . . .
>
> A nurse said, "Where's the crash cart?" I didn't know what a crash cart was, but it sounded important. They started CPR. I was sad they were so upset, but I was FINE.
>
> Even as I had lifted out of my body, there were Beings on both sides of me—HUGE, POWERFUL Angels, with even more powerful white feathered wings. *Oooo, feathers,* I remember thinking. I wanted to touch those wings so much; they looked so soft. As I reached, the Angels started to escort me. That was their job—to keep me safe (*from what?* I wondered).
>
> We floated down through a tunnel that had opened up to us. Once we got to the end, the Angels disappeared. I then saw hundreds, maybe thousands of people, all dressed in a soft white, simple, plain, long clothing, each with a gold sash at the waist. All were smiling and accepted me just as I was in my humanity. No one had a fault-finding or critical attitude. The meeting was joyous, not scary.

Over to one side, on my right, was something amazing. I moved (floating not walking) over to look. There were steps, ivory, glowing steps. At the bottom of the steps were tiny spirit beings—cherubim? They were constantly singing the praises of God: "HOLY, HOLY, HOLY TO THE LORD OF HOSTS; GLORY, GLORY, GLORY TO GOD; HOLY IS HIS RIGHTEOUSNESS, TRUTH AND POWER."

My Soul welled up within me to worship God with them; oh, how I wanted to kneel down and stay with them! The Light permeating everything was especially strong there. The steps led up to God, and such was His brightness, that I could not look directly at Him. I was allowed to see Jesus, smiling at me. I was so overwhelmed, but happy, too, I could hardly react!

Suddenly, a podium appeared. Yes, the hundreds of beings were still watching me. I had turned to my left and somehow moved slightly forward (although there was no real "direction"). I was in some sort of Courtroom, and an Entity had appeared. After he appeared, my Life Review began. I was given to understand this was what it was. This was awful.

EVERYTHING I ever thought, did, said, hated, helped, did not help, and should have helped was shown in front of me. The crowd of hundreds and everyone watching made it seem like it was a movie. How mean I'd been to people, how I could have helped them, how mean I was (unintentionally also) to animals! Yes! Even the animals had feelings. It was horrible. I fell on my face in shame. I saw how my acting, or not acting, rippled in effect toward other people and their lives. It wasn't until then that I understood how each little decision or choice affects the World. The sense of letting my Savior down was too real. Strangely, even during this horror, I felt a compassion, an acceptance of my limitations by Jesus and the crowd of Others.

During this Review, the Evil being was there. I looked at him; he was handsome, not ugly. Black hair, medium build, dressed in a brown robe with a black cord at his waist. His eyes caught my attention. They were a black void! There was no life or goodness in them. Intense in every way, his only Purpose was to possess, own, control my very Soul and make me suffer!! I shrank back in horror. Every time during the Review that I erred or failed, he enjoyed it immensely. He would shout out, "THERE! See how she messed up?" He would accuse me, "Why didn't she do better? Or help more? She ought to be punished!" I was desolate. My few, little good works didn't and couldn't measure up to God's perfect standard.

Then, when it was over, a huge deep voice boomed out: "IS SHE COVERED BY THE BLOOD OF THE LAMB?"

"YES!"

With that, Jesus looked at Satan and declared: "SHE'S MINE!"

The courtroom disappeared, and the evil being, Satan, screamed! He hissed like a snake, turned and whirled like a tornado, but got smaller and smaller. He shrunk down to a pile of dust and poof! He disappeared completely, after screaming in anger the whole time.

Everything in that setting was gone, except the Heavenly crowd and Jesus Christ. He gazed at me with INCREDIBLE love! He held out his nail-pierced hands and wrists, that although healed completely, had the outline of the crucifixion marks. This was no wimpy Jesus. He was strong, powerful, tall as a ceiling, and shining all over! His long, white hair was nothing compared to his burning, liquid-gold eyes. They burned with Purity, Joy, and Purpose. He opened his mouth, and I heard a loud sound like a freight train! The rushing and roaring sound that came out was almost deafening. He spoke of who He was, and that he was my advocate with God the Father. I fell down in awe and worshiped Him with my very Soul. I cried with Joy like a baby as I gazed up at His glorious, loving smile. He loved and accepted me—totally. I was filled with peace and contentment.[29]

In the book of Revelation, John writes about hearing angels declare of Jesus, "Your blood has ransomed people for God from every tribe and language and people and nation" (Revelation 5:9). John also heard Jesus declare, "All who are victorious will be clothed in white. I will never erase their names from the Book of Life, but I will announce before my Father and his angels that they are mine" (Revelation 3:5).

Although this courtroom setting is not common among the life review NDErs describe, maybe God used it to teach Alexa, and us, because it also mirrors this description from the Old Testament book of Job: "One day the members of the heavenly court came to present themselves before the LORD, and the Accuser, Satan, came with them" (Job 1:6).

The voices of evil want to accuse us, guilt us, and constantly condemn us in our minds. But Jesus died to set us free to walk daily with God in confidence, without fear, forgiven so that he can help us grow into kind, loving, life-giving people. "We know how much God loves us, and we have put our trust in his love," writes the apostle John (1 John 4:16). He goes on to say,

> So we will not be afraid on the day of judgment, but we can face him with confidence because we live like Jesus here in this world. Such love has no fear, because perfect love expels all fear. If we are afraid, it is for fear of punishment, and this shows that we have not fully experienced his perfect love.
>
> I JOHN 4:17-18

Do you live with this confidence, safe and secure in his perfect love? God wants that for you. God wants you free from living under the weight of condemnation, accusation, or obsessive guilt. His grace truly sets us free. As we will see, living free of fear enables us to live openly and honestly before God, tapping into his strength and guidance to grow into more and more of our true selves—the people he always intended us to be in his great love story.

PART 3

GOD'S MYSTERY
AND MAJESTY

8

THE MYSTERY OF A TRIUNE GOD

WHEN HEIDI'S HORSE FELL OVER ON HER (chapter 3), she was a sixteen-year-old Jewish girl raised by atheist parents. She had no concept of a triune God. She just knew intuitively that God existed, and she prayed to God every night. Yet in her NDE, Heidi experienced God's mystery as three persons—Father, Son, and Holy Spirit. She explains what happened as she continued her intriguing journey after floating thirty feet above the accident with Jesus:

> Before Jesus and I left the scene, I became aware of something else—I had no more questions. I hadn't asked any questions; I simply became aware that I knew the answers. Of course, if you ask me, "What are those answers?" I can't tell you. I only knew that I'd known the answers when I was dead, and I realized that everything made sense . . . but here on earth,

it is in seeking God that we become truly humble, truly human; we become the people he intends us to be.

Jesus and I took off. We went faster and faster until we reached what I guess would be the speed of light. Before we reached the speed of light, things were still separate. I could differentiate one object from another. After we reached the speed of light, we crossed a threshold, and on the other side, everything became One Thing, one undifferentiated thing that contained all of life. Jesus and I were individuals, yes. I could still see him and feel the warmth of his hand clasping mine, but all around us there was only One Thing. I knew that One Thing was God. The simplest way I can describe this realization is to state that there is no corner, no place, no space God does not occupy. He contains everything and everything is contained in him. He is in us. We are in him. What I experienced is difficult to translate into words. I am reminded of John 14:20 [NRSvue]: "On that day you will know that I am in my Father, and you in me, and I in you." Yes, Jesus was in the Father, and he was in me, and I was in him. I wish I could explain this better, but I simply can't. He was one, and he was himself, but he was in me too. There was a part of him in me. There really aren't any words to describe this awareness.

Jesus had smiled at me. He'd been so pleased I'd recognized God's immensity. Believe me, God's immensity will bring you to your knees. Our human brains can't grasp him without tripping the circuit breaker. The Israelites were right to fall on their faces at Mount Sinai. . . .

As we crossed the threshold, I saw a light. The light took up my entire field of vision. It was a perfect, white, blemishless light, and it was infinite in its scope. There was no end to the light, no beginning. The light was alive, and the light was love. Jesus took me directly into the light, and I found myself sitting on God's lap—God the Father, but yes, Jesus, too. They were one and the same, yet separate—but again, still one. See how difficult this is to explain?

So, there I was, sitting on God's lap, kicking my legs like a little girl. I had my arms wrapped around his waist. I buried my face in his chest. Talk about a perfect love. . . . Love incarnate. All love. Every single smidge of love in existence. That was God. He had his arms around me too. He held me tight. And he's a big God. I was like a toddler sitting on her father's lap. I had a sense I should not look at his face; certainly not in the way I had glued my eyes to Jesus' face. I snuck a quick glance upward and then just as quickly buried my face against his chest. I couldn't see his face. It seemed to be shrouded in clouds, obscured somehow. . . .

I was humbled, but I felt no fear, only awe in the truest sense of the word. I had come home to my real Father. He loved me. He loved me with all the love in the universe. What my [earthly] dad had told me wasn't true. It was a lie. My life was not less significant than the most microscopic speck of dust in the universe. My life had significance to God. God knew me. God comforted me. God accepted me. God loved me. God filled every single corner of me. He filled my heart. . . .

Picture an infinite God/Light wearing a pure white robe-type garment of light, also infinite in size. Picture this infinite God/Light pulling back a corner of his robe, the corner of his robe infinitely far away. It was only by withdrawing a portion of himself that I was able to see what it was he wanted to show me. Keep in mind that here on earth, in this life, I was nearly blind [without glasses]. When I was dead, I had perfect vision. Keep in mind too, that what God wanted to show me was infinitely far away . . . [yet] I could see every single detail as if it was inches from my face.

The first thing I saw was grass, green grass. The grass was like the grass on earth, and the green was like the green of earth, but it was different as well. I realized that all the colors we experience here on earth are mere reflections of the colors of heaven. . . . The most beautiful perfect day on earth, while

worthy and worthwhile and lovely, is still a pale reflection of
every day in heaven. . . .

I could see every single blade of grass. The most amazing part?
The grass was singing! I will never ever forget what I saw and
what I heard; what I witnessed. Each blade of grass was singing
the praises of God. The music the grass made was astonishing,
amazing, gorgeous, heavenly, awesome. The flowers and the
trees were swaying in time to the song of the grass, and all were
moving in the light of God. It was God's light flowing through
everything, animating everything. As I watched this remarkable
sight, I noticed a path through the meadow. I heard singing,
people singing. They too were singing the praises of God.

Jesus took my right hand in his. He seemed serious,
concerned. "You didn't die," he said. "You have to go back." I
pulled my hand from his and wrapped my arms around God's
waist. I buried my face in God's chest. "I'm not going back,"
I said. Jesus again took my hand. "You didn't die. You have to
go back."[1]

Heidi told me that as Jesus put her back into her body, she was having a hard time adjusting. He said, "Your life is in good hands." Then
she suddenly felt his presence in her body. "I didn't have the theological
language at the time," Heidi says.

I believe this was God's Holy Spirit. Jesus left, but he left me
with his Presence. I couldn't see him, but he was there. I felt
his Presence and his Presence reassured me. Over the years, his
Presence made me want to know more—to seek Jesus. To seek
him physically in Israel, and then to seek him in Scripture, and
ultimately in community [a synagogue and a church]. What I
would now call the Holy Spirit changed my present life.[2]

Though Heidi had no expectation of meeting the Father, Son, and
Holy Spirit, she did in her NDE. She even understood they were somehow one God—but how could three be one?

THE PARADOX OF THE TRINITY

There is only one God. That truth is revealed consistently in the Old and New Testaments of the Bible. And yet, throughout the Bible, God also reveals himself as three persons—Father, Son, and Holy Spirit. How can three persons be one God? While it may feel like a contradiction to most of us, NDErs who have been in God's presence also experienced God's triune nature.

What theologians refer to as the Trinity,* or the triune God, is actually not a contradiction. Rather, it is a mystery or paradox that makes sense on the other side of our finite three dimensions of space. If that seems far-fetched, consider that science has already discovered other extra-dimensional mysteries. For instance, Einstein's theory of relativity perfectly explains gravity and the motion of large objects, such as planets; quantum mechanics perfectly describes the behavior of subatomic particles, such as electrons and quarks. However, the two scientific theories don't work together in a unified way—in fact, they seem like incompatible descriptions of reality. This has baffled scientists for decades.

Theodor Kaluza and Oskar Klein, two scientists who were contemporaries of Einstein, came up with a theory that showed mathematically that a fifth dimension, hidden from our sight, would unify the theories of gravity and electromagnetism.[3] It was a precursor to string theory, which suggests there exist many more unseen dimensions to reality.

The point is, humans are bound by three spatial dimensions and by time. If there are more dimensions we can't see, we will experience them as paradoxes to nature (and God's reality) when reduced into three-dimensional terms. Quantum mechanics is discovering many such paradoxes. So, the Trinity is not the only mystery for us to grapple with, and given what science is discovering, this paradox should not surprise us.

Okay, but hang on a second. If Jesus was the one true God, how did God die on the cross? Who was running the universe if God was dead? Skeptics often pose such questions. Let's think about it. If God exists

---

* *Trinity* is the word theologians use to describe the mystery of one God in three persons revealed in the Bible. Although the word *Trinity* is not used in the Bible, this aspect of God's nature is evident in various ways throughout the Old and New Testaments.

outside our dimensional understanding, then we can only imagine the Trinity, in part, by analogy.

Imagine I create a flat world of only two dimensions and populate that world with flat people. We'll call it "Flatland."[4] The people in Flatland would only be able to move forward and backward or side to side because there's no third dimension—no up or down. Since I am a three-dimensional being,* they cannot even conceive of what I'm like, what I can do, or where I exist in a third dimension. Now, let's say I put three fingers into their world (Figure 1). The people of Flatland would see me as three round slices in their two-dimensional world (Figure 2).

Figure 1

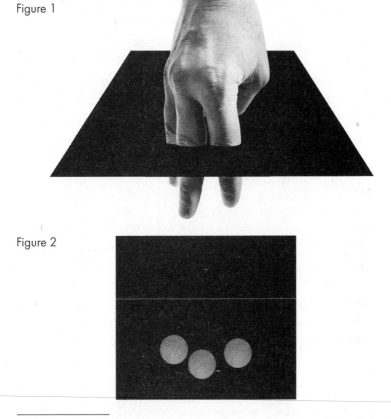

Figure 2

---

* Technically, according to Albert Einstein, we exist in four space-time dimensions (three spatial dimensions and one time dimension), but since we speak of the three-dimensional space we live in, I'm using this convention.

But what if I told the people of Flatland that I'm not actually three separate beings, but only one being? And that these three round slices are not three different entities, but three representations of the one me in two dimensions? That would be a paradox to them—three circles can only exist side by side in their world. Three circles can never be "one" because there's no third dimension in their world—no reality in which the three circles join up my hand and arm into my one, three-dimensional being.

Using this analogy, perhaps we can imagine that three persons—Father, Son, and Holy Spirit—can somehow connect "up" in higher dimensions, or beyond all dimensions, as one being. I say *perhaps* because all analogies for the nature of the infinite God are still finite, and therefore incomplete (for commentary on other analogies see the endnotes).[5]

So back to the skeptic's question: "Who ran the universe while Jesus died on the cross?" God continued to exist and sustain all things, even though his "arm" reaching into humanity's "Flatland," through Jesus, died on a cross. But don't be confused, there is only one God.

ONE GOD WE WORSHIP

Crystal McVea had a rough beginning. Her parents divorced, and she was molested by a babysitter who took care of her every week while her mom got high upstairs. Her alcoholic stepfather was abusive. So, Crystal struggled with the idea of God the Father, but Jesus intrigued her. Jesus was a person, and he had suffered too, so she felt he could relate. Plus, she'd heard he came to save us. When she was nine, Crystal got baptized because she wanted Jesus to save her. And while she did feel cleansed from all the shame she'd felt, the abuse continued. She spent her teen years angry at God, convinced he didn't love her. That led to years of rebellion, which she describes as breaking all the Ten Commandments.

Then at age thirty-three, Crystal went to the hospital for pancreatitis, and due to complications, she coded—no heartbeat or brain waves for nine minutes. She found herself outside of her body, with two guardian angels in front of her on her left.

I was also aware of a being on my right, and instantly I knew who this was, too. And what overcame me was a profound, endless desire to praise and worship this being, for I knew immediately I was in the presence of God.

I have always referred to God as a him, and I guess I always will. But the being on my right was not a him or a her; it was just God. Nor did I make any distinction between God, Jesus, and the Holy Spirit, as we sometimes do on Earth. They were all One—the One before me now . . . a blinding profusion of brightness. . . .

I'd spent my life doubting His existence and disbelieving His love for me, but in that instant I knew God had always, always been there—right there with me. . . .

In heaven we don't have just five senses; we have a ton of senses. Imagine a sense that allowed us to not only see light, but also to taste it. . . . To touch and feel light. . . . That is what I experienced in the presence of God—a beautiful new way of receiving and sending love. . . .

The sheer ecstasy of it! The beauty of it, the joy and the grace, the way my spirit soared and my heart burst—how I wish I had the words to convey just how miraculous this was. . . .

With every fiber of my existence I wanted to praise and worship God, and that's *all* I wanted to do. And I wanted to do it *forever*. . . . What drove my praise was the intensity and immensity of my love for God. There is simply no other love remotely like it.[6]

It's so interesting to me that people on earth who are not inclined to worship or praise God can't help but do so in his presence—and, in fact, they wish they could do so forever! Even as a pastor, I find the thought of Sunday worship for eternity to sound boring and laborious. Yet, the kind of worship NDErs describe from being in God's presence sounds like living in joyful love and ecstasy. Worship is not merely singing songs; it's expressing gratitude, love, wonder, and awe.

As Crystal said, there is only one God, not three Gods. The creed of the Israelite people given by God to Moses makes it clear: "The LORD is one. Love the LORD your God with all your heart and with all your soul and with all your strength" (Deuteronomy 6:4-5, NIV). This was and still is the core belief of Judaism—there is only one God; love God only.

Jesus affirmed that there is only one God when he stated, "The Scriptures say, 'You must worship the LORD your God and serve only him'" (Luke 4:8). Yet, Jesus' final prayer on earth for his followers also acknowledges the mystery of this one God: "And this is the way to have eternal life—to know you, the only true God, and Jesus Christ, the one you sent to earth. . . . I pray that they will all be one, just as you and I are one—as you are in me, Father, and I am in you. And may they be in us so that the world will believe you sent me" (John 17:3, 21). So Jesus affirms there is only one God, in all and through all, but with a twist.

The apostle Paul states the twist: "There is one God, the Father, by whom all things were created, and for whom we live. And there is one Lord, Jesus Christ, through whom all things were created, and through whom we live" (1 Corinthians 8:6). So there are not three Gods; there is only one God, revealed in three persons. In heaven, NDErs experience this mystery.

GOD IN THREE PERSONS

"When I first came upon Jesus," Dean Braxton recalls after his NDE due to sepsis, "I knew all of a sudden that the Holy Spirit, Jesus, and the Father are one."

> It was just an inward knowing that I was not speaking to one, but all three at the same time. And most of the speaking was not verbal, but thought-to-thought, and as I was speaking in my head, I was aware of each distinct person there hearing, but they were one. Not like we would think of one; I knew the fullness of Jesus was in the Father, and the fullness of the Holy Spirit was in Jesus—I could not separate them there. I have to separate them now, so it sounds like I was just talking to Jesus, but I knew I was talking to Father and Holy Spirit.

I did experience Jesus, the glorified man, and then the Father on his throne, but I realized there is a box we've built around it that the actual experience transcends our words. God the Father is, as the Bible says, a Spirit. He is pure Spirit. He is pure love, and he is pure life, and he is pure light! . . . All I can say is there is no end to God the Father. He is bright like Jesus with many colors coming off of him. Jesus and the Father God light up everything. . . . They live outside of every being and inside every being. Every being shines because of the Father and Jesus.

God the Father was singing back to each and every being giving him praise before the throne. He was singing an individual love song to each of his creations. Like in the Song of Songs in the Bible. There is an exchange of love words between God and each person. The only time I saw beings open their mouths was when they were singing praises to the Father at the throne. Every living being and creature praises the Father and Jesus. Every part of God's creation praises God all the time. To hear the flowers praise the Lord is wonderful. The birds sing praise to the Lord. Water praised the Lord. Mountains praised the Lord.[7]

I always thought it was just metaphor when Isaiah wrote, "Sing for joy, you heavens. . . . Burst into song, you mountains, you forests and all your trees, for the LORD has redeemed [his people]" (Isaiah 44:23, NIV). However, hearing Dean and many other NDErs speak of this has convinced me otherwise. All creation praises the Father, Son, and Holy Spirit. Imagine all the awesome wonders and mysteries we have ahead of us as we experience eternal life in God's presence. Maybe imagining such heavenly wonders can help us join all creation in praising him now!

Manifestations of God in the Bible

God is one God in three persons. That revelation makes sense when we remember that God *is* love. Yet, love is always relational. So, before

God created anything, whom did God love? The answer is found in the persons of God: The Father loves the Son loves the Holy Spirit loves the Father. God *is* a relationship. The Creator of everything is a relationship of love. And this understanding of the Trinity of love is not a recent discovery but something that shows up from the beginning of biblical history. Allow me to walk you through just a few of the ways the three persons are evident throughout the Bible.

The angel of the Lord. Scripture tells us that God appeared visibly around 2000 BCE to tell Abraham and Sarah they would have a child to bless all nations: "The LORD appeared to Abraham near the great trees of Mamre. . . . Abraham looked up and saw three men" (Genesis 18:1-2, NIV). They turned out to be two angels plus the angel of the Lord who reiterated his promise: "Then the LORD said, . . . 'All nations on earth will be blessed through [Abraham]. For I have chosen him'" (Genesis 18:17-19, NIV).

In the Old Testament, when Yahweh, the one true God, appeared visibly in human form, he was often referred to as the "angel of the Lord." While angels refuse to be worshiped, saying, "Worship only God!"[8] the angel of the Lord at times accepts worship, and his words are often equated with those of Yahweh (see Judges 6:11-27). Theologians call this a *theophany*,[9] a visible manifestation of God, possibly as the preincarnate son of God. Here, we could be seeing the first glimpses of the triune God revealed, though not explained, four thousand years ago.

A child. Then around 700 BCE, Isaiah made things a little clearer, writing that a great light would come to the region of Galilee: "For to us a child is born, to us a son is given. . . . He will be called Wonderful Counselor, Mighty God, Everlasting Father, Prince of Peace" (Isaiah 9:6, NIV). Isaiah prophesied that Mighty God would come as a child and live in Galilee, the land where Jesus grew up and ministered.

The Son of Man. Later, around 500 BCE, the prophet Daniel had a vision of God on his throne: "His throne was flaming with fire. . . . Ten thousand times ten thousand stood before him. . . . There before me was one like a son of man, coming with the clouds of heaven. He approached the Ancient of Days [God] and was led into his presence.

He was given authority, glory and sovereign power; all nations and peoples of every language worshiped him" (Daniel 7:9-10, 13-14, NIV).

What? They worshiped "a son of man"? There's only *one* God—and the Jewish creed says to worship God only. So why is this Jewish prophet Daniel talking about a "son of man" to whom Yahweh will give all authority and saying all nations will worship him? Unless this "son of man" *is* the one true God incarnate!

When Jesus was on earth, "Son of Man" was a name he often used for himself. Jesus was referring to himself when he said, "The Son of Man has authority on earth to forgive sins" (Matthew 9:6, NIV). When Jesus took Peter, James, and John up on a mountain and showed them his glory, "Jesus' appearance was transformed so that his face shone like the sun. . . . Jesus commanded them, 'Don't tell anyone what you have seen until the Son of Man has been raised from the dead'" (Matthew 17:2, 9). Clearly, Jesus equated himself with the Son of Man mentioned in Daniel, who is worshiped by all nations as the one true God.

The God of Abraham. Jesus also equated himself with the God of Abraham. Confronting the hypocrisy of the religious leaders who were plotting to kill him, Jesus said,

> "Some of you are trying to kill me because there's no room in your hearts for my message. I am telling you what I saw when I was with my Father. . . .
>
> Your father Abraham rejoiced as he looked forward to my coming. He saw it and was glad."
>
> The people said . . . "How can you say you have seen Abraham?"
>
> Jesus answered, "I tell you the truth, before Abraham was even born, I Am!" At that point they picked up stones to throw at him.
>
> JOHN 8:37-38, 56-59

The religious leaders clearly understood what Jesus claimed when he used "I Am" to refer to himself as the same God revealed to Abraham and Moses. They tried to stone him to death for blasphemy because he was equating himself with the one true God. Their own prophets had long foretold his coming, but the religious leaders of Jesus' day were blinded by their ambition and lust for power. As Jesus said, there was no room in their hearts to let God be God.

The Father, Son, and Holy Spirit. In his NDE, Bill Smith recalls,

> There is a difference in the two identifiable characters who are one and the same God, one comes out of the other. The Spiritual Person who unites each one, God's Spirit, moves from the Son to the Father. There is no separation between them. We finally see Jesus as who He is, wrapped up in unity with the Father. There's God Himself—single, only one. He reveals Himself in time through the incarnation. Jesus is all that comes from the Father. . . . He serenaded me and sang me to His throne.[10]

What about the Holy Spirit? Is the Holy Spirit just a New Testament revelation of God? Not at all. The Holy Spirit was also there from the beginning: "In the beginning God created the heavens and the earth. . . . And the Spirit of God was hovering over the waters" (Genesis 1:1-2, NIV). And to Isaiah, God conveys his threefold nature in very personal terms:

> [God] said, "Surely they are my people, children [of a Father?] who will be true to me"; and so he became their Savior. In all their distress he too was distressed, and the angel of his presence [the Son?] saved them. In his love and mercy he redeemed them; he lifted them up and carried them all the days of old. Yet they rebelled and grieved his Holy Spirit.
> ISAIAH 63:8-10, NIV

The Holy Spirit is a person, not an "it," not "the force." The Holy Spirit has feelings, can love, and can be grieved.

After his resurrection, Jesus confirmed God's triune nature, saying to his followers,

I have been given all authority in heaven and on earth.
Therefore, go and make disciples of all the nations, baptizing
them in the name of the Father and the Son and the Holy
Spirit. Teach these new disciples to obey all the commands
I have given you. And be sure of this: I am with you always,
even to the end of the age.

MATTHEW 28:18-20

Jesus confirms there is one God, revealed as Father, Son, and
Spirit. In this statement, Jesus reminds us that God does not manifest
himself in thousands of gods, but as three persons, one God—no
more, no less.

We've just scratched the surface of all the ways God reveals his true
nature as one God in three persons. And consider this: If this were not
God's true nature, why would human writers preserve this paradoxi-
cal description of God across 1,500 years of writing? Why not "fix it"
to eliminate confusion? And why would people like Heidi and other
NDErs, with no previous understanding of the biblical view of Father,
Son, and Spirit, say the same thing? I think the answer is clear: God is
in fact a triune God, one God in three persons, just as he has revealed
all along.

Manifestations of God in NDEs

So what do we make of the giant God some NDErs see? At first hearing,
I struggled with NDErs saying God was giant. It felt like something
from a fairy tale. Yet, so many NDErs said the same thing about their
encounter with the Father. "When the Lord appeared like this, He was
a giant; He was a giant maybe seventy feet tall," Santosh said.[11] A giant
man in a white robe came to Bibi Tahereh in her NDE declaring, "I AM
HE WHO IS." She said, "He was so tall and his robe very long, but he
was enormous. I was trembling and shaking. There was a presence of
power and strength about him."[12]

A man named Matthew, who was not a believer at the time of his
NDE, thinks his wife's prayers moved the hand of God to rescue him
from hell:

The hand descended to me with the light shining about it, emanating from it. . . . This hand gently wrapped itself around my whole body, my back and waist lying somewhere in the palm area of the hand. I began an ascent as soon as I was grasped by this hand. . . . then I heard a commanding voice that came from everywhere all at once. . . . "It's not your time."[13]

Dean shared, "When I came back to the planet and tried to define the magnitude of God, as I try to quantify or define the size of the Father, he was huge; but I can't tell you because things like distances and sizes work differently there."[14]

As I've studied what NDErs convey, it seems the God who is Spirit can show himself to us in many ways—sometimes in grandeur of size, sometimes in simplicity, like the human Jesus. To NDErs, Jesus comes in various manifestations—from an ordinary human being to a larger-than-life, glorified Son of God. Jesus appeared on earth as a man, yet his followers also saw him transfigured, bright as the sun (Matthew 17:2). When the apostle John saw Jesus in his vision of heaven, he wrote, "He was wearing a long robe with a gold sash across his chest. His head and his hair were white like wool. . . . And his eyes were like flames of fire. His feet were like polished bronze refined in a furnace, and his voice thundered like mighty ocean waves. . . . And his face was like the sun in all its brilliance (Revelation 1:13-16)." So I imagine God can reveal himself in various manifestations, though he has never identified himself in Scripture as anyone other than the persons of the Father, Son, and Holy Spirit.

RELATING TO THE TRIUNE GOD

We've covered a lot of theological content, but what does it actually mean? How do we use what we've learned about the Trinity to relate to God and to love God better? You may wonder, as I have, which of the three you should focus on—the Father, Jesus, or the Holy Spirit? To whom should you pray, or does it even matter? Here's my pastoral wisdom: Don't stress about it. God knows our finite nature. Whatever best helps you to connect with and trust God is probably where God would want you to start. But as you grow in faith, stretch your imagination to include interaction with all three persons of the one triune God.

God the Father loves us better than any earthly mother or father loves their children. Jesus says the Father is infinite, eternal, all powerful, and a faithful provider. And when God's children get lost in life, Jesus says the Father searches for them, runs to his wayward children, embraces them, and throws a party every time even one of them comes home to him (see Luke 15:11-32). Do you need to be reminded that God is all powerful? Do you need reassurance that he is sustaining the universe and you're safe in his perfect plans, free to run into his arms to find comfort, protection, and love? That's the Father—the one true God.

Or maybe it's Jesus you need to spend time with, the Son who shows the unseen God in human form. Jesus shows us that God *gets us*. He has "been there done that." He was tempted as we are, he suffered as we do, and so he knows the struggle is real. Do you need a God who understands? That's Jesus, the one true God, and as you'll see, you've never had a closer friend.

Or do you need to experience the Holy Spirit—not an *it* or a force, but a person. The Holy Spirit is God's very presence, God's power, God's comfort, and God's wisdom with you always to guide you into truth. Jesus promised the Spirit to empower you to live your best, most fruitful life. You are never alone. God's Spirit, the one true God, is with you always.

AWESOME GOD AND FATHER

TWELVE-YEAR-OLD SUSANNE SEYMOURE COULDN'T wait to hit the ski slopes in the Poconos. Her family had bought a cabin, and the snow had fallen early that year. It wasn't Vail or Park City with fancy chair-lifts and groomed slopes, but the tow rope ski lift would pull her to the top—good enough! Flying down the mountain was all Susanne cared about that day as she and her family hiked up to the ski hill.

"Closed." They couldn't believe their eyes. Susanne and her brother had so looked forward to the start of the season. Her dad couldn't stand to watch his kids' disappointment. It was a small-scale operation; maybe there was still a way. Dad found the ski lift operator and talked him into turning on the tow rope. How perfect! They had the mountain to themselves.

Earlier that morning as they were getting ready to leave, Susanne's mom had insisted she wear a scarf to keep out the Pennsylvania cold. She tied a loose knot around Susanne's neck, never anticipating how much she would later regret that decision. After a few runs up and down the mountain, Susanne waited close to the spiraling rope for the next tow rope handle. She looked back at her brother and then suddenly felt a horrible tug on her neck. Her long scarf, she quickly realized, was caught and winding around the two-inch rope as it twisted its way up the mountain, suddenly dragging her along by the neck.

Susanne tried to get herself free, but the knot tightened. She put her hand between the scarf and her neck, but the twisting tow rope had no mercy as it led her by the neck up the ten-minute climb toward certain death. Susanne had seen the rope pass through the small opening housing the gearbox at the top. She knew her head would either make it through the hole only to meet the grinding gears or, if not, she would be decapitated.

But God is merciful, and Susanne does not remember either horrific scenario. A good reminder for anyone who has lost a child in an accident. "I think I died right before I hit the gearbox," Susanne told me. "I was choking, and my neck would most certainly have broken." No one witnessed what actually happened. What her parents and grandparents did see was her scarf coming down the mountain, perfectly straight, hanging from the rope and without any holes or tears, even after going through all those gears. Miraculous! Here's what Susanne does recall:

> What I remember just before I hit the gearbox is finding myself lying in the snow, and on the side of me I'm seeing birch trees and pine trees, because I'm drawn to a human figure in a white robe and light all around him. At first, I thought it was my dad. There were two others behind him I thought might be my mom and grandmother. I thought it was my dad because he felt so loving. And I just knew he was going to help me, and rescue me, and come and get me. I felt there was a sense of urgency. As soon as he came close, he put his hands out and looked at me, and through his eyes he just tells you exactly who he is. "I'm Jesus." And I just felt all this love and light, and I'm thinking, *I don't really know Jesus*, but he felt so loving. And next to him were these two angels, but I didn't know to call them angels.[1]

There was a calm and a comfort that is hard to find the words for. I felt no fear; he was like the most loving parent multiplied by a thousand. The hardest thing is to find the words for something that is so amazing. It was so remarkable that to this day there has not been a single experience that could ever compare.[2]

Jesus had longer brown hair, his eyes were a brown-hazel with a golden color. His hands were what I really noticed— something with his hands. He was wearing a white robe. Nothing I'd seen before. The light was his light. The light immediately came around me, and then my focus was on Jesus and his hands. He put out his hands, and all this information was conveyed: "Everything is going to be all right." If you've never met Jesus, he tells you everything about himself in an instant. There's no question. And it's like he lets your whole body know [that] he knows everything about you. Everything. Just feeling that understood—my mind, my heart, everything felt so understood. It felt like he knew my whole life in a second. So, there was no fear because we had this instant "I've known you all my life" connection.

He picked me up, scooped me in his arms. He was holding me, and the angels were shielding me on either side. And I was in a state of joy—home, bliss, happy. There's just so much joy. I never felt more loved or more joyful—and happy, euphorically happy. And suddenly, we're flying. I remember looking at the angel's wing over my right shoulder, and then I heard this scream—it was so chilling.

I looked back and it was my mother at the bottom of the hill. She was running around screaming hysterically. My grandfather was on his knees by a tree clutching his chest, and my grandmother was holding him. So, I could see what was happening at the bottom of the hill, even though there's no way you could see the bottom of the hill from the top, not unless you [were] lifted up above the tree line. I told my parents what I saw when I revived, and they confirmed. My grandfather actually had a terrible chest pain, fell to his knees, and my grandmother was holding him.

My mother's pain broke my happiness and joy. I said to Jesus, "I think I have to go back." And I remember the angels thinking, *What? . . . We weren't really planning on that.* Jesus was just calm as we continued. I kept saying that to him, "I don't think I can stay here."

We came to a place that was very similar to earth. It looked very familiar, but I knew it was somewhere very, very special. It was heaven, it was beautiful. I remember being by a big tree, larger than the sequoias. And I could see much farther. Your vision goes for miles. We sat down under this tree, and I sat on Jesus' lap as he answered all my little questions spinning in my mind. As I looked into his eyes, I knew the answers. I knew he was very superior to me. I knew he knows everything, and so this trust just happens.

I was worried about my family, and my dog, and the scream from my mom. And he gave me understanding that everything will be all right. Not like we say it, but with a complete understanding that he knows—he's not just saying comforting words. You feel the magnitude of his love that carries wisdom, and knowledge, and trust. There's nothing he's not going to know about you, down to your DNA. Billions of people are nothing to him, he knows them all personally. Just like a speaker in a stadium can reach personally to every person, God can reach in even more personal ways to each person. And I'm just a kid, but I felt so personally known and special; I'm *his* kid.[3]

Susanne felt so comfortable with Jesus, like any child would with a loving dad or a best friend, but then he showed her who he is in all his splendor.

I'm sitting with Jesus among this landscape of rolling hills of green with mountain peaks like the Rocky Mountains in the distance. He was talking with me and just hanging out with this kid like he was just a very comfortable, relatable dad. Then he let me know, "I'm a lot more powerful and awe inspiring than I've let you see until now." He showed me Reality.

Imagine if, as a kid, your neighbor is this kind, grandfatherly figure who loves to just be with you, play games with you. He's so relatable. But then one day, you find out who he really is—he's the president of the United States—he's the most powerful man in the world. That's like a tiny fraction of the majesty and power Jesus showed me.

Over the rolling hills, I could see this golden light growing. I thought it was a city behind the mountains. I knew there was a city and a throne, but I was focused on this beautiful, golden glow, growing and increasing, coming over the hills. I was captivated by this light because I just knew something magnificent was there. This was the presence of Almighty God. It felt like a hand, but it wasn't because it was light, but I felt it reaching toward Jesus and toward me.

Each time I had met people in heaven, I felt a different level of awe, like, "Whoa!" Jesus had held the greatest sense of awe or wonder for me up until then, but he showed me a side of himself he had not shown—who he really is—the power and glory of it all. When the golden light came, that was the biggest "whoa" of all.

I watched in awe as this beautiful, beautiful light—all these points of golden light—kept coming up over the hills, coming together to form this enormous golden hand larger than the whole sky. It covered everything. The golden light was the ultimate of every great word, "The Almighty," "Sovereign," "All-Powerful," "Holy." I've since learned that all those words are meant to convey something, but that Something was more than all words can express . . . just, "Whoa!"

The gigantic hand of light reached for Jesus and the golden light "touched" or merged with the whiter light of Jesus, and I knew intuitively in an instant—this is one light. This is

God, and there was no question in my mind. Jesus was letting me know, "That's me, that's my glory, that's my power, that's my light." There was a separation, a distinction of Jesus from Almighty God, but Jesus was also showing me they were one and the same.

All that overwhelming glory and power are hard to connect with as a child, so he first came to me as a man, like a dad, but then he showed me that he was so holy, so mind-blowing in size and awe and grandeur—the ruler of the universe— nothing is greater. Jesus became part of the golden light, and he let me know, "I am God, I am the light, I am the truth, and I am your Father." And all that came to me, and it was just blow-my-mind exciting to me at the time.

After that, Jesus brought me back to the scene of the accident, and he stayed with me as I went back into my body. He gave me a mental picture of a bird, like a dove with wings open, and he pointed to my chest, and it's like he put a dove in my chest and said, "I will always be with you." And I realized coming back that God is always with us, and he let me know his Spirit is for everyone, but not everyone receives him or accesses his Spirit's availability. But we don't ever have to be alone, he wants us to know he's always with us to love and guide us.[4]

The emergency rescue team found Susanne's body lying in the snow in front of the gearbox. She miraculously survived, healed, and became a follower of Jesus. I find it remarkable that Heidi and Susanne—two teenagers with no understanding of God as Father, Son, and Spirit— experienced God that way in their NDEs. Both women became nurses and are still inspired today by the awe and wonder of God they encountered.

GOD'S AWE-INSPIRING CHARACTER

There are things about God's character that have been revealed—in nature and in Scripture—so we can know him, love him, and follow him, but not *everything* is revealed. Some things remain mysterious. Moses notes, "The secret things belong to the LORD our God, but the things revealed belong to us and to our children forever, that we may follow all the words of this law" (Deuteronomy 29:29, NIV). And the apostle Paul said of his visit to heaven, there are things that "cannot be expressed in words, things no human is allowed to tell" (2 Corinthians 12:4). One NDEr said, "I gained access to a wealth of knowledge, a complete knowing and understanding. . . . No, I wasn't allowed to bring back the knowledge itself. Why, I don't know."[5]

If you feel certain you understand everything about God, and if there is no room for mystery beyond your current comprehension, then the God of your understanding is finite. There is an *incomprehensibility* to God, theologians say. Not that we can't know anything about God—we can—but God is also *beyond* finite words or concepts. So, as we imagine God, we must leave room for mystery. Otherwise, we cannot love and revere God in truth.

Jesus said, "True worshipers will worship the Father in spirit and in truth. The Father is looking for those who will worship him that way. For *God is Spirit*, so those who worship him must worship in spirit and in truth" (John 4:23-24, emphasis added). What God desires, like anyone in love, is that the people he loves would long to connect with him as he really is—in truth—and that includes the mysterious qualities of his nature that are hard to comprehend. Let's look at some of the mysterious, awesome aspects of God the Father's character so we can better love him.

God Is Spirit

What did Jesus mean when he said, "God is Spirit" (John 4:24)? When we think of "spirit," we often imagine something ethereal or wispy, such as a hologram or vapor—something less tangible than our physical reality. But when Jesus says "God is Spirit," he doesn't mean God is a wispy vapor: He means God is the very *foundation* of all reality. Everything physical and material was created from and is sustained by this great Spirit.

When the apostle Paul traveled to Athens and saw all the altars and shrines to the people's Greek gods, Paul observed what many missiologists have also found—in most ancient civilizations is the memory of the one true God.[6] Paul tells them:

> One of your altars had this inscription on it: "To an Unknown God." This God, whom you worship without knowing, is the one I'm telling you about.
>
> He is the God who made the world and everything in it. Since he is Lord of heaven and earth, he doesn't live in man-made temples, and human hands can't serve his needs—for he has no needs. He himself gives life and breath to everything, and he satisfies every need. . . . His purpose was for the nations to seek after God and perhaps feel their way toward him and find him—though he is not far from any one of us. For in him we live and move and exist. As some of your own poets have said, "We are his offspring." And since this is true, we shouldn't think of God as an idol.
>
> ACTS 17:23-25, 27-29

Paul points out that God made everything, and he is not far away from any one of us. God sustains our very being. We live and move and continue to exist *in him*, Paul says. In his letter to the church at Ephesus, Paul states that there is "one God and Father of all, who is over all and through all and in all" (Ephesians 4:6, NIV). This means God is the life force within each of us, the very breath of life. "The Spirit of God has made me; the breath of the Almighty gives me life" (Job 33:4, NIV). And Moses reminds Israel that "the LORD is your life" (Deuteronomy 30:20, NIV). The New Testament writer of Hebrews equates this sustaining life force with Jesus: "The Son is the radiance of God's glory and the exact representation of his being, *sustaining all things* by his powerful word" (Hebrews 1:3, NIV, emphasis added).

God is with every living person, but he is with us in different ways. For those who reject God's leadership over their lives, he is still the sustaining force of their physical lives, loving them and providing glimpses of his goodness, in hopes they will turn back to him (Acts 14:16-17). For believers, God is the sustaining force of their spirit as well as their physical body. So when a believer's spirit separates from her body (final physical death—not just an NDE*), her spirit lives on by God's Spirit (believers have spiritual life—there is no second death[7] or spiritual separation from God).

Jesus explained it this way: "No one can enter the kingdom of God unless they are born of water [from the womb] and the Spirit. Flesh gives birth to flesh, but the Spirit gives birth to spirit" (John 3:5-6, NIV). When a person says yes to God's forgiveness and guidance offered through Jesus, they are spiritually "born" by his Spirit, and their life will continue in God's presence after they die. So, God is Spirit, living in and through all, and yet God is far beyond all of his creation.

God Is Immanent and Transcendent

God as Spirit is both *immanent* (very near) and *transcendent* (far exceeding humanity and nature) at the same time. Father Cedric Pisegna recalls in his NDE how the glory of God overwhelmed him:

> I was standing before the throne of God! I was experiencing the pleasure all humans seek all our lives, the joy for which we were made. God's presence is the ultimate pleasure for which we long. . . . What I encountered when I stood before God was glorious and electric. I wasn't allowed to see a form, but what I did see was light. It was as if I were looking at the sun with my eyes closed, yet even more luminescent. Psalm 104:1-2 tells us the truth that God is "clothed with honor and majesty, and covers himself with light as with a garment." I didn't just see the light, the brightness embraced me. The light was somehow alive. In addition to the brightness, there was an overwhelming glory. . . . God's glory is not just something I observed, it was an electricity and ecstasy that I felt. It was a rhythmic powerful surge that ran all through me. I was experiencing the beatific [blissfully happy] vision![8]

---

* As I've mentioned, an NDE is not a final, biological death in which a person crosses over the border or boundary between life on earth and eternal life. Jesus even says to some NDErs, "You have not died yet, go back." So NDEs do not reflect a person's eternal destiny (heaven or hell). But I do believe God gives the NDE as a teaching for that person and as a witness to all of us.

Father Pisegna experienced the magnificent glory of God, yet when he came back, he realized that God is not just far away on his throne (transcendent), he is also simultaneously with us (immanent) and even in us through the Holy Spirit.

> I experienced the Holy Spirit when I came back. The same glory I felt in God the Father's presence I also felt, but to a much lesser degree, in prayer and everyday life. Remember what Jesus said, "Behold, I stand at the door and knock. If anyone hears my voice and opens the door, I will come in to him and eat with him, and he with me" (Revelation 3:20, ESV). I believe that the door talked about is the portal to eternity residing in our heart. . . . Opening that door takes work and discipline and grace. Usually, we are far from it, unaware and living in sensuality and carnality. But if we can slow down and get centered, we can begin to transcend time itself and enter the place of rest, God's glorious presence within us.[9]

Holding God's immanence and transcendence in tension can be challenging for our finite minds, yet God has revealed both aspects of his mysterious character. "'Am I a God who is only close at hand?' says the LORD. 'No, I am far away at the same time'" (Jeremiah 23:23). It sounds like a contradiction because in our world, you can't be simultaneously near and far. But this near-yet-far revelation of God is a paradox, not a contradiction.

Science is revealing many mysteries in nature that are paradoxes rather than contradictions. For instance, ever heard of the quantum double-slit experiment in physics? Light behaves as both particles and waves when a beam of light passes through a horizontal metal plate with two vertical slits. Yet, even though light *cannot* be both particles and waves, the same light does sometimes act as particles (like photons or dots of light passing through the slits) and sometimes act as waves (with interference patterns revealing wavelike behavior). Weirder still, what determines whether light acts as particles or waves depends on whether it is *observed* by a person. Scientists don't understand it, but they acknowledge it. Eminent theoretical physicist Richard Feynman says the double-slit experiment puts us "up against the paradoxes and mysteries and peculiarities of nature."[10]

It's important to hold the paradox of God's immanence and transcendence in tension. When we lean too far one way or another as we imagine God, we fall into error. Those who see God only as immanent (in all and one with all), but not transcendent, will sometimes say that God is not only in nature or sustaining nature, but that God *is* nature and nature is God. Or they will say, "I am god, and you are god" and "God is just the sum of all creation"—which is pantheism. But that's not who God revealed himself to be. God is in all, and yet God also transcends nature and all creation. The prophet Isaiah wrote,

> In the year that King Uzziah died, I saw the Lord, high and
> exalted, seated on a throne; and the train of his robe filled the
> temple. Above him were seraphim, each with six wings: With
> two wings they covered their faces, with two they covered their
> feet, and with two they were flying. And they were calling
> to one another: "Holy, holy, holy is the LORD Almighty;
> the whole earth is full of his glory."
> ISAIAH 6:1-3, NIV

God's glory fills the earth (he's immanent), but God is also high and exalted beyond his creation (he's transcendent). NDErs sometimes experience God the Father as ruler of all, seated on his throne and giant in size (as Isaiah implies, saying God's robe filled the temple). Just as Jesus revealed God locally to earth, I believe seeing God on his throne is also a local manifestation of God the Father for the inhabitants of heaven. Needless to say, the throne of God is mind-blowing in grandeur and wonder!

The Awesome Throne of God

Commercial airline pilot Captain Dale Black was in a twin-engine plane that hit a seventy-foot-high monument at 130 mph just after takeoff. In his book, Dale includes photos of the wreckage printed in the *Los Angeles Times*.[11] Though no one else survived, Dale miraculously came back to tell of the majestic city of God with God's throne at the center:

> I was fast approaching a magnificent city, golden and gleaming among a myriad of resplendent colors. The light I saw was the purest I had ever seen. And the music was the most majestic, enchanting, and glorious I had ever heard.[12]
>
> I got this descending, airborne view of the City of Gold. It's a city. It's a city that's walled. . . . Over the city were majestic mountains that were as gorgeous as any that could ever be seen. However, they did not look that different than earth. . . . The wall was gigantic. It looked like it was a couple hundred feet high. It was made of very dense stone, yet it was translucent. You could see through it. The light from the throne room of God was permeating through the stones, giving life to everything. . . . The light which came from the city center was holy and thick and pure. . . . There was a stairway that was near a glass sea, which did look like a sea; and a stairway that went up [to the throne]. . . . I was beginning to recognize that I'm being infused with power, like there's some nuclear power plant on the inside of me, but the power is coming from the light, and that light is giving energy.[13]
>
> There was a huge gathering of angels and people, millions, countless millions. They were gathered in [the] central area . . . Waves of people, moving in the light, swaying to the music, worshiping God. . . . The worship of God was the heart and focus of the music, and everywhere the joy of the music could be felt. The deepest part of my heart resonated with it and made me want to be a part of it forever. I never wanted it to stop.[14]

Richard Sigmund, whose NDE followed a terrible car accident, recalls,

> [The throne area] was wider and higher than I could even imagine—hundreds of miles, with massive arches and pillars. Everything in Heaven comes out of the throne. . . . As I got nearer to it, the air became electrically charged with the power and presence of God. . . . The closer I got to the throne, the more everything became transparent. Everything is absolutely transparent, with purity closest to God. I saw Jesus walk up to the throne and disappear into the enfolding fire that surrounds the Being on the throne. . . . He is a very big God![15]

God the Father's transcendent majesty manifests in the center of the city of God. In God's awesome presence, all becomes solid and visible, yet transparent, as the apostle John also reported of his experience of heaven (see Revelation 4:6; 21:11).

Around the throne, the worship of God the Father is not a "should" or an "ought," but something that erupts out of a joy and ecstasy that NDErs say they just can't contain. They never want to stop—that's how wonderful it is to be with God. In heaven, God the Father and the throne of God create the most beautiful and majestic place in the universe. Yet, God still transcends even the locale of the throne.

Dean Braxton felt the magnificence of God and his throne in exhilarating ways:

> No matter where I went in heaven, God was there. I could also look to the throne—it's the center of everything—but no matter how far I was from the locale of the throne, I could look at him and be up next to him from anywhere. And I always felt he was there with me. The focal point was the Father, and all else surrounds him. The throne is not like we picture, it looked more like a cloud than a chair. Like [the cloud] at the Transfiguration of Jesus or at Mount Sinai,[16]

the throne goes with him—it's part of him. It's not a room or building; it seemed to be more open. The Father was on his throne, but it was open, like all of heaven, not one little place. The columns seemed like pillars.

The glory of God is shining out of everything, so it kind of looks translucent. The glass sea is different; it's blue but mingled with fire, and it's changing and growing greater and greater. The whole realm of the Father was so beautiful and intense; everything was like beautiful artwork growing in intensity. God's creative power makes everything increasingly more and more beautiful in heaven. Just as everything on the earth is deteriorating and falling apart, everything in heaven is growing and getting better—they're moving in opposite directions. But the Father held the attention fully. It was just overwhelming wonder. . . .

In heaven, I experienced "the fear of the Lord" [described] in Scripture. It is a sense of awe and respect. He's so pure—all these words don't seem right—so clean, nothing wrong, no evil, all so pure. It is holiness, but it's a "what you see is what you get" purity that is so wonderful.[17]

The presence of the Father at the throne of God constitutes the most glorious, powerful, awe-inspiring sense of wonder we could fathom. Yet, God is greater still.

The Unseen, All-Powerful God

God in his fullness cannot be seen. God is described as *omnipresent* (everywhere at once) and *infinite* (not confined to a location). The apostle Paul describes God as "the King of kings and Lord of lords, who alone is immortal and who lives in unapproachable light, whom no one has seen or can see" (1 Timothy 6:15-16, NIV). No one can see God (because we cannot "see" or "comprehend" an infinite presence), yet God has manifested himself in knowable ways for our benefit.

Isaiah saw God on his throne, and people saw Jesus. NDErs claim to see God today. Yet, no one "sees" all of God. The apostle John wrote, "No one has ever seen God, but the one and only Son, who is himself

God and is in closest relationship with the Father, has made him known" (John 1:18, NIV).

God is the *unseen, omnipotent* (all-powerful) Creator of everything. During his NDE, Dr. Ron Smothermon encountered the immensity of God's power. He realized that the only response to God's all-powerful presence is awe and respect (this shows in how he capitalizes God's qualities).

Amin's right arm is drawn back, and the knife is aimed at my chest. Meanwhile, time has stopped, and in an instant out of time, I see the qualities of the LIGHT, His qualities. However, the experience of these qualities is not something I can give you, for their essence cannot be rendered in words. . . . Imagine trying to describe the Grand Canyon, the Milky Way galaxy, or an atomic bomb blast to a blind person. . . . GOD's LIGHT appeared like a sudden silent fusion atomic bomb blast, pure white and full of His POWER.

His qualities project themselves with perfect clarity and you are better able to receive Him than eyes can detail vision or ears define hearing . . . [giving] awareness that we call "charisma" in humans. In the case of GOD, this quality is infinitely magnified. I could feel the presence of His KNOWLEDGE. I had an image of a universe made of libraries, and He wrote every book. With His LOVE came certainty of INFINITE POWER. If encountered without INFINITE LOVE, His INFINITE POWER would provoke pure terror; you would surely "fear" GOD. . . . The response His POWER calls forth is Surrender. In the smallest space of time, perhaps outside time, I knew: This is the One who created universes of unfathomable dimensions, the One who created reality, time, you, and me. . . . He has the moral right to use His POWER, for it comes wrapped in His INFINITE LOVE. . . .

The Scriptures tell us to fear GOD. When you meet Him person to person, fear transforms into respect. If you cannot respect GOD, you do not know Him, and then you had best fear Him.[18]

The power of God reminds us just *who* this infinitely kind, loving being is—the one who deserves utmost honor, respect, awe, and even fear if it were not for his great love. It's not that we *should* or *ought* to feel awe and respect, but that we *will* on the day we experience God as these NDErs have. And properly imagining God in all his power helps us to grow in loving awe and respect for God today.

Karina Martinez had an overwhelming encounter with God's power during her NDE. When her heart stopped due to a failed pacemaker, she cried out the Lord's Prayer and found herself with Jesus in a beautiful landscape beside a river. He took her to the throne, where she felt the power of God the Father's presence. The apostle John wrote, "In front of the throne there was what looked like a sea of glass, clear as crystal" (Revelation 4:6, NIV). Karina didn't know that what she experienced was in the Bible until after her NDE:

> I was prostrated on this glass floor—it was all glass, but it was
> bright, light coming out of it, and I was on my hands and
> knees, pushed down by the sheer power of some presence, and
> I lifted my head up just enough to see this white gown coming
> towards me. There was a gold belt and a purple sash around
> the robe. I couldn't see clearly his face; it was all white—so
> bright—the light.[19]

Karina experienced a tiny fraction of the power of God's glory. God's power is unlimited—nothing is greater. Let that give you confidence, knowing how much he cares about you.

Can you imagine a God who is present with you always, sustaining everything, yet also infinitely beyond all he's created? God's overarching power has no comparison, yet this supreme power is used only in love.

The awesome Father we just read about loves and cares for you, knows you perfectly, and is able to do anything necessary for your ultimate well-being. This truth can give you great reassurance and confidence when life feels chaotic or uncertain. God is infinitely greater than all your problems, troubles, trials, and tribulations. He is with you, and he cares for you, so you can trust that you're going to be okay in his mighty hands.

JESUS,
OUR BROTHER AND FRIEND

AS RANDY KAY LAY IN A SAN DIEGO HOSPITAL, his mind was flooded with worries and concerns for his family. Having been a medical company executive most of his life, he knew the critical concerns of a pulmonary embolism combined with an MRSA (staph) infection. He knew his body was shutting down. He worried that his wife, Renee, and his two young kids would have radically different lives after his death, and he was anxious about how his death would affect their futures.

Randy had been the CEO of several companies. He was the executive responsible for launching a new "cure" for Alzheimer's, and *Time* magazine featured his company for developing a possible breakthrough treatment. But the breakthrough Randy needed this night didn't happen. His body went into septic shock, and Randy clinically died. His medical records show that his heart stopped beating for thirty minutes. As he felt his soul being sucked out of his body, he cried out the name of Jesus.

I was being pulled up, and I could see my body below for just a short period of time. But I was in a vacuum being pulled up into a light that was streaming down from above. And the light was illuminating my environment. I had peak senses. I could breathe where I couldn't before. I was able to see things far out in the distance. As I rose, I witnessed some kind of cosmic battle going on across hillsides far away, in a world I realized was some other dimension all around us.

I continued my ascent, and at some point, I settled on soft ground. The light that was streaming from above was now illuminating everything around me. I had touched down in some heavenly paradise. I had senses there I don't have here—not just sight, sound, and smell—but I could sense everything growing. In this life, you know things are alive and growing around you, but there you have a new sense that can actually experience the life and growth of everything. And nothing was dying or dead, everything was alive and growing.

I felt someone wrap his arm around my torso, and I could feel the soft, cottony garment he was wearing. He was pulling me tightly to him, and instantly, I knew it was Jesus Christ. I knew it was the Lord. Comfort surged through me with an assurance I had never felt before. And I was overwhelmed—by the love—and being in the presence of the Lord.

So this is love.

I distinctly remember that one overwhelming thought. Yet, I could not tell you exactly what I felt since no words could adequately explain it.

Jesus tenderly embraced me. As I began to turn, he pressed his cheek gently into mine and wrapped his other arm around me and hugged me tenderly. I felt his beard softly against my face, and I could see his left eye and long nose out of the corner of my right eye. When Jesus hugged me, he ripped away all of the cares that encumbered me. Every concern melted away like ice, leaving behind the snuggling feeling of a warm blanket on a cold night. I snuggled with him like a two-year-old formerly lost, now comforted by his parent. I could literally see his figure, smell his fragrance, and feel his smooth skin against my face. He was altogether familiar as a friend and as a loving father in one.

I wasn't inclined to look around because I just wanted to be in that place, in the person of Jesus Christ. And this was before he said anything, but I just knew. One of those extra senses in heaven is a sense of knowing.

He said, "Have no fear. Trust me. You are going to be okay, and you're not going to stay here. I'm going to return you."

When I turned to look at him, his eyes just tunneled through me and exposed everything dark within me. I looked into the eyes of love itself. I have to choke back emotion thinking of it. I don't know any other way to explain it, but I saw into the eyes of love. I'm not a romantic; I'm a realist. I'm the doubting Thomas. I've always been the guy saying, "Prove it." So for me, just trusting in the Lord had been hard for me previously, but there it felt absolutely right. Comfortable. I knew! I knew that I knew that he had taken care of all I was worried about.

So there was such comfort in his presence—everything was as it should be. Time became irrelevant when I met him in this place, this . . . heaven! In awe, I bowed down before Jesus Christ, wanting nothing but to please him, worship him, venerate him with every fiber of my being. I tried to tell him, "You are perfect in every way and so above my ability to worship you with any semblance of worthiness. My Lord! . . ." And then I broke down in tears, unable to control my wellspring of emotion.

Jesus reached down to softly lift me from my prostrate position. With tenderness, he wiped the tears running down my eyes, and as he did, an impartation of assurance consumed me. "I have been waiting for you, my beloved child." I was overcome with breathless excitement and awe. I was so excited and giddy that my shaking would not stop. My lips quivered as I shook in awe of Jesus' absolute love.

"I'm going to send you back. You have yet to fulfill your purpose." We started walking together. Now I was noticing the environment around me. Paved roads—or rather pathways you might find through rolling hills, were spectacularly golden. They gave off a radiant glow resplendent with colors I'd never seen before. . . . Waves of hills and majestic mountains lay nested on a flowing river. These waters gave life, glorious life. Everything touched by the waters sprouted life. I noticed that the river flowed from Jesus himself. What a spectacular sight!

"I feel at home," I said. I did not want to return to the world. I had become so enthralled and embedded in this place of wonder. At no time in my wildest imagination could I fathom such beauty. That paradise danced with joy. Even while I thought those words, I knew Jesus was reading my mind.

"You are with me always, my beloved," he responded. "I have known you from before you were born, in all ways and in all things." His words kept comforting me. I felt so at home, so known, so comfortable with him. "I am sending you back, my beloved. Many have prayed for you, and my purpose for you is not yet complete."

"But, I have to go back? Please, no. I want to stay. This is home. Please!" Jesus looked at me with his graceful, passionate eyes. I did not want to go. Everything was so perfect, so . . . and there I thought again, comfortable.

What was my purpose? I wondered. Jesus answered, "The life each lives on earth is a process of discovery, my beloved. My truth is imparted to those who know me."

"But now I have to go back—to complete my purpose?" I asked incredulously. I felt like a little child waking up Christmas morning only to be summoned back to his bedroom.

I had questions, "Your Kingdom, Lord, what is your Kingdom?"

Jesus' eyes glistened with joy as he spoke: "My Kingdom is within each believer, and within me, beloved. It is my impartation of who I am. . . . My Spirit can only be manifested in my children, and without my Spirit, people are dead to my Kingdom, my presence. . . ."

"So, the secret is in being, more than doing? More about getting close to you?" I so loved that smile Jesus gave me when I was on to something deep. It was better than a warm fire on a freezing night.

"My Spirit has revealed this to you, my beloved."

The illuminating light that effused [came out from] all of heaven began turning colors of orange mixed with purple and yellow and other brilliant colors I had never seen before— a kind of heavenly storm was underway. Only, this storm produced rains of refreshment intermixed with a hallowed sense of wonder. Every living thing cried out praises to God!

Jesus whispered into my ear, "You must go now, but remember, I will never forsake you, my dearest one." With this, he kissed me on the forehead, and I began to fall from my Lord's embrace back to the harsh dryness of the world. I remembered the songs of the angels—how beautiful the sound—and as I revived, I heard this couple at my bedside singing the same song of praises to God.[1]

A FRIEND IN JESUS

When I contemplate the fact that the Creator of the universe, the most powerful, majestic being in existence, took on human skin to relate to us, it blows my mind. Not only that, but God's love for you and me is so great that he chose to intertwine himself with humanity *forever*. Jesus still has skin, scars, and a human body (though a resurrected human body), and he will have this body for eternity. It's a great mystery.

Jesus is not limited by his resurrected body. He sometimes appears to NDErs in ordinary human form, just as he appeared on earth; other times, he appears in glorified form, as we've discussed. This may explain the varied descriptions NDErs have of Jesus' eyes. You may have noticed some NDErs say blue, others a golden, brown-hazel color. Perhaps the color changes depending on whether Jesus appears in his earthly form or his glorified form. NDEr Dr. Mary Neal told me she saw all the colors in his eyes, and many described eyes that color alone cannot explain.

Regardless, Jesus is still the climax of God's story across human history. God became one of us! God gets us. He can relate to us in every way. He's like a best friend or devoted older brother—someone in whose presence we can feel so comfortable, so known, so loved, and so understood. No one knows us better. Imagine it!

I recently spent a week with some longtime friends—one of whom I've known since I was ten, and the others since high school. We grew up together. We know everything that shaped us—our families, secrets, successes, sins and failures, triumphs and tragedies—yet despite knowing the good and bad, we've remained close friends for decades. It's amazing how quickly we pick up where we left off, no matter how long we've been apart, because we've traveled all of life together— we understand each other and we're for each other. Time has proven that.

Even though it might be hard to imagine, this is also true about you and Jesus. He has been with you all along the journey of your life—he knows you better than you know yourself. He's seen the highs, the lows, the victories, the defeats, the good and bad—he's been there through it all. And he is still for you. He's proven that. His love for you is immeasurable. I think that's why NDErs such as Randy and others feel so comfortable and at home with the Lord. He's like a combination of a best friend or a big brother and the wisest, most loving parent, all at the same time.

In her NDE, Pepi from Spain noticed,

> Someone was waiting for me where the path ended. I knew it was Jesus. He was tall and strong, with long dark hair and a wonderful tender smile. His eyes were unforgettable, immense, dark, so loving and full of wisdom. He was wearing a long white tunic and sandals. He was there all by himself and smiling, just waiting for ME. He welcomed me. He didn't say a word, I didn't either, but we were communicating without talking. . . .

When I was getting comfortable and ready to stay there, he took me out again. "You must go back," he said (no words), and his smile has since then accompanied me throughout my life. . . . He was my friend and my boss, no doubt about that.[2]

Jesus' disciples experienced the same comfortable friendship with him when he walked the earth. Jesus said, "I do not call you servants any longer. . . . Instead, I call you friends" (John 15:15, GNT). Like Randy, who snuggled up against Jesus in his NDE, the apostle John "leaned back on Jesus' chest" during the Last Supper (John 13:25, NASB). Just picture the approachability, the relatability, the comfort, love, and closeness John must have felt in Jesus' presence. The tender friendship of Jesus was true for his followers then, it's true for the NDErs who meet him in heaven, and it's true for you while you live on this earth. That God would descend from heaven to enter human suffering and misery, just to be with us forever—it seems too good to be true. Maybe God knew we'd need some proof of this radical love, so he marked a date on the calendar when his love would come down.

AT JUST THE RIGHT TIME

In God's great love story, at just the right time in history, Jesus appeared on the scene. Paul said, "There is one God and one Mediator who can reconcile God and humanity—the man Christ Jesus. He gave his life to purchase freedom for everyone. This is the message God gave to the world *at just the right time*" (1 Timothy 2:5-6, emphasis added). At the right time, Jesus came not only to save us, but also to teach us, heal us, and to do life with us starting now, and forever.

"The right time" turned out to be fairly early in the history of the total human population. It's estimated that about 170 million people lived during Jesus' lifetime. The population doubled by the Renaissance during the fifteenth and sixteenth centuries, but it didn't reach one billion until 1800. In the last two hundred years, we've added nearly seven billion souls.[3] We forget that most of humanity has lived since the time of Jesus. Maybe Jesus came "at just the right time" for that reason—because most of the world's population would live after he walked the earth. Or maybe it was "at just the right time" because the *Pax Romana* (Roman peace) had descended across the Mediterranean, bringing with it a common language and paved roads that enabled the gospel message to spread more rapidly. Or maybe it was "at just the right time" because hundreds of years before, God had foretold the arrival of the Messiah at that exact moment in history.

In the sixth century BCE, the prophet Daniel had been in Babylonian captivity for almost seventy years when he read Jeremiah's prophecy about the first scattering of Israel: "Israel and her neighboring lands will serve the king of Babylon for seventy years" (Jeremiah 25:11). The seventy years were coming to completion, so Daniel prayed, asking God about the future destiny of the Jewish people. Daniel says the angel Gabriel appeared to him with a prophecy (Daniel 9:20-23). Recall that the way the Jewish people would bless all nations was through the Messiah. Gabriel gave the rebuilding of Jerusalem as the start of the countdown until the year of the Messiah's coming. This is incredible— the angel Gabriel reveals *exactly* when Messiah will come.

> Now listen and understand! Seven sets of seven plus sixty-two sets of seven will pass from the time the command is given to rebuild Jerusalem until a ruler—the Anointed One [in Hebrew "Messiah"]—comes. Jerusalem will be rebuilt with streets and strong defenses, despite the perilous times.
>
> After this period of sixty-two sets of seven, the Anointed One [Messiah] will be killed, appearing to have accomplished nothing, and a ruler will arise whose armies will destroy the city and the Temple.
>
> DANIEL 9:25-26

Gabriel says the clock starts "from the time the command is given to rebuild Jerusalem." After that, there will be seven "sevens"[4] plus sixty-two "sevens" until Messiah comes. It's a little cryptic—what are the sevens? Given the context of history Gabriel's referring to, along with the fact that sevens of years made up the Jewish sabbatical year cycle, it must be sevens of years.[5] Assuming it's years, there would be 483 years from the time the decree is issued to rebuild Jerusalem until Messiah comes (7 x 7) + (62 x 7) = 483. The question is, 483 years from what starting date?

Years after Daniel's prophecy, the Persians had conquered Babylon, and King Artaxerxes began to rule Babylon in 465 BCE. The Jewish priest Ezra, also a scribe in King Artaxerxes's service, records exactly when the decree to rebuild Jerusalem was made. Notice these are known rulers and historical dates, not mythology:

> [Ezra] came up to Jerusalem in the seventh year of King Artaxerxes.
> Ezra arrived in Jerusalem in the fifth month of the seventh year of the king. . . .
> This is a copy of the letter King Artaxerxes had given to Ezra: . . .
> Artaxerxes, king of kings,
> To Ezra the priest, teacher of the Law of the God of heaven:
> Greetings.
> Now I decree that any of the Israelites in my kingdom, including priests and Levites, who volunteer to go to Jerusalem with you, may go. . . . Do whatever seems best with the rest of the silver and gold, in accordance with the will of your God.
> EZRA 7:7-8, 11-13, 18, NIV

Artaxerxes's decree *is* the starting date. In the Hebrew Bible, this decree is written in Aramaic, the trade language of the ancient Near East (which the Persian king would have used)—so Ezra copied the exact Aramaic decree into what became the Hebrew Bible.[6] After the letter was read, complaints came back to King Artaxerxes: "The king should know that the [Jewish] people . . . have gone to Jerusalem and are rebuilding that rebellious and wicked city" (Ezra 4:12, NIV). They cited this decree that started the rebuilding. This is confirmed in history with known dates, giving us the date to start the countdown until the Messiah.

Encyclopedia Britannica says the rule of Artaxerxes began in 465 BCE.[7] Ezra said the decree was issued almost halfway into the seventh year of Artaxerxes's rule, so 457 BCE is the year of Artaxerxes's decree that starts the countdown until Messiah. The angel Gabriel had specified 483 years from that 457 BCE decree, which means Messiah should have come in 27 CE.* This coincides with the approximate time of Jesus' baptism and the beginning of his public ministry.[8] At "just the right time," Jesus came to earth. The following chart briefly summarizes the dates when these events occurred and when the biblical prophecies were fulfilled.

457 BCE	457 to 27 CE	27 CE	70 CE
Artaxerxes issues the decree to restore and rebuild Jerusalem (Ezra 7)	Prophetic timeline to the Messiah: [7 x 7 = 49] [62 x 7 = 434] [49 years] + [434 years] = 483 years (Daniel 9:25)	The Messiah comes in 27 CE not 26 CE, as there is no year "zero" (Daniel 9:26)	Romans destroy the second Temple and Jerusalem (Daniel 9:26)

Even if we set aside the date calculations, the angel Gabriel says to Daniel that the Messiah, the "Anointed One," will be killed, and then Jerusalem and the Temple will be destroyed (Daniel 9:26). In 70 CE, the Roman general Titus leveled Jerusalem and scattered the Jewish people a second time. The Jerusalem Temple has still not been rebuilt to this day! Remember, the angel Gabriel said that the Messiah would come before the destruction of the Temple in 70 CE, and Jesus did! He came at just the right time to save us, and to connect with us as a friend, mediator, brother, and teacher.

HOW JESUS RELATES TO US

Jesus relates to us as a friend, but he's much more than just a buddy. Jesus plays various roles in our relationship to God. The more we understand what Jesus has done for us and how we are related to Jesus, the

---

* Subtracting 483 years from 457 BCE would be 26 CE (457 – 483 = -26), but because there is no "year zero" between 1 BCE and 1 CE, we add one year to bring us to 27 CE when the Messiah comes.

deeper our love and trust can delve into this supernatural friendship. Let's look at how NDErs experienced Jesus in these same ways Scripture spells out.

Jesus Our Mediator

Many NDErs experience Jesus as a *mediator* between them and God. They don't necessarily even understand what that means, but they are intuitively clear that he mediates on their behalf. A mediator is a go-between, someone who helps two parties in a conflict come together to resolve their differences. We have all turned from God and followed our own will against his will. Jesus is our mediator, the one who advocates for us before God.

Micki, who experienced the maternal love of God during her NDE, found herself at the bottom of a huge stairway that led to a throne with a brilliant light radiating from it that she knew was God. She recalls how Jesus advocated for her: "Jesus was standing at the right hand of God. . . . telling God how much I loved him and believed that he died for my sins. God then spoke mentally to me and told me how much he loved me. (Jesus was the mediator between God and me.)"[9]

As we explored in chapter 6, God's love and God's justice met on the Cross of Christ. All those who admit their need for God's forgiveness and accept that Jesus paid for their wrongs stand guilt free and blameless before God (see Ephesians 1:4). But even when we are reconciled to God, we still struggle with sin. We still go against God's will and God's ways. But now we don't have to let our sins or failures separate us from God; instead, he takes our mistakes and helps us grow through them. As the apostle John explains, we can confess and return to God, knowing Jesus paid our debts, understands our struggles, and advocates for us:

If we claim we have no sin, we are only fooling ourselves and not living in the truth. But if we confess our sins to him, he is faithful and just to forgive us our sins and to cleanse us from all wickedness. . . . My dear children, I am writing this to you so that you will not sin. But if anyone does sin, we have an advocate who pleads our case before the Father. He is Jesus Christ, the one who is truly righteous.

1 JOHN 1:8-9; 2:1

We don't have to fear confessing or being honest with God because Jesus has our backs. He has been through all the trials, the temptations, the betrayals, the sufferings, and even the tortures of humanity. Yet, he did not sin. That's what qualifies him to be our perfect mediator—our perfect High Priest—to reconcile us to God. The author of Hebrews writes:

> Nothing in all creation is hidden from God. Everything is naked and exposed before his eyes, and he is the one to whom we are accountable. So then, since we have a great High Priest who has entered heaven, Jesus the Son of God, let us hold firmly to what we believe. This High Priest of ours understands our weaknesses, for he faced all of the same testings we do, yet he did not sin. So let us come boldly to the throne of our gracious God. There we will receive his mercy, and we will find grace to help us when we need it most.
>
> HEBREWS 4:13-16

Do you realize that you can confidently, boldly go to the throne of God for help—even as you're struggling in an addiction, or lashing out in anger, or giving in to lust or envy? That is exactly when we need to humbly seek God's help for power to change and grow. Fortunately, because Jesus is our understanding mediator, we can turn to God for help and receive it, even at our worst moments.

Jeremy,* a lead software engineer, met Jesus in his NDE and intuitively knew that Jesus was his mediator. Here is what he wrote to me about his NDE:

> I was standing in a room with a few people. I will refer to this room as a waiting room but only because I don't have a better

---

* Jeremy is a pseudonym.

explanation for its purpose. It had two opening entranceways to a large courtyard. Everyone knew exactly who I was, and they were definitely waiting for me to arrive. I didn't recognize anyone, but I knew they all knew me and loved me. There was one person that was in the room who never said his name, but I knew everything I saw in the building and garden was his.

I am a shy person, so he wanted to show me around, and we went for a walk in the garden section of the courtyard. He introduced me to people in small groups. He knew everyone we met, and they all loved him. I probably was introduced to ten to fifteen people. I remember feeling like I was loved and a sense that everyone longed to meet me.

The whole time, I knew exactly who this man was, and I was so sure of it. He never said who he was; I just knew it. I recognized him as Jesus, not by name but by function. I am terrified of blaspheming, so I hesitate to use this name if there is any evidence that I could be wrong. When I looked at him, I knew he was the mediator to God, [and] the creator, and God. But most of all, I absolutely knew he was the mediator to God in a way that I can't describe. It was just true, and it was so obvious that he was a mediator to God. I don't even know what a mediator to God looks like, but it looks like what I saw.[10]

Jesus eternally functions as our mediator to a holy God, and because of him, we have nothing to fear in boldly approaching God. He is the perfect mediator, and the perfect brother.

Jesus Our Brother

Jeremy knew that Jesus was his mediator, but he also experienced Jesus as his brother during his NDE:

Later, one of the people in the waiting room introduced Jesus as my "brother." I never understood this part until a few months ago. When I looked at my "brother," I knew this "brother" of mine was the mediator between me and God, but he was certainly not my biological brother. So I was confused until recently, when I read in the New Testament about Jesus saying, "Whoever does the will of my Father in heaven is my brother and sister" [Matthew 12:50, NIV]. Now, when I think about this, it brings tears of joy to me, and I don't cry often.[11]

Jesus revealed this inconceivable truth: He is our brother. During his earthly ministry, when someone informed Jesus that his mother and biological brothers were looking for him, Jesus looked at the crowd he was teaching and said, "Who is my mother? Who are my brothers? . . . Anyone who does the will of my Father in heaven is my brother and sister and mother!" (Matthew 12:48, 50).

The writer of the book of Hebrews expounds on this mystery of Jesus as our brother:

> It was only right that [God] should make Jesus, through his suffering, a perfect leader, fit to bring them into their salvation. So now Jesus and the ones he makes holy have the same Father. That is why Jesus is not ashamed to call them his brothers and sisters. For he said to God, "I will proclaim your name to my brothers and sisters."
> HEBREWS 2:10-12

This is exactly what David had written a thousand years before, foretelling the crucifixion of the Messiah, who says, "I will proclaim your name to my brothers and sisters" (Psalm 22:22). Jesus came not only to pay the price to restore us to God, but to make God relatable as a kind, caring older brother.

While Julie was in the ICU of a San Antonio hospital, her organs shut down. She found herself in the presence of Jesus near the river of life. There, she gained new understandings of Jesus as both her mediator and her loving older brother.

> There were things that I talked about with Jesus that I did not know or believe at the time [like] . . . a person cannot under

any circumstances be in the presence of God or anywhere near
the throne of God without Jesus. It is just not possible. God
wants us to be near him and desires it greatly. Jesus is truly the
doorway to the throne of God . . . .

We then walked over next to the river, then Jesus took
both my hands, turning my palms upward. While holding my
hands, he said, "I want you to remember something. You are of
a royal lineage. You are a child of God. The Most High God.
You live in the world but are not of the world. Your rightful
place is in heaven with the Father."

I said, "Yes, I understand." The whole while he was telling
me this, I felt like I was the most precious, most loved, most
beloved person in existence. Next, I asked, "Just what is your
relationship to me?"

Jesus said, "I am your brother."

I said, "I know that's what the Bible says, so it's true then?"

Jesus said, "Yes, I am your brother. We have the same blood
running through our veins. I will never leave you or forsake you.
I will always be there for you. Never ever forget who you are."

I just stood there looking around us for a while. He then
said, "Now go back to your bed and wake up."[12]

Do you realize that you are of royal blood if you've given your life
to God? Jesus and you are related, and he can relate to all you're going
through. He's family. He's there for you, and he longs to guide you and
teach you.

Jesus Our Teacher

Many of those who deny the divinity of Jesus nevertheless respect and
affirm the wisdom and moral soundness of his teaching. But Jesus did
not claim to be just a wise teacher; he claimed his teaching was from
God himself. Those who heard him teach were amazed and asked,
"'How did this man get such learning without having been taught?'
Jesus answered, 'My teaching is not my own. It comes from the one
who sent me. Anyone who chooses to do the will of God will find

out whether my teaching comes from God or whether I speak on my own'" (John 7:15-17, NIV).

"The Way" of Jesus, as his first followers called it, is the way to live a life of "love, joy, peace, patience, kindness, goodness, faithfulness, gentleness, and self-control" (Galatians 5:22–23). This is how we enjoy the moments of life in the unburdened, worry-free way of Christ. Have you studied Jesus' teachings and actually tried to live them out? If you do, you, too, will see how they enable you to live the life your soul longs for.

It's not difficult to summarize the teachings of Jesus because he already did it for us. When the religious leaders asked Jesus, "Teacher, which is the greatest commandment in the Law?" Jesus replied,

> "Love the Lord your God with all your heart and with all your soul and with all your mind." This is the first and greatest commandment. And the second is like it: "Love your neighbor as yourself." All the Law and the Prophets hang on these two commandments.
>
> MATTHEW 22:37-40, NIV

Everything Jesus taught reveals what it means to love God and to love people.

Studies show that most people think they are, in fact, kind and loving people. Yet, the world is far from a kind and loving place. The truth is, Jesus fully expects those who follow him as Lord to both *know* what he taught and to *do* what he said to become the kind and loving people God intended. "Jesus said to the people who believed in him, 'You are truly my disciples if you remain faithful to my teachings. And you will know the truth, and the truth will set you free'" (John 8:31-32).

Jesus' aim is to lead us into freedom and life, but there's a requirement. We must know his teachings and take them seriously—as seriously as Jesus did: "Heaven and earth will disappear," Jesus said, "but my words will never disappear" (Matthew 24:35). I find it intriguing that sometimes Jesus even quotes himself to NDErs.

Kevin Zadai had a near-death experience during dental surgery. He recalls how Jesus corrected him. "He started to speak to me about how I had been very careless about my words," Kevin says. Jesus referenced his own words in Matthew 12:36, saying, "You will be held accountable for every idle word that comes out of your mouth." Then he said to Kevin, "You know I meant that."[13]

Dr. Mary Neal, whose NDE happened during a kayaking accident, told Jesus, "This is wonderful. Why don't you do this for everyone, and everyone would believe?" Jesus quoted himself, "You see and believe, but even more blessed are those who don't see, yet believe."[14] He paraphrased his own response to "doubting Thomas" as recorded in John 20:29.

NDErs who clinically die as followers of Jesus often convey how much Jesus expects us to read and study and follow his teachings. Dr. Richard Eby was a medical doctor and surgeon who fell headfirst from two stories, cracked his skull open, but miraculously revived after ten hours. During his NDE, he said, "Jesus and I walked in heaven together, but it was more like flying than walking. We were talking while suspended in midair. . . . Communication is so far superior than anything we can imagine down here. Space is also limitless."

When Dr. Eby asked Jesus about the life that people experience in heaven, Jesus replied, "I only give them the desires of their heart," echoing Psalm 37:4. Then he said, "I put it in My book. Didn't you read My book? Everything in it is explanatory of what a child of Mine needs to know." Dr. Eby recalls, "Several times I asked a question and He answered, 'Didn't you read My book?'"[15]

It's a good question for all of us who claim to follow Jesus: "Did you read my book?" It's one of the ways we love God—by knowing his teachings and doing what he said. Jesus said, "All who love me will do what I say. My Father will love them, and we will come and make our home with each of them" (John 14:23). Salvation and relationship with God is not dependent on our deeds, but it gives God joy when we follow his commands, and it grieves him when we ignore them.

In the conversation Dr. Gary Wood had with Jesus during his NDE, Jesus reminded him of the truths of Scripture and how it hurts him when we ignore them:

Jesus looked right at me with those piercing blue eyes and said, "Don't ever buy the condemnation of the devil that you are unworthy. You are worthy. You have been redeemed by the Blood of the Lamb." He said, "Why do my people not believe in me? Why do my people reject me? Why do they not walk in my commandments? . . . Remember what I say, for the Father and I are one. When I speak, the Father has spoken. Above all else love one another and always be forgiving towards each other."[16]

Jesus expects us to follow his teachings. He is the wisest counselor ever, and the only one who truly knows how life works. We can follow what he said and what he did while on earth.

BE LIKE JESUS

Jesus understands us like no other. He's the best friend, brother, teacher, and role model we could ever hope to find. He came to save us, to heal us, and to teach us the way to life. When we study the life and teachings of Jesus, we see what humanity is supposed to be like under God's leading. If we could all be more like Jesus, our world would be a much better place.

You may recall Dr. Ron Smothermon's description of how all the qualities of God—his infinite power, love, kindness, compassion, justice—exploded into him like an atom bomb during his NDE. But of all of those qualities, he identified one that had the most impact on him: "Humility is what really got to me. He is so humble." Ron's voice quavered with emotion as he continued, "Just thinking about being with him sometimes, I break out in tears. He's so kind and humble; he's not proud or boastful. I've been full of pride yet have no reason to be. He has every reason to be, and yet he's so humble."[17]

"Let me teach you," Jesus said while on earth, "because I am humble and gentle at heart, and you will find rest for your souls. For my yoke is easy to bear, and the burden I give you is light" (Matthew 11:29-30). We can all live in the peaceful, unburdened way of Jesus, fulfilling our God-given purpose on earth by following his teachings. And he's given us his Holy Spirit to guide us as we learn to hear his voice.

GOD'S SPIRIT
SPEAKS

AS A CRITICAL CARE NURSE, Penny Wittbrodt knew her body was shutting down from anaphylactic shock, but the nurse at the rural Kentucky hospital thought the EpiPen would be enough to treat her allergic reaction. When a resident walked by the waiting area and saw Penny in distress, he rushed her into the ER just as she stopped breathing. That's when Penny found herself outside her body, watching as they intubated her.

The next thing she knew, Penny traveled at the speed of thought and found herself in the back seat of her sister's car. It was pouring down rain, and her sister had pulled over into a gas station to send a Facebook message. Penny, still not realizing she was dead, noticed her sister's outfit and thought, *What is she wearing? She looks ridiculous; her clothes don't match. Why is she driving in this pouring rain? Something's wrong!*

Penny couldn't get her sister to respond to her—it was like her sister had no idea she was there. She read what her sister wrote in Facebook,

"Hang in there, kiddo, I'm coming." It would be five days later, when Penny came out of her death-spiral coma, that she told her sister all she had observed. Her sister freaked out but confirmed she had quickly grabbed whatever clothes she could find to rush to the hospital, pulling over in the blinding rain to send Penny the Facebook message.

Penny then popped out of the car and found herself in a dark void. She didn't know how long she stayed in the void. "Time gets away from you on the other side," Penny recalls. Finally, Penny felt a rumbling, thundering presence she said shook everything that had ever been or ever would be. "Every planet in the cosmos was rumbling with this energy," she recalls.

I could feel it in my bones, and I knew Something Big was coming. I never saw a person. I refer to Him as "He," but He was this mix of masculine and feminine because He was very nurturing, but that power makes me think of a man. There was this Light and Energy—I could tell it was Father, Son, Spirit all in one. I knew the Holy Spirit from when He had given me words of knowledge.

He came to me, and I heard Him say this telepathic thing, "I Am." And I had read that in the Bible so many times . . . and that's all He had to say. And I remember thinking, *Man, you're the STUFF. You can just come up to someone and say, "I am," and they're like, "Yeah, you are!"*

And this Light . . . it had a vibration to it that was alive, that just went through me, coursing through every part of me. And I'm there with Him, and immediately I got kind of scared. I was like, *Oh, no, He's going to look at all the stuff I've done wrong, that I'm so ashamed of.* And He wasn't judging me, He was super loving, but I was just wanting to hide. And He soothed me about that, and I knew we were going to go through my life. But all those things that I was dreading never came up. I think I had probably beaten myself up enough about those. But these other things came up.

First, He showed me the good. The things that I had done that I felt really good about did not come up. But the things that came up were like a scene in the grocery store that I had forgotten about. There was a woman in line in front of me, and she was short just a couple of dollars. She was trying to figure out what to put back . . . and I said, "It's okay, it's okay—I've got it." And I gave her the money. And so, I'm seeing this scene like I'm there, and immediately it flashes forward, and I see this [same] woman working in a food pantry. She's blessing these people with food. And God said, "I want you to see the ripple effect of every little act of kindness."

And then we went through some of the negative things, and the one thing that really stuck with me was that, of all the things I've done in my life that I'm not proud of, the thing shown to me is probably the hardest thing to never do again. And it was to control my thoughts about other people. God showed me the negative thoughts I carried, and He said, "Let me explain something to you. A thought has a certain energy to it. A word has even more. And an action has even more than that. But it all starts with a thought." There's something in the Bible that says, the mouth is like the rudder of the ship.* The way you speak is the direction you go. And there's life and death in the tongue. Well, it's the same thing with your thoughts. What you think about is what you talk about is what you end up doing. It starts in the mind.

He showed me these negative thoughts I had about people, and they were deserved, let me tell you! These were some really jerky people. But He said, "When you spend your energy on this and you're thinking these negative thoughts, it hurts you, because the energy impacts you."

Then He showed me how my negative thoughts about

---

* See James 3:4-6.

them is like energy that attaches to them and only increases their tendency to be that way. And this is why forgiving is so important. . . . When I forgive you, that energy is able to be redirected. So it's really important to that other person's journey for you to forgive them, and it's really important to you because that negative energy attaches to you.[1]

Penny's husband had abandoned her when their three children were very young. She had watched the hurt and rejection seep into their little souls year after year as he would promise a birthday gift but never send it; promise to call or come by but rarely show up. The hurt and pain of watching her children internalize their father's lies—believing there was something wrong with them for their father to reject them so—tore at the fabric of Penny's faith. The hurt caused her own bitter isolation from humanity. And while she was there in God's presence, she realized something else:

I am with this loving Creator who has let the big stuff go, stuff that I was all worried about, and then I suddenly become angry with Him. And I realized I'd been angry with God for a long time. And I told Him so. It's amazing how comfortable and yourself you can be with Him. I told Him, "You say You're so loving, but I call bull crap—how could You let a dad do that to his kids?" God said, "Oh, you've completely misunderstood Me. Let Me show you something."[2]

God showed her a flash forward of her adult son sitting with her, watching her grandson, Cole, playing soccer. Her son leaned over and said, "Mom, I'm going to be the dad to him that I deserved to have." Penny realized then that God was going to make something good out of something bad.

The thing I learned there is [that] we have this really screwed up view of good and bad. To us, "good" is when nothing is wrong. "Bad" is when it doesn't go our way. In the spiritual realm, good is forward motion. No matter how awful it feels. If you're moving forward, growing, positively affecting the lives of other people—even if you're doing it through grief or trials—if you're still doing good work, you're moving forward and it's good. But the day you stop interacting with the world and you're only doing what makes you comfortable—that's bad, even though nothing bad is happening. That's not what we're on earth for.

So, I'm there with God, talking about the kids, and I needed more healing. I'm in this Light, and this healing process begins where the Light comes through my feet, creeping up through my body, spiritually healing every cell . . . and I feel like when I get to this core part of myself, . . . God is there! It blew me away, I'm like, "Whoa! You mean to tell me, You've been in there all the time? You're not this external thing?"

And He said, "Well, I'm kind of both."

And I said, "So in all of us, even the people who don't believe, God is in there?"

He said, "You can't take Me out any more than you can take out your own father's DNA. I made you. I'm in there.* You can choose to not acknowledge Me, but I'm in there. And I'm just waiting to love you, even through all the difficulties you're going to go through."[3]

Penny felt all the hurt, bitterness, and anger at God melt away in his light and love. She knew she had been avoiding the things she was supposed to do, and she needed to go back to her life on earth, but she was so heartbroken to leave God's presence. She was crying, "At least let me remember this, or I don't think I'll have hope."

Three years after her NDE, Penny was sitting in the bleachers with her adult son, watching her grandson Cole's soccer game. Her grandson had been two years old at the time of her NDE, and now he was five. Her son leaned over and said, "You know, Mom, I'm going to be the

---

* "God created human beings in his own image" (Genesis 1:27).

dad to him that I deserved to have." Penny's heart overflowed with hope. God was with her.[4]

God is with us to lead us. As Penny realized, allowing God to guide our thoughts, words, and actions is key to becoming our best selves. He does that by his Holy Spirit. But who *is* the Holy Spirit, and how does he guide us?

THE ONE THING

The night before his crucifixion, Jesus explained to his disciples how he would guide them when he was no longer with them, giving an analogy of the one thing that matters most for spiritual growth:

> A branch cannot produce fruit if it is severed from the vine, and you cannot be fruitful unless you remain in me. Yes, I am the vine; you are the branches. Those who remain in me, and I in them, will produce much fruit. For apart from me you can do nothing.
>
> JOHN 15:4-5

A branch does not need to work hard to produce fruit; it simply must stay connected to the vine (the source of nutrients) and fruit grows naturally. Focusing on this one thing, staying connected to the Source (God), affects every other area of our lives in a positive way. And as Jesus said, without this we can do nothing of spiritual value. It's how we become who God created us to be and how we accomplish our God-given purpose. That night, Jesus explained that we stay connected to God (the Source) by the Holy Spirit.

> I will ask the Father, and he will give you another Advocate, who will never leave you. He is the Holy Spirit, who leads into all truth. The world cannot receive him, because it isn't looking for him and doesn't recognize him. But you know him, because he lives with you now and later will be in you. No, I will not abandon you as orphans—I will come to you. . . . When I am raised to life again, you will know that I am in my Father, and

you are in me, and I am in you. . . . It is best for you that I go away, because if I don't, the Advocate won't come. If I do go away, then I will send him to you.

JOHN 14:16-18, 20; 16:7

The prophets had foretold God's coming in human form as the Messiah. What could be better than to walk, talk, interact, and experience the love and character of God in a relatable human form? We tend to think, *If God would just show up, tangibly, that would be the best.* Yet Jesus said, "No, it's *better* for you if I return to the Father and I send the Holy Spirit of God." But *why* is that best?

Those who walked and talked with Jesus on earth experienced Jesus within his human limitations. He could be in only one place at a time and give attention, guidance, and teaching only to those in close proximity. But now that Jesus resides with God in heaven, all of us who have received God's love and forgiveness have the Holy Spirit in us always—not just as a life-sustaining force, but within our very spirits to guide us into life. As Jesus said, the Holy Spirit "lives with you now and later will be in you" (John 14:17). This, too, God foretold through the prophet Joel: "I will pour out my Spirit on all people. . . . Even on my servants, both men and women" (Joel 2:28-29, NIV).

Jesus tells us that God will live in us *by* his Holy Spirit, and he also says, "I will not abandon you as orphans—*I will come* to you," and, "All who love me will do what I say. My Father will love them, and *we will come* and make our home with each of them," because "I am in my Father, and you are in me, and I am in you" (John 14:18, 23, 20, emphasis added). So the triune God lives in us *by his Spirit.* As we stay connected to God (the vine) by his Spirit, good fruit grows in our lives as a natural outcome, blessing not only ourselves but all those around us.

MOMENT BY MOMENT DEPENDENCE

Randy Kay, the CEO from San Diego, was taught by Jesus during his NDE that moment by moment dependence on the Holy Spirit is the way we live connected to God and accomplish our purpose on earth.

But we must also understand that we live in a world at war, a clash of kingdoms. It is a spiritual war being fought with God's truth against the lies of evil. This includes evil in the form of deceptive thoughts that often attack our minds. Randy saw this spiritual battle raging in another dimension as he left earth's vicinity. When Randy asked about it, Jesus explained:

> "The warfare you see is the fighting between my angels and those [angels] who have fallen. . . . My angels direct my beloved to me, and when a person receives truth, he or she is freed to receive my impartation. The demons you see spread lies. They want to confuse my beloved so that they cannot hear the truth, and in so doing, they blind their victims to me. My Spirit can only be manifested in my children, and without my Spirit, people are dead to my Kingdom, my presence. . . . My Spirit speaks truth and the demons speak deceit and lies, seeking to confuse. . . ."

The next question festering within me caused me to become anxious, as though I would insult Jesus by asking it. Yet, I had to ask it! "Dear Lord, why can you not reveal my purpose to me now?"

"My dear child, each person in the world must discover their purpose each day. If I were to reveal your purpose in full, leaving nothing to question, you would not rely upon me. . . . You must trust me and continually seek my revelation, so that you will not only know your purpose, but also so that you will be empowered by my Spirit to fulfill your purpose."[5]

Jesus also explained to Randy, "When I speak to my children in the world, it is my Spirit that speaks."[6] The Greek word translated as "Advocate" in John 14 is *parakletos*. This word can also be translated as "Comforter," "Counselor," and "Helper." Jesus promised to send his Spirit as an Advocate, Comforter, Counselor, and Helper to walk with us through life. And he said that having the Spirit is better than if we had lived, walked, and talked with him during his short period on earth.

Jesus did not save us just so we could one day be in heaven; he made a way for heaven—God's Kingdom—to invade earth through us today as we depend on the Holy Spirit moment by moment. Let's look closer at the person of the Holy Spirit, and some of the ways the Holy Spirit helps us in life, so we can cooperate with his work in us.

YOUR OWN LIFE COACH

It's helpful to remember that the Holy Spirit is God with us and in us. The Spirit has intellect, a will, and emotion, and we can bring joy or sorrow to the Holy Spirit by how we live (see Ephesians 4:29-32). The Spirit is a separate person, yet still one God. He has personality distinct from the Father and the Son, which is why we see the Spirit at Jesus' baptism: "As Jesus came up out of the water, the heavens were opened and he saw the Spirit of God descending like a dove and settling on him. And a voice from heaven said, 'This is my dearly loved Son, who brings me great joy'" (Matthew 3:16-17). "Then Jesus was led *by the Spirit* into the wilderness" (Matthew 4:1, emphasis added). Jesus was the perfect human and God's representation incarnate. As a man, Jesus followed the Spirit just as we must do.

NDErs find it hard to describe the Holy Spirit, probably because the Holy Spirit is God's presence distributed. One NDEr described the Holy Spirit as a more "feminine" presence of God. When Jeff, a water well technician, was working in a twelve-foot-deep trench, an entire wall of shale came loose and buried him alive. He found himself at the throne of God, in awe. When Jesus sent him back, he recalls, "When I came to, I was being cradled in this huge energy-like ball that felt endless and was truly feminine in nature. Like the best-est mom in all the universe. I knew that it was the Holy Spirit. . . . And we can tap into this any time we need to. I continue to grow closer to the Spirit within me each day."[7]

I've wondered about this feminine aspect of God's nature, since the Holy Spirit is equated with wisdom, and wisdom is often personified as feminine in the Old Testament. For example, Isaiah writes, "The Spirit of the LORD will rest on him—the Spirit of wisdom" (Isaiah 11:2). And Proverbs says, "Do not forsake wisdom, and she will protect you; love

her, and she will watch over you" (Proverbs 4:6, NIV). Yet, to differentiate God's masculine/feminine characteristics into separate persons of
the Trinity divides God's essence, so it's probably not accurate to say the
Father is more masculine or the Holy Spirit is more feminine; God is a
unity of masculine and feminine.

During his last night on earth, Jesus explained that the Holy Spirit
will be with us forever (John 14:16). He assured us the Holy Spirit will
lead us into all truth (John 14:17). He will teach us and remind us of
the words of Jesus (John 14:26). He will point people to Jesus and help
us also explain Jesus' love to the world (John 15:26-27). He will convict
people by prompting their consciences about sin and the right ways of
God so that people will turn back to God (John 16:8). He will guide us
into life by telling us God's will (John 16:13-15). And the Spirit does
so much more.

Just think about how much we pay for instructors, therapists, and
life coaches to give us wisdom and guidance. They can be helpful, but
Jesus says the ultimate Counselor, Therapist, and Guide is already with
us, ready to help. Do we consult him? Do we seek his guidance? Learning
to quiet ourselves and listen for his guidance is the single most important
thing we can do. I believe this is what Jesus meant when he said that we
will bear spiritual fruit when we remain connected to him, like a branch
to a vine. This is the one thing we must do to grow spiritually.

The apostle Paul expressed this same idea of staying connected
when he wrote, "It is for freedom that Christ has set us free. Stand firm,
then, and do not let yourselves be burdened again by a yoke of slavery"
(Galatians 5:1, NIV). Jesus wants you living in a newfound freedom. So
many people believe the lie that following God restricts their freedom,
but it's the opposite. God wants us living with freedom from the law
(Romans 6:14-15) because all the "shoulds," "oughts," "dos and don'ts"
are unnecessary when following God's Spirit. We can live free from shame,
worry, anxiety, addictions, and from plaguing bad habits. We can live free
to enjoy the moments of life in profound love, peace, and joy. And all this
growth and forward movement comes as we keep doing the one thing that
matters most—staying connected moment by moment to God's Spirit.

Paul calls this "walking by the Spirit" and explains the spiritual fruit that grows as a result: "So I say, walk by the Spirit, and you will not gratify the desires of the flesh [old sin-habits]. . . . But if you are led by the Spirit, you are not under the law. . . . The fruit of the Spirit is love, joy, peace, forbearance [patience], kindness, goodness, faithfulness, gentleness and self-control" (Galatians 5:16, 18, 22-23, NIV). Do you see what this says? Do this one thing—walk by the Spirit daily—and you don't have to white-knuckle in your own effort to "stop this" or "try harder" to quit that, or muster up more religious effort to "be good." God grows good fruit from within, naturally. It doesn't mean it's always easy, or that there are no struggles, but this one thing is the key to growth. It's a very freeing way of life.

Remember when Santosh stood before God and asked about the narrow door? God told Santosh that what he really wanted was a sincere and honest relationship with him that would be daily, 365 days a year, not just once a week. His instruction was, "Walk with me." He explained to Santosh that this would involve surrendering himself fully to God each day. Santosh didn't have a background to know exactly what "walk with me" meant, but he realized later that God meant, "If [God's] going forward and I'm going backward or sideways, we're not walking together."[8]

Walk through life with the Spirit in daily honesty and surrender, willing to do God's will, and as Jesus said, spiritual fruit will grow naturally. You don't have to "do" a bunch of religious deeds or focus on changing yourself—you simply focus on walking with God's Holy Spirit. It's simple, but not easy.

In fact, staying focused on this one thing is probably the hardest thing to do. But as you practice getting better at it, you will move toward fulfilling your purpose, and those old "sin-habits" will begin to fall away. What will grow from within is more love, more joy, more peace; more ability to naturally replace outbursts with calm patience; replace old addictions with self-control; replace lust, envy, fear, or anxiety with spiritual peace and contentment. No amount of religious "trying harder" heals us and changes us from within. The Holy Spirit does for us what we cannot do for ourselves. And to follow where he leads, we must first learn to recognize and hear the Spirit's voice.

HEARING THE HOLY SPIRIT'S VOICE

We all want to hear the audible voice of God. Personally, I never have. Yet, God has very clearly guided me for the past forty years, and I have journals full of the amazing proof of God's leading. But I had to learn to recognize and hear the Spirit's voice. Let me explain with an illustration.

Suppose I am talking with you, explaining my learnings about God. I'm limited, which means I must use language, my voice, and your ears to communicate verbally. I wish I could just place all my thoughts in your mind at once—that would be more direct communication. Of course, you could still dismiss all my thoughts or ignore my thoughts, but at least you'd have all my thoughts directly.

I can't do that, but God can! Heaven's communication is thought-to-thought, feeling-to-feeling, with impressions put directly from the spirit of one person into another. And that's exactly God's preferred mode of communication with us here on earth—by his Holy Spirit, "we have the mind of Christ" available to us (1 Corinthians 2:16).

Kaline Fernandes, the civil engineer from Brazil who experienced God's fatherly voice, said the voice she heard in her NDE is the same voice she "hears" today. Not an actual voice, where you'd worry about "hearing voices," Kaline explains, but more like thoughts:

> [Sometimes] it also warns me of certain things, and a few days later it actually happens. . . . It's that same voice I heard in my experience when I was having that surgery on January 8, 2020. The same [voice], not another. . . . Like yesterday, it was almost midnight, and I called my mother, "Is there something wrong?" And there was. There really was. . . . [God] said—as if they were his final words before he left—that my duty now, coming back, was to free myself from certain things that made me angry with people in my own family, [and] it would be difficult. But he emphasized this issue of interpersonal relationships . . . and that I had to learn at times to remain silent, to hold my tongue, and to not speak.[9]

Kaline's NDE helped her learn to recognize God's voice, but the promise of Scripture is that we can all learn to listen to the guidance of the Holy Spirit.

Jesus said, "Anyone with ears to hear must listen to the Spirit" (Revelation 2:7). This may seem strange because most of us have physical ears. But Jesus clearly meant we need a spiritual kind of hearing to discern the prompting thoughts of God's Spirit. When he speaks of "ears to hear," he's talking about the willingness of our hearts to listen. Jesus explained, "For the hearts of these people are hardened, and their ears cannot hear" (Matthew 13:15). Jesus implies that the more willing our hearts are to hear and respond obediently to the Spirit's promptings, the more clearly we will hear.

I accidentally discovered God's voice one day in college as I was praying. I had a random thought enter my mind, *Call Alison.* Alison is my younger sister, who was in high school at the time. I wasn't thinking about or praying for Alison, so I ignored the thought. Several minutes later, the thought came again. It felt like my own random thought, so again, I ignored it. The third time, I had this feeling I should call Alison, so I asked, "Lord, is that you? You know Alison is at school; she won't answer." (This was before mobile phones.) But I decided to act in faith and just call. Alison surprised me by answering, and I discovered she had stayed home from school, depressed about being bullied. I was able to encourage her, and I was able to experience the Holy Spirit's guiding voice.

I've never had mystical spiritual experiences, but I have found that as I respond in faith, doing what I think God's Spirit is prompting me to do, I can often look back and see evidence of his guidance. And the more willingly I respond in faith, the more promptings I seem to get.

When I worked as an engineer in California, I had a Christian friend who was a professional communication coach. He kept encouraging me, saying, "You have a teaching gift from God." He said that because he saw my love for learning and how excited I was to share what I learned with others. At the time, I was terrified of public speaking and had zero desire to ever learn to speak in public. But Dave kept saying,

"Let me coach you in public speaking. You have a gift. Just do one talk—I'll set it up." "No," was always my response. "It's not going to happen, Dave," I told him over and over for months.

Then one day while praying, I had a very obtrusive thought: *When you resist Dave, you resist me.* It was just a thought, like other thoughts in my head, but I knew I hadn't generated that thought. That was the last thing I wanted to think. *When you resist Dave, you resist me.* I said yes to Dave that day. And since then, I have communicated to over two hundred thousand people in more than thirty countries—it's crazy! God and I both know what a miracle that is! But that's what the Holy Spirit does. God's Spirit prompted me, I obeyed the prompting, and step-by-step the Holy Spirit helped to develop the teaching gift he gave me. The Holy Spirit will do the same for you as well, as you are willing to listen and act in obedient faith.

GIFTS OF THE HOLY SPIRIT

In addition to providing guidance, the Holy Spirit also gives us gifts and helps us develop them as we follow God. The apostle Paul writes, "There are different kinds of gifts, but the same Spirit distributes them" (1 Corinthians 12:4, NIV). God has gifts for each of us to develop and use as we follow the Holy Spirit.

Erica McKenzie, the nurse whose heart failed, floated in outer space with God as he began to teach her about our words and our gifts.

> I went up and up, and I knew I was going to Heaven. . . .
> While I could not see a physical image, I distinguished this
> brilliant Presence as the voice I had heard all my life. . . . He
> brought me close to Him like a parent about to tell a child a
> story. We stood together with our backs towards Heaven and
> looked out at the stars . . . .
>
> God told me to look to my right. Suddenly, His right arm
> and shoulder appeared in human form. They were the size of
> a semitruck . . . and resting in His palm was a massive rock.
> Emanating from this rock was the most brilliant light. God
> turned to me and said, "You are the rock. You are the Light.

The Light is of Me, and·I AM with you." At once, God let loose the rock and together we watched it fall. . . . I saw a vast body of water appear. It was greater than the largest ocean and into the water the rock plunged. Together, we watched as a single ripple of water appeared. God said, "Mankind is the water. You are the ripple." I watched the single ripple expand until I could no longer see it. I repeated, "I am the ripple." And then God turned to me and said, "Like the ripple affects the water, so too do man's words and actions affect mankind." . . .

I began to comprehend its significance. Every word, thought, and action, no matter how small, affected everyone and everything. I had no idea of the power and consequences of my thoughts, my words, and actions. . . .

God asked me to look once again. To my right . . . were the most amazing, multidimensional shelves. The shelves reached high into the stars until I could no longer see the tops of them. . . . On the shelves appeared gifts, presents, like those we give and receive at Christmas. There were so many gifts on all of the shelves that they filled each and every space available. But not one gift looked like the other. . . .

God said, "When you are born, I give each of you gifts. When you were born, Erica, I gave you the gift of patience and the gift of beauty." Immediately I thought, "Oh no, God, that can't be right!" I recalled the kids in school. If I were truly beautiful, I wouldn't have been judged. . . . He so lovingly corrected me by saying telepathically, "Erica, I gave you the gift of patience, and I gave you the gift of beauty." God added, "In life, I have more gifts for each and every one of you. All you have to do is ask, and then be prepared to be quiet and listen, to be able to receive these gifts."

Sometimes it's hard to see the gifts we possess. I thought of my gift of beauty and realized how impossible it was for me to see it in myself because I looked to mankind for my value instead of God. . . . It took dying to make me realize that my uniqueness was my value, and my value was my contribution on this Earthly Journey. As we stood together in silence, God filled me with the knowledge that it was important to share these lessons with others. . . . I understood it's never about one person using their gifts or uniqueness alone. Rather, it is God's plan for us to embrace our uniqueness and come together to embrace and empower each other.[10]

The Holy Spirit will lead us to use our words to build up and empower each other's gifts, working together for the common good.* Dave used his words and gift of communication to develop my latent gifts of speaking and teaching. Erica realized in her NDE that the words and actions from others had sowed lies into her heart and almost disabled her gifts and development. That's why we must pay close attention to the thoughts we carry in our hearts.

GROWING THOUGHT BY THOUGHT

If you have trusted in Christ, the Holy Spirit resides in your spirit. That happens once for all time when you believe, or trust, in Jesus (Ephesians 1:13-14).† But we can still choose to listen and respond willingly to his Spirit moment by moment or choose *not* to listen and respond. Paul notes that we can grieve the Holy Spirit when we ignore his promptings and do our own will anyway (Ephesians 4:30-31, NIV). It happens first in our thoughts before our actions, so we must pay attention to our thoughts.

Scripture contrasts being controlled by alcohol with being controlled by the Spirit: "Don't be drunk with wine, because that will ruin your life. Instead, be filled [keep on being filled] with the Holy Spirit" (Ephesians 5:18). Just as you can give your mind over to drunkenness drink by drink, you can give your mind over to following the Holy Spirit thought by thought. And God's Spirit does not force behavior, but rather guides and empowers, as much as you are willing. Evil tries to force and control, but God's Spirit always respects your free will.

---

* This has always been God's plan for his community called the church (see 1 Corinthians 12–13).

† We are sealed and given the Holy Spirit when we believe (Ephesians 1:13, ESV), but we can be "baptized" or "filled" with the Spirit at a later time in ways that more fully manifest the Spirit's presence, power, and gifts.

The way we walk by the Spirit, filled with the Spirit, begins by paying attention to our thoughts. As God told Penny and Erica, thoughts have a certain energy or power that affect people, words have more, and actions have even more. But it all starts with our thoughts—thoughts lead to words and actions. So, the apostle Paul instructs, "We take captive every thought to make it obedient to Christ" (2 Corinthians 10:5, NIV).

Paul explains that Jesus' payment for our wrongs not only gets us into heaven, but also frees us from fear of judgment, so we will feel safe to let the Spirit into our thoughts every moment:

> There is now no condemnation for those who are in Christ Jesus . . . [so] that the righteous requirement of the law might be fully met in us, who do not live according to the flesh but according to the Spirit. Those who live according to the flesh have their *minds set* on what the flesh desires; but those who live in accordance with the Spirit have their *minds set* on what the Spirit desires.
> ROMANS 8:1, 4-5, NIV, EMPHASIS ADDED

Here's the key question: What do you set your mind on? All through the day, do you let God's Spirit into your thoughts? Do you talk over your thoughts with God's Spirit? Or do you give your attention to old ways of thinking, such as lies and negative or condemning words that may have shaped you in the past or are shaping you now?

As Kevin Zadai went under anesthesia during dental surgery, something went terribly wrong. Next thing he knew, Kevin was watching the surgery from above as Jesus taught him about his mindset and the words that had shaped him. "Kevin, this world we live in down here is limited," Jesus explained, "but your words are very, very powerful." Kevin recalls,

> [Jesus] started to teach me about words. He had this plain robe on, but he had this presence about him that he was a king. And he talked to me about his Kingdom and about how I was part of that. . . . And he started to speak to me about how I

had been very careless about my words. . . . And Jesus said, "You're supposed to be speaking where you're going." And it was very uncomfortable at first because he said that I wasn't being careful with my words . . . [but] he cared about me, and he showed me how my life up to that point had been going in a zigzag. . . .

Then he said, "When you [were] born again, Kevin, the Spirit of God inside of you made you new. You're a brand-new creature now. Now that your spirit is new, you have to speak from your spirit. . . . Kevin, when you pray in the Spirit, when you speak the right words, the demons have to listen to you." And I realized, *Oh my gosh, this is what's been going wrong in my life. I haven't been speaking the right things. . . .*

[Jesus said], "Kevin, there's a part of you called your soul that is hindering you." And he showed me my spirit. My spirit was lit up [with light], and I had this robe of righteousness on me, but I also saw this black part of me, and he said, "Kevin, do you see how that's obscuring your beauty?" And I said, "Yes." He said, "That's your soul. Look real closely." And when I looked really closely, I saw all these words, these phrases and statements that were spoken. And I remember them being spoken to me when I was a little child. People said things, and they actually cursed me, and they said things that weren't true about me. And they changed the way that I perceived God, and my whole observation of this life was tainted by the enemy, because people had spoken wrong [untrue] words over me. People would say things like, "You're never going to amount to anything."[11]

Kevin recalls growing up feeling blamed for everything. He believed their words, and always felt like the world was coming against him. This formed his mindset. Kevin comments, "That's why having our minds set on the Spirit is so critical, so we can live out the desires of the Spirit." While Kevin was out on the table for forty-five minutes, Jesus showed him his spirit and his soul, and how things in his soul needed to be renewed, to be transformed. "[Jesus] said, 'We've got to take care of this. . . . You need to build yourself up, praying in the Holy Spirit and staying in the love of God. And then you need to always meditate on the Word of God, and you need to allow your mind to be changed.'"[12]

The apostle Paul says letting God into our thoughts is key: "Don't copy the behavior and customs of this world, but let God transform you into a new person by *changing the way you think.* Then you will learn to know God's will for you, which is good and pleasing and perfect" (Romans 12:2, emphasis added). You live in the Spirit when you make it a habit to go through your day, moment by moment, inviting the Holy Spirit into every thought, every decision, every action. You listen for the quiet prompting of the Spirit, allowing him to align your thoughts with the truths of Scripture, so you can know what is true. Then you can follow his lead when he prompts you to keep quiet, speak up, or take action.

The Holy Spirit is the triune God living in you. He wants to guide you, comfort you, counsel and teach you so that day by day you become the best version of you—activating the gifts he's given, growing in the fruits of his Spirit. The one thing you must do: stay connected, walking by the Spirit. The more you act in faith on the Holy Spirit's promptings, the more you'll look back and see God working in your life. Of course, this also requires developing the habit of listening to God in prayer and understanding how prayer works on earth and in heaven. This is what we will tackle next—how our prayers work in moving God's heart and drawing us closer to him.

PART 4

DOING LIFE WITH GOD TODAY

HOW PRAYER WORKS
WITH GOD

LORRAINE WOODFORD PLEADED WITH her brother-in-law on the phone, "David, I need you and Shelley to pray; Jim didn't come home last night, and I feel something is horribly wrong."

David replied with confirmation of the seriousness of her concern: "Shelley woke up in the middle of the night several times with an urge to pray. Now we know why."

Another of Lorraine's sisters later reported that she, too, had been awakened with an urgent sense to pray. Lorraine and her sisters believed in Jesus, but her husband, Jim, had stubbornly ignored God for years. He had no interest in God, even after contracting Guillain-Barré syndrome, a severe autoimmune disease that attacked his nervous system, causing excruciating pain. The disease also permanently grounded him from his lifelong passion of flying.

Jim Woodford had flown forty-two different types of aircraft, including a 737, which he piloted around the globe. Flying was his love, having logged thousands of hours as a commercial airline pilot. Though he grew up in a Catholic family in Newfoundland, he never prayed. Jim admits, "My one goal in life was to have things. I had a yacht, an airplane, and nineteen British sport cars that I kept in the garage on my horse farm. I enjoyed things, but never once did I even have an urge to talk to God. My sole goal was the accumulation of wealth, and I was good at it."[1]

But as the intensity of the pain from his disease increased, so did the need for relief. Jim drove out to his horse farm that night to check on a broken fence. As he sat in his truck watching the sunset, he popped the last two pills in the bottle. He had lost count of how many opioids he'd taken that day—too many, as it turned out. Jim's head hit the steering wheel as he died. Medical records later documented, "Eleven hours with no sign of brain activity."[2]

> I'd never asked God for anything, but as I saw the setting sun with my hands shaking violently, from somewhere deep inside was this feeling, "Acknowledge God. Thank him for the life you thought was your own doing and ask forgiveness." I said, "Jesus forgive me." And with that, I collapsed.
>
> I woke up, sat back up, and immediately I felt incredibly well. I got out of the truck, walked about fifteen feet away, and it was as if I'd taken off a heavy wet overcoat and all the pain with it. I looked down, and I could see through my feet to the ground, but I dismissed that as the effects of the drug. But I felt like I was twenty years old again. And I thought, "I got it right; you have to take the whole bottle."
>
> I looked back at the truck, and I felt outraged—someone was sitting in my truck, sleeping on the steering wheel! When I looked at the body in the truck, that moment seeing the blood gushing out of the mouth, I realized: that body on the steering wheel is mine! Suddenly, I began to rise.[3]

Meanwhile, that next morning, Lorraine, her three sisters, her brother-in-law, and her nephew gathered in her kitchen. Two officers of the Royal Canadian Mounted Police collected information on where they might search for Jim. Afterward, the six family members joined hands and prayed, never imagining that Jim could actually *see* their prayers.

After traveling swiftly through a tunnel of light, Jim landed gently on beautifully manicured grass. To his right, he saw a heavenly atmosphere. To his left, he saw what he described as an eternity without God, and before him appeared to be a final choice:

I knew the tunnel behind me was closing and I had to step out of the tunnel. I stepped and felt something solid. The tunnel closed, and I could see grass, the most beautiful grass imaginable. Each blade lit up as I walked on it. I looked out on the most beautiful scene ever. I've seen Hawaii, the savanna, Arizona—nothing compares. As a pilot, I tried to find the sun to get my bearings, but there was no sun. I had never read the Bible, so I didn't know it says there is no sun in Heaven. But the rolling hills and mountains were covered with flowers, with colors beyond description. I'm breathless by the beauty, but as I looked toward the left, the beauty went from green to brown to scorched to an ugly black rock dropping off into a deep crevasse probably three hundred yards away. It was like a visual dichotomy. I was confused by the difference between the beauty to the right and the emptiness to the left, so I made my way over toward the crevasse out of curiosity. I got to the edge and looked down, and what I saw was like a distant campfire in a deep, dark valley at night.

I'm both in terror and fascinated as I notice this thing, this creature, that is fifty feet high, obese, sniffing around in the bottom of this pit, and its body was on fire. The creature turned and looked up over its squat neck, and I looked into the eyes of this creature. Words fail me to describe the sheer hatred for me I felt in its eyes. It looked like the face of a hyena on a body on fire. It snarled, and it breezed up the canyon walls, coming for me. I could smell the stench of death.

The worst part is that you feel the pain of all the hurt you caused. I experienced that pain. I was ruthless in business. I gave young women false ideas. I was poster boy for success, but I had no regard for anyone's feelings. This creature was calling my name. To hear this demon call my name was the ultimate wake-up call. I know this sounds like a cheap Hollywood movie, but that's what Satan wants us to think. When the demon spoke to me it said, "Jim, we are here for you. This is your time. You belong here. Come, Jim, join us. We are here for you." I turned around and dropped to my knees. I could feel its breath on the back of my neck. I had cried out, "God forgive me," in the truck, but when I felt its talon clawing down my back, I begged, "God, help me, help me." And I expected nothing. I had ignored God all my life. I deserved nothing.[4]

As soon as Jim cried out for God's help, he saw three points of light appear in the distance, rapidly approaching. The three lights converged, strafing Jim's head like three fighter jets doing a flyby. He turned his head just in time to see the convergence of the three lights strike the hideous creature, which shrieked and darted back down the crevasse.

I turn, and I'm looking at three of the most magnificent creatures anyone could imagine. The first was ten feet tall. I found out he had been assigned to me from conception. Another was thirteen feet tall, and another fifteen feet tall. I say "he," but to me they were a combination of the strength of a man with the gentleness and wisdom of the feminine. Imagine this beautiful being of light, with flowing robes that shimmered as they walked. They came right up to me, smiling at me. They had very light, silver hair, and two spires of light, which were the shoulders of the wings folded in. The spires came up from their shoulder blades, and they caused a golden refraction [that] we see as a halo. Their eyes were the most incredible violet color. Their eyes never blinked, but their look was a look of absolute love and protection for me.

I looked up into [one of] the angel's violet eyes, and I realized he was about to speak, but his lips didn't move. I felt the words, "Fear not, James, for we are your constant friends." Then he smiled. I found out later the ten-foot one had been my guardian. He told me I was the 2,031st soul he had protected. The thirteen-foot angel looked really studious, with some sort of paper and quill, and I later found out he was a scribe. The fifteen-foot one was a warrior angel, unmistakable, wearing armor.

The tall warrior angel, with a voice much deeper than the other two, said, "James, would you walk with us?" And as he turned, a gravel path through a field of flowers opened up, and we began to walk. As I walked, it was like I had omni-vision, 360 degrees. I could look off at the mountains of Heaven and see the petals of a flower on the mountains, while also seeing other things simultaneously. At the same time, I was asking the angels questions with my thoughts, and as I'm thinking the questions, I'm feeling their answers. I'm looking around me and seeing paradise—just like earth but ten thousand times more beautiful.

"The flowers are so beautiful," I said, and I stopped. The Guardian motioned toward the flowers, and I kneeled to look closer. As my knee hit the ground, light ripped out from my knee. I heard something coming from the flowers, like a tinkle of small bells, but then to my amazement, I saw a melody wafting up from the flowers. In Heaven, color has sound and sound has color. "Is that music?" I asked. A big grin came across the Guardian as he said, "James, the flowers of Heaven are so happy you are here, they are singing to you." I was in awe.

I looked up in the sky, and it was a cerulean blue—it was a sunless sky, deep, deep blue, and I spotted something like streaks of brilliant light going straight up. [To me] as a pilot, they looked like the white contrails of ice left behind by jets. I thought, *Are those contrails?* I was stunned, seeing six contrails across the sky. I asked the Guardian, "What are those?" And he said, "James those are the prayers of your family for your soul, as we speak." When I got back, I found out my family all came to the house and six of them prayed, "If it be the will of Jesus, please send Jim back." And I was in Heaven seeing those prayers.

I said, "The prayers for me?" And the guardian angel went on to say, "Sadly, mankind is losing the will to pray. Your grandparents would make time to pray after the day was over, but sadly, again, mankind has become a culture of instantaneous gratification. With your devices, you watch something instantly. People go to church, pray to God on Sunday, [and] if it doesn't happen by Tuesday, they say, 'God doesn't care.' Every prayer that has ever been uttered by anyone ever conceived, every prayer is recorded in Heaven, Jim. Your prayers are recorded to show you during your life review all the things that you prayed for that didn't happen. God will one day show you, when a prayer was not answered, it was because God knew it would not be good for you. And yet, you can power through with your own free will to try and make it happen."

The Guardian explained to me that God has absolute respect for our free will because love can never be taken, it can only be given. He will not violate our free will because free will is necessary for love.

The Guardian said, "James, touch my robe." I did and instantly we were in the sky, and I wondered if this was for me because I was a pilot. I was looking down on this golden city, and instantaneously I knew I was looking down on God's celestial home.

I saw immaculately laid out concentric circles of golden streets, with greenbelts between them, and they intersected to form crosses. Streets of gold, but not like we think of gold.

There was a translucent gold that you could see into almost like glass, but with a golden tint. Everything flowed to a brilliant light that appeared to be the throne of God. As the golden streets grew nearer to the throne, their color became more transparent, as some kind of crystal. The buildings I saw were in the Greek/Roman style, but not hewn from stone, hewn from blocks of light.* I could see these buildings in all their glory. The buildings were magnificent in scope and size, but there was a warmth to them—it felt like I had come home.

I'm looking down on this populace of people, all tribes and nationalities—they're beings of light, but they have the features of men and women and children. They acted like normal people, and you could see families who had just been reunited in the holy city, and they were walking around describing things to the newcomer—it was so relatable and stunning.

"Am I seeing this correctly?" I asked the Guardian, "because it seems everybody appears to be in their early thirties or younger." He said, "Yes, James, you are correct. No one in Heaven is older than Jesus was when he died." It was explained to me that people can show themselves to their loved ones as they last remembered them. If you want to remember your child younger, that's how they'll appear. I started to point to buildings. The Guardian described the halls of learning and the halls of music.[5]

We came upon a beautiful building made of the same shimmering material as the others. I asked the angel, "What is this magnificent building?" He replied, "James, this is the hall of knowledge. It is the repository of all the prayers and petitions that mankind sends to Heaven and the throne of God." I was reassured again that nothing is ever lost to God. So the knowledge spoken of is God's knowledge of the heart

---

* I'm fascinated by the way NDErs describe what the city is made of. Dr. Mary Neal told me the city gate was made of "old Roman block arches . . . seemingly solid-looking but not. They were really woven together with love, which is nonsensical." Jim said they were made of light, but remember, he described the light he saw as love. Santosh said the city was made of "otherworldly building materials." And John, in Revelation, says it was made of "pure gold," yet "clear as glass" (Revelation 21:18).

of man and his deepest longings, which are cataloged there. Along with prayers, there were accounts of the deeds of people both good and evil. Again, nothing is lost to God. The halls of knowledge are where the books of each of our lives are kept.[6]

Jim miraculously revived and went from agnostic to fervent follower of Jesus. Jim saw the power of our prayers firsthand, and if we're going to do life with God, the first thing we must understand is how prayer works and why it's so important to God.

YOUR PRAYERS MATTER TO GOD

"How in the world can God hear billions of prayers at once? Impossible!"

"My prayers just fall on deaf ears, they don't work."

"God only hears the prayers of the Mother Teresas, the saintly people, not mine."

These are some of the many misconceptions about prayer that deter people from praying, which is why I'm eager for us to imagine how prayer works with God. NDEs can shed light on what the Scriptures have taught all along.

Your prayers matter to God. As I hope you can now imagine, God is with you always. He is infinite Spirit, so time and distance do not limit God as they do humanity. NDErs attest to this. God not only attends to every single prayer of every person; God answers our prayers in such a way that the outcome works together for our good *and* for the good of all those who love him. Scripture assures us and NDErs testify that in God's presence, all things work together, and it all makes sense.

I find it encouraging to know that we don't even have to "do it right" for God to hear or answer our prayers. Prayer is not a puzzle or a formula, something we have to figure out with precision before God will hear us or give us what we ask for. Prayer is simply communicating with God—silently in our hearts or out loud. In prayer, we have a conversation with God, our Creator, who loves us and wants to guide us through life by his Holy Spirit. We don't have to be good at prayer, we simply have to be willing to do it! God promises his Holy Spirit will help us—aligning our will to God's will as he works all things together for good.

The Spirit helps us in our weakness. We do not know what we ought to pray for, but the Spirit himself intercedes for us through wordless groans. And he who searches our hearts knows the mind of the Spirit, because the Spirit intercedes for God's people in accordance with the will of God. And we know that in all things God works for the good of those who love him, who have been called according to his purpose.

ROMANS 8:26-28, NIV

In heaven, every heartfelt prayer goes to God the Father on his throne. That means God hears your every prayer and apparently his angels record each one.* Why are all our prayers recorded? Perhaps it's so that humans and angels forever remember the role prayer plays on earth, and why every prayer is so precious to God. Or maybe, as the angel told Jim, God will one day reveal to us in our life review how all his answers worked for our good, even if it didn't seem good to us at the time. Never doubt that your prayers matter to God—and so do your sufferings.

Not one tear, struggle, question, or heartache taken to God in prayer is lost on him. In fact, the promise of Scripture is this: "You keep track of all my sorrows. You have collected all my tears in your bottle. You have recorded each one in your book" (Psalm 56:8). He holds our tears as treasures when we call out to him in prayer through the valleys of life.

Dr. Gary Wood witnessed this promise firsthand when he died in a head-on car accident. In heaven, he was led to the throne of God by his deceased childhood friend John:

I saw angels carrying golden bowls filled with a liquid substance. I asked John what it was, and he told me it was the tears of the saints below. Every time a child of God prays so earnestly that a teardrop falls, an angel is there to catch that tear and deliver it to God. The tears are stored in golden bowls at the base of God's throne. I saw other angels carrying golden

---

* See Revelation 8:4; 20:12.

vials filled with a vaporlike substance. I asked the angels what it was, and they replied, "It is the praises of the people on earth presented to God as sweet smelling incense."[7]

While in heaven, NDErs see firsthand how our prayers are not just *important* to God, but *substantial* and *effective*—they set things in motion, including the angels of God. When we pray on behalf of others, we may not always see how our intercessions play out because God works with the free will of each person, but our prayers do have effect.

Steve Kang, a former Buddhist, got into drugs during college. He smoked a "death bowl," consisting of marijuana mixed with many powerful psychedelic drugs. As a result, he attempted suicide slashing his neck and stomach. He believes Jesus rescued him from hell because his Buddhist mother called on her Christian friend, who brought eight people to the ICU to pray for Steve. Today, Steve's mother is a follower of Jesus and Steve is a pastor.[8]

Likewise, God honored the prayers of Ian McCormack's mother. As Ian was thousands of miles from home dying from multiple box jellyfish stings, God awakened his mother in the middle of the night to pray for Ian, and simultaneously gave Ian a vision of his mother telling him to pray the Lord's Prayer.[9] The prayers of mothers—and fathers too—never miss God's attention.

Ivan Tuttle, now a minister, credits his mother's prayers for saving his life. At age twenty-six, Ivan found himself in a hellish NDE after partying for days until the drugs killed him. Then, he said, "I heard a voice like a mighty roar of thunder that said, 'It is not his time yet. His mother has been praying for him since he was a little boy. You must release him now; I made a promise!'" Ivan told me, "The voice said my mother had prayed over twenty-eight thousand times for me, and it was her faithful prayers that saved me."[10] A parent's prayers are never forgotten by God. They are powerful and can move the hand of God, but on their own, they cannot change a human heart. Ivan got a second chance, but just like Steve and Ian, he still had a choice of whether to follow God or not. No matter what, our prayers for others are powerful.

Dean Braxton told me that in his NDE, he was traveling very fast on his way to heaven, "Yet, the prayers of people who were praying for me were moving faster than I was . . . they were like shooting stars passing me." Dean knew the prayers he saw that were closest to him were prayers for him, and the "shooting stars" (or "contrails," as Jim Woodford described them) that were farther away were prayers for other people. When Dean went before the throne of God, he noticed something else:

> The prayers went straight to the throne and the Father. Not only did they go to Father God, but they went inside him. To try to understand this, you will have to realize that the throne of God is not a seat. It is a place. He is the throne! There were millions upon millions of prayers entering the Father. I saw these lights of prayers like shooting stars entering the Father. I came to understand that he answers our prayers with himself.
>
> Jesus downloaded information into me about prayers. I saw mighty warring angels, and I knew that prayer is what moved them. God hears our prayers and sets angels into motion in response.* I understood that our prayers must come from our hearts. Our God is a heart God, and he is looking for us to talk to him from our hearts. He hears us if we are praying from our hearts. He hears your heart. He understands your heart. He only hears prayers from the heart.[11]

HEARTFELT PRAYER

What does it mean that God "only hears prayers from the heart"? As I pondered this in light of what Jesus teaches in Scripture, I realized that it all goes back to the fact that God is a relational God. I'll explain with an illustration.

My three-year-old granddaughter, Sophie, and I had "Papa Camp" several months ago. She spent two days with me while my wife, Kathy, was with our daughter as she gave birth to our second granddaughter, Bella. Near the end of our first day together, completely out of the blue, Sophie gave me a big hug and said, "I love you, Papa." Then she kissed

---

* In Daniel 10:12 an angel was sent because Daniel prayed.

me. My heart melted, as you might imagine. Sophie's "I love you" was truly from her heart. That's why it meant so much to me. If her mom had said to her, "Go say to Papa, 'I love you,'" and Sophie had just parroted the words, that wouldn't have been from the heart. This is the same in talking with God. Our authenticity matters, and prayer from our hearts is what means the most to him.

What I hope you can imagine by now is that God truly wants a relationship with you, and that comes from the heart or not at all. Prayer is heart-to-heart communication. So what's the difference between heartfelt prayer and other prayers? Heartfelt prayer is sincere and honest. To be sincere doesn't mean your prayer has to be emotional or always positive, it just needs to be genuine. It's part of what Jesus tried to teach us when he said, "When you pray, don't be like the hypocrites who love to pray publicly . . . where everyone can see them. I tell you the truth, that is all the reward they will ever get" (Matthew 6:5).

Saying flowery or beautiful prayers might impress some people, but not God. He desires honesty, as God told Santosh in his NDE: "I want to see how true, how sincere, how honest you are with Me . . . that's the relationship I want."[12] Tell God what's in your heart and on your mind. That counts with God, and Jesus even indicates that God rewards that kind of forthright communication.

In contrast to the hypocrites, who wanted recognition from others watching them pray, Jesus taught us to pray for God's recognition alone: "But when you pray, go away by yourself, shut the door behind you, and pray to your Father in private. Then your Father, who sees everything, will reward you" (Matthew 6:6). Does this mean we should never pray in public or in groups with others? Not at all. Jesus said that when two or three pray together in agreement, that's even more powerful, like when Jim Woodford's six family members prayed together for him (Matthew 18:19-20). But God also longs for intimacy with you, and when you make time to be quiet and alone, talking with God from the heart—about all that troubles you, about your joys and gratitude, about your wants and desires, about the needs and concerns of others—God promises to reward you.

Jesus also explained the difference between prayers of the heart and empty words, which are just noise to God: "When you pray, don't babble on and on as the Gentiles do. They think their prayers are answered merely by repeating their words again and again. Don't be like them, for your Father knows exactly what you need even before you ask him!" (Matthew 6:7-8). In other words, prayer isn't about manipulating God into giving us what we want; it's about aligning our heart with God's heart.

If we are just babbling words with no heartfelt connection to what we're saying, it's not what the Father wants. This does not mean, however, that memorized or written prayers cannot also be prayed from the heart. In fact, Jesus taught his followers to pray from the heart using a prayer we refer to today as the "Our Father" or the "Lord's Prayer" (Matthew 6:9-13). And for Karina Martinez, this prayer was powerful.

PADRE NUESTRO (OUR FATHER)

Karina grew up Catholic in Colombia. She had memorized the Our Father as a child, but the prayer was just meaningless words to her—until the day her heart failed. Now in her forties with a family, Karina had been misdiagnosed with a heart condition, and doctors had installed a pacemaker. A year later, during the COVID-19 pandemic, she went to the hospital with elevated blood pressure. They gave her new meds and sent her home to rest. As she lay on a lounge chair on the back patio of her home, she knew her heart was failing. She called her husband and three children and started apologizing profusely for past wrongs. "I told them, I'm going to heaven," Karina recalls, "but I feared I was going to hell because of all the bad things I had done in the past. It felt like heaven and hell were fighting for me."

Karina's father and stepmother had moved from Colombia to New York and abandoned her to her grandmother and aunt when she was sixteen. She felt unwanted, filled with anger, always trying to prove her worth. She had been a singer in a band, a fashionista, a swimsuit model—anything to be famous so she'd feel worth something. Partying and promiscuity led to a pregnancy at nineteen. She wanted to keep the baby, but the cousin she lived with said, "Get an abortion, or I'm kicking you out." She called her parents, and they, too, refused to let her live with them while pregnant. Distraught, she got the abortion. She felt so lost.

In the years that followed, Karina went to multiple churches search-ing for redemption and healing but never felt welcomed. She felt like an outcast. But God hears the prayer of the heart, and when Karina's heart failed, he heard her sincere prayer for forgiveness and help. Here is how Karina describes what happened after her heart stopped and her spirit rose above her body.

> In the blink of an eye, I started dropping into this blacker-than-black place, head down, going fast into this black tunnel. And it was really, really cold. I had a fear in me, and I knew I was going to hell. I started praying in Spanish, "I'm sorry, God, please forgive me." And I was repeating in Spanish, "Our father in heaven, holy is your name, your kingdom come, your will be done. Forgive us our sins." And I would say, "I'm so sorry, I'm so sorry for those things I knew were wrong." I was repenting, though I didn't know what *repent* meant.[13]

With that prayer of the heart, a golden light shot down into the darkness. Karina felt her spirit body flip and start moving up into the light. As soon as the light touched her, she said,

> A shower of love came over me, something that I had never felt before flooded my being. This intense love, not only love, but everything that came with it—peace, no pain, [no] anger, nothing. Even right now, I just want to go back to it.
>
> I knew this was heaven, but I felt so unworthy. I felt, *This is not good; I don't belong here.* I felt like God should send me back to the dark place because I'm such a bad person. But his voice just said, "Come, come, you're home." And I could see all these people in the light, and they were saying, "Come, come." And they were celebrating . . . me! I was overwhelmed. And the voice said, "You're home." And I was so full of joy, I just went right in. I was so happy. Before sending me back, Jesus said to me, "You're awesome!"[14]

Out of a wounded heart, Karina had spent much of her life trying to find her worth and value in the eyes of other people. Jesus showed her she didn't need people's approval. To God, she was already awesome! Karina came back to her body after a full-blown experience of all the beauty of heaven, including the city of God and God's throne. Today, she calls herself a prayer warrior for Jesus. Beginning with her first heartfelt prayer during her NDE, God has been healing her of the wounds and lies that led her into all kinds of self-destructive behavior. That's why prayer matters. Jesus gave us the Lord's Prayer as an outline of what to pray from the heart.

LEARNING TO PRAY THE LORD'S PRAYER

Here is the prayer Jesus taught his followers to pray:

> Our Father in heaven,
>   may your name be kept holy.
> May your Kingdom come soon.
> May your will be done on earth,
>   as it is in heaven.
> Give us today the food we need,
> and forgive us our sins,
>   as we have forgiven those who sin against us.
> And don't let us yield to temptation,
>   but rescue us from the evil one.
>
> MATTHEW 6:9-13

I believe Jesus intended the Lord's Prayer to be a model, an outline we can follow as we learn to communicate with God heart to heart.

Our Father in heaven, may your name be kept holy. As you pray, Jesus says, first honor God and worship God for who he is: your heavenly Father. Put God in the right place in your mind—he's holy—he's to be loved, respected, and honored. Tell him so.

May your Kingdom come soon. May your will be done on earth, as it is in heaven. Surrender your will to God's will. The joy and harmony in heaven come from God's will being done perfectly there, but that's not the case with earth. In our fallen world, God's will only comes to earth through you and me, as we are willing. Pray for God's will to be done through you today.

Give us today the food we need. Pray for the things you need. For Jesus' first-century audience, many lived in poverty, relying on God each day for food. But you can ask God for anything. Remember, God is not stingy. He's not trying to make you barely scrape by; he's a good father. Jesus said, "For everyone who asks, receives. . . . If you sinful people know how to give good gifts to your children, how much more will your heavenly Father give good gifts to those who ask him" (Matthew 7:8, 11). So ask!

And forgive us our sins, as we have forgiven those who sin against us. Admit your sins, or wrongs, to God, who eternally forgives you in Christ. We confess our sins so that we don't continue to turn away from God. And we must also forgive anyone who has wronged us, even if it was years ago. If we refuse to forgive, it's not that the gift of salvation is taken back, but we will not experience God's forgiveness and intimacy in the present. God forgave us for every wrong when Jesus died on the cross, so he expects us to forgive others.

Douglas had led a life of crime, which made him both rich and famous. But Douglas discovered none of that mattered when his car hit a parked semitruck on the side of the highway, and he died. In his NDE, he saw his name in the Book of Life from when he had accepted Jesus as a child, but he also saw the book of his deeds that were not pleasing to God. When he came back to his earthly life, he changed his ways and started following Jesus. However, he discovered following God's will was not always easy, even after having an NDE. It was a struggle for Douglas, just as it is for all of us. For Douglas, his thoughts were dominated by anger and a desire for revenge against those who had betrayed him.

> I was trying desperately to change who I was and what I had become, but as hard as I would try, I could not escape myself. . . . My hope of forgiving others for what they [had] done to me was another impossibility and the word *forgiveness*

would get stuck in my throat when trying to recite the Lord's Prayer, I couldn't even finish the prayer. My "walk" towards God had hit a roadblock. . . .

I began to pray to God asking Him for help in becoming able to forgive those people who had wronged me. . . . What God did show me was that even though I myself (the old man) never would forgive, Jesus Christ existed in me as a new person and had done all the forgiving that has ever needed to be done. However, He was also telling me that I had to allow him to become me.[15]

God forgave us for every wrong when Jesus died on the cross, and he expects us to forgive others. We can ask God to give us the power to forgive when it's difficult.

And don't let us yield to temptation, but rescue us from the evil one. Not every thought you have originates with you—some thoughts are yours, some thoughts come from God, such as promptings from the Holy Spirit, and some thoughts come from the evil one as temptations. You don't need to feel bad about having a tempting thought; it wasn't yours in the first place. As I like to say, "The first thought is free, the second will cost you." Sin enters the picture when you choose to *keep thinking* about something against God's will. When you realize you're yielding to temptation, or nursing thoughts against God's will, ask God to help you redirect your thinking.

Jesus answered his disciples' request, "teach us to pray," with the Lord's Prayer as an outline. We can pray for all these things from the heart. But don't forget, prayer is just conversation, and conversation in a loving relationship is ongoing.

PRAYER AS UNCEASING CONVERSATION

Prayer can take many forms, but I believe one of the most important and most overlooked forms of prayer is what the apostle Paul described as continual or unceasing prayer: "Rejoice always, pray continually, give thanks in all circumstances; for this is God's will for you in Christ Jesus" (1 Thessalonians 5:16-18, NIV).

Unceasing prayer is how we walk through life with the Holy Spirit moment by moment, day by day. We begin as we wake up in the morning and then continue until we go to bed at night, discussing with God every thought, every decision, every event, and every meeting or encounter that comes our way. That's God's desire—that we talk everything over with him, we thank him along the way, and we listen for his guidance through the Holy Spirit's promptings. Unceasing prayer is how we stay connected to God.

As we discussed in the previous chapter, this is the *one thing* Jesus said we must do, and it's really the *only thing* we have to do to become all God intended. When we practice unceasing prayer, staying connected to God's Spirit with a willingness to obey every prompting, Jesus says we will "bear much fruit" (John 15:5, NIV). The challenge is, most of us have developed the habit of ignoring God most of the day. From the moment we wake up, all we're thinking about is, "What do *I* have to do today?" "How do *I* get *my will* done in all things?" So we must develop new habits to help us remain in constant connection with God's Spirit, willing to do his will.

Our willingness is key! God's Spirit does not intrude on our thoughts and will. He humbly waits for our willingness. The more willing we are to talk over things, to let him into our moments, to listen to his guidance, and to act in faith, the more clearly we will experience the Spirit guiding us through life. And the result, Jesus says, is our "joy will overflow!" (John 15:11).

Randy Kay, the CEO, was told by Jesus he had to go back to earth to fulfill his purpose. Jesus gave Randy insight into staying connected to the Holy Spirit in unceasing prayer.

> I remember I didn't have to say, "Don't leave me." [Jesus] knew. He knew I was thinking it. He said, "I won't. I won't. Never. Never."
>
> I said, "Why am I going back?" because I knew my children would be taken care of. I knew he loved them more than me. I knew that everything was good.
>
> He said, "Because of your purpose."

I said, "Tell me my purpose, then. I want to know what it is."

He said, "I won't tell you your purpose. I'm going to return you, and your purpose will be revealed one moment at a time, because if I were to reveal your purpose in full, you would not be dependent upon me. You must trust me and continually seek my guidance."

I pleaded with him, "Please tell me, please. I'm leaving paradise. I don't want to go."

He said, "I love you." Then he said, "Trust me. Your purpose, that's why you're going back, and there are others praying for you."

The Lord was telling me I needed to get quiet and still with him in order to stay in my purpose. If I remain still and listening and steeped in his presence on earth, then wisdom will be my guide.[16]

What Jesus told Randy is also true for us. We can fulfill the purpose God has us here to do as we stay attentive, listening to the Holy Spirit's guidance in a practice of unceasing prayer. For me, the same lesson came a different way.

THE 60:60 EXPERIMENT

When my wife, Kathy, and I started Gateway Church in Austin, Texas, over twenty-five years ago, nothing was going as I had planned. The first two years were especially rough because we had no facility of our own. We had to rent, and we kept getting kicked out of one meeting place after another—six different places in two years. People would attend, find faith, and then we'd move and lose them. Honestly, I got very frustrated with God, wondering why he didn't answer my prayers for a facility. I felt let down by God. When I would get quiet and listen during prayer, I started to have the same question from God's Spirit intrude into my thoughts: *Am I enough? Am I enough for you, John?*

After several months of processing this in prayer, I realized that what God was asking me was this: "John, is it enough to love me, love your family, and love and serve the people who *are coming*? Am I enough, or do things have to go your way?" And that's when I realized I was not okay with things not going my way. I was addicted to "myself," to "my will be done."

During this time, I started praying this prayer when I woke up each morning: *God, today I want to do life moment by moment with you, willing to do your will as you guide me.* And as I would go through the day, I tried to stay connected to God's Spirit by continually pausing to ask, "Is this what you want me doing? Is this what you want me thinking?" Or, as I would interact with a person, "Lord, is there something you want me to say or do for this person?" And when I sensed God prompting me to do or say something, I tried to radically obey the prompting.

After about a year of doing this, I was blown away. I had *joy*! Even though none of my "bad circumstances" had changed, I began to experience a joy that would bubble up from within at the strangest moments, often for no reason at all. It was what Jesus promised about staying connected—that his joy would be in me, and my joy would overflow (John 15:11)!

One day as I was mowing the lawn and talking to God about how fantastic this experience of his joy had been, I told God how I wished everyone coming to our church could experience it. And a strong thought entered my mind: *Do an experiment. Do an experiment to get people to try to stay connected over a sixty-day period and let them see for themselves how good it is.*

And so we did! We called it the 60:60 Experiment, and our church has done the 60:60 every few years for over twenty years now. We keep doing it because people are amazed when they experience the joy of staying connected to God's Spirit. They experience his personal, unique, and relational guidance moment by moment throughout the day. I encourage you to give it a try.

I wrote a book called *Soul Revolution* to teach and illustrate the experiment, but it's really simple. To do the 60:60 Experiment, devote sixty days to staying connected, moment by moment, in an unceasing conversation with God's Spirit. To help keep you on track and form a new habit, set an alarm or reminder on your phone for every sixty minutes during your waking hours for sixty days (or download our app*). The reminder is not so much an hourly "call to prayer" as a reminder to briefly take inventory and process with God what you observe about the practice. "Lord, how did I do staying connected to you this last hour? How can I remain in your love right now? How well did I let you in on my thoughts, decisions, and interactions? Is there anything you want me to do right now?"

Spoiler alert: You *will* fail at this—definitely more than you succeed. But just as a toddler falls more than walks at first, you'll get stronger as you stumble along. And the more you walk with God, the better you'll get at staying connected to him. Be willing to fail forward. What you will find is what thousands of people who have done this experiment before you have found: God really does care about all the details of your day. He wants to help you with work, with kids, when you're impatient, when you're in a fight with a significant other, and when you struggle with temptations. And every time you choose to remain in him, he lovingly guides you from that moment to the next.

When you practice staying connected to God's Spirit, you'll find that God takes care of a lot of things you could never make happen on your own. You'll be guided by God's wisdom, love, joy, peace, and many other God "winks" throughout the day.

I hope you'll experiment with this prayer of constant conversation with God. And use Jesus' model prayer as an outline of things to pray about. But above all, remember, God is crazy in love with you, and prayer is simply communication with the one who loves you most!

---

* We developed a free smartphone app called "Soul Revolution 60:60" that sends alerts every hour with a verse to help you remember to stay connected to the Holy Spirit throughout the day.

13

THE PERFECT PLANS
OF GOD

DR. MARK MCDONOUGH IS A PLASTIC SURGEON with a passion to help burn victims, especially children. Mark has a unique appreciation for what they must endure—and few people have seen the confusing sufferings of this world juxtaposed against the certainty of God's perfect plans as Mark has.

It was in the wee hours of Tuesday morning, August 3, 1976, when sixteen-year-old Mark awoke suddenly to feelings of intense heat and the sound of roaring, like tornadoes, outside his bedroom door. The oldest of five boys, Mark had been told by his father that day, "Watch out after your mother and brothers while I'm gone," and then he left on a business trip.

Mark darted through his door into the hallway, only to be knocked back by the searing heat and billowing black smoke coming up the stairs. Mark yelled to his three younger brothers to get out, watching as each jumped from one of three different second-story windows. His mother and youngest brother, Toby, were in rooms opposite the flame-engulfed stairwell, distance and noise precluding them from hearing Mark's screams.

I have to get to them! Mark's mind raced. He screamed into the inferno, "Fire! Get out!" He raced around, looking for a pathway to his mom's room. With the fire now cutting off his escape route, he plunged down the stairs, feeling his skin blistering and oozing from the nearby flames. Hoping to climb from the outside to her balcony, he grabbed the brass knob of the front door and pulled with all his might, but the metal door had swollen shut. His only option was to duck and run through the kitchen to a door leading out to the garage. Covering his face, he was only conscious of the need to get his mom and Toby out. Just as Mark reached the back door, the smoke overtook his lungs and he dropped to the ground.

Firefighters found Mark unconscious with burns over 65 percent of his body. He was aware of paramedics scrambling to revive him as he went in and out of consciousness on the way to the hospital. Overcome by pain, he begged, "God, please take me. Just take me." The pain was too much for Mark to withstand. "This is absolutely unbearable; I won't tolerate another second of it. Take me," young Mark pleaded with God. But another second would pass, then another, and another. Mark kept asking the paramedics, "Did Mom and Toby get out?" No one answered him; the trauma of knowing his mom and brother were gone would be too much for this young kid to bear.

The first ten days, Mark's body was physiologically unstable, and he was on a ventilator. When his father returned, he could barely recognize his oldest son, the burns had so blistered and swollen his face. Mark would lie in bed screaming for relief from the inexplicable pain, as every nerve under every centimeter of skin fired its torturous alarm. Finally, after ten days, Mark stabilized enough for surgery. During surgery, Mark suffered what doctors call "intraoperative awareness." He was actually awake, feeling severe pain with each cut. But medications given to cause paralysis prevented him from blinking an eye, let alone screaming. That's when Mark's heart stopped.

> All of a sudden, I had this feeling that everything was okay. I was in complete peace and tranquility. I was in a position as though I were in a La-Z-Boy recliner and just sort of floating and hovering above my body. I felt the presence of God—a love that is just so

difficult to put into words, but a sense of love and security that's almost indescribable. Everything is okay. It always has been, it is now, and it always will be, and there's nothing to be afraid of.[1]

It had seemed like time stopped. Now I didn't want time to start. . . . I just wanted to linger in this blissful state. . . . All things—past, present, and yet to be—had a specific purpose and reason. . . . Everything was perfect, exactly as it was intended from the beginning of time and would remain so forever. And all of this was so plainly apparent that I felt like giggling at the simplicity and impeccability. *Oh . . . God! Of course! Who else?* It was wonderful to be free from pain, but even that which I'd experienced did not matter anymore. And it was hard to even categorize it as bad. . . . *No suffering is ever in vain. All pain has its purpose and is part of the plan.*[2]

The euphoria, the happiness, the laughter—as quickly as I could think of a question, the answer was there. And the answers were so simple, so joyful, and so clear. I thought, *Oh, yes, of course—that makes complete sense. It all fits together and makes perfect sense. And I'm right where I should be, and things are just the way they should be. It's going to all work; it's all going to be okay.*[3]

Mark sensed the presence of angels and people around him. He drifted up toward a "square-shaped tunnel ascending a gentle slope" toward the light, but then Mark sensed a border or boundary.

Somehow, I knew . . . that to go beyond was to cross to some other side, and it's not my time. I felt the presence of my mom, my brother, and my grandfather who had died when I was one. I felt their very presence as if we were all comfortably cozied up in blankets on the couch watching TV. We were completely aware of each other's thoughts. And I knew that God was saying, "This is a difficult challenge, but it's one we can do together, and I'm with you. I won't leave you." [With] the provision of the Father, and my buddy, Jesus, we're going to make this. It's not going to be easy, but we're going to do it together.[4]

When young Mark came out of the surgery, he told his dad, "I think I met Jesus, and it's going to be okay."

Mark did go on to become a plastic surgeon, helping many other trauma and burn survivors of all ages. He experienced the perfection of God's plan while in God's presence, but he also had to endure the confusing truth of God's words when God said to Mark, "It's not going to be easy."

GOD'S SOVEREIGN PLAN

Perhaps you've wrestled with some questions like these: Does God have a plan for my life? If so, why am I going through all this pain and suffering? Am I on the right road? What if I miss his plan with bad choices—will I just have to settle for "off-roading" my whole life? Is it possible to make choices that get me back on the right road, back to his path and purpose? But wait, if God knows the future and has a plan laid out for me, then what difference do my choices make anyway? Is everything predetermined? Am I just a robot? And if people can choose good or evil, and God doesn't control them, how can God be in control and know the future?

This is the dizzying merry-go-round of questions many of us have about God's sovereignty (God's all-powerful, all-knowing rule over all he created) and human free will (our ability to decide and choose freely). The debate about sovereignty versus free will has been raging for over five hundred years, typically between Calvinist theology (which tends to emphasize God's sovereign control) and Arminian theology (which tends to emphasize free will), and now Open Theism (which says God determines some of the future, but he has chosen to leave the future partly open to free choice). We won't solve this longtime debate in one chapter. But Scripture offers some insights, and maybe the experiences of NDErs can shed some light on why this is still a debate and how we might live in the tension instead of being derailed by it.

Maybe you are thinking, *Who cares? What difference does it make anyway?* Actually, it makes a lot of difference! Not in the debate itself, but in how you and I imagine God. For example, maybe you turned away from God because people made evil choices and God didn't stop them, causing you to believe God can't be trusted. Or maybe you have prayed and prayed but things didn't go as you'd hoped, so you concluded prayer is useless and God doesn't care. And yet, consider what God declared to the prophet Isaiah:

> I am God, and there is no other; I am God, and there is none like me. I make known the end from the beginning, from ancient times, what is still to come. I say: "My purpose will stand, and I will do all that I please." From the east I summon a bird of prey; from a far-off land, a man to fulfill my purpose. What I have said, that I will bring about; what I have planned, that I will do.
> ISAIAH 46:9-11, NIV

God makes it very clear that he has a plan and purpose—and what he has planned will happen. Knowing the loving character of God, that should give you and me lots of assurance about the future as we follow him. Personally, I find nothing more convincing of God's *sovereignty* than the way he foretold the events of Israel and the coming Messiah thousands of years in advance, as we have seen.

You are secure in Christ because nothing can thwart his will or his ultimate plans and purpose. In fact, even when someone is hell-bent on opposing him, God will use what that person intends for evil to accomplish his plan for good. The Old Testament story of Joseph provides a perfect illustration of this. Joseph's brothers betrayed him and sold him into slavery in Egypt, yet God ultimately elevated Joseph to a position of great power—second in command only to Pharoah—in order to save lives from a famine. When his brothers came to Egypt pleading for food during the famine, they were unaware Joseph was alive, much less in power. Yet Joseph told them: "You intended to harm me, but God intended it all for good. He brought me to this position so I could save the lives of many people" (Genesis 50:20).

When you're intent on following God, stories like Joseph's should give you great comfort and peace. Nothing and no one can thwart God's plans for you, and God's plans are good. They will succeed. Through the prophet Jeremiah, God said, "For I know the plans I have for you, . . . plans to prosper you and not to harm you, plans to give you hope and a future" (Jeremiah 29:11, NIV).

God has a plan for all who will turn to him, seek him, and call on him—and his plan is to prosper us, to give us hope and a future. But that does not mean all circumstances go our way. God's promise spoken to Jeremiah is often quoted to encourage us that God has a good plan, but the larger context sometimes gets left out. God is telling his people they will be in Babylon as exiles for seventy years. These are circumstances they do not want to endure, yet God is reassuring them that his plan for them is good even through the difficulties.

We may go through hard times, as Joseph did, but they aren't intended to harm us. God wants to benefit us, but not only us; his plans are for the good of others also. And his plans to prosper us are not just materially on earth, but spiritually and eternally. In his timing, God fulfills his ultimate plan for good in our lives, and in the lives of others, despite the circumstances we may have to endure.

The apostle Paul reiterates this truth, saying, "In all things God works for the good of those who love him, who have been called according to his purpose. For those God foreknew he also predestined to be conformed to the image of his Son" (Romans 8:28-29, NIV). Even when our circumstances are confusing and life is not going the way we hoped, we can rest assured that God's plan for us is good, and ultimately it is to help us become more like Jesus. So we should pay attention to what God is doing *in* us, not just around us.

When I interviewed Dr. Mary Neal, she explained how Jesus showed her this truth in her life review.

Mary Neal: My life was laid bare for all its good and bad. And one of the things we did was look at many, many, many events throughout my life that I would've otherwise called terrible or horrible or sad or bad or tragic. And instead of looking at an event in isolation or looking at how it impacted me and my little world, I had the most remarkable experience of seeing the ripple effects of the event when seen twenty-five, thirty, thirty-five times removed.

John Burke: What do you mean? The impact of one life to another?

Mary Neal: No, the impact an event had on me, on my little world, but then also on other people in the world. And looking at how an event that I would have said was bad changed me and changed others such that again and again and again, I was shown that indeed it's true that beauty comes of all things. It was really a life-changing experience.

John Burke: You know, there's that verse that always gets quoted when bad things happen, right? "God works all things together for the good of those who love Him" [Romans 8:28, BSB]. Was it like seeing that?

Mary Neal: Yes. It was being shown very concretely again and again. . . . I had this absolute sense of understanding the divine order of everything. And I also had this, for me, very profound understanding of how it can be true that God actually knows each and every one of us—all the billions of us on the planet—and loves each and every one of us as though we are the only ones, and how he has a plan for each and every one of our lives that's one of hope. God's plans for us are always greater than we can imagine.[5]

Through all of our interactions together, God is working his marvelous plan for each one of us to accomplish the most good for all people. He's using it to shape every willing person into the masterpiece he intended.

To the prophet Jeremiah, God makes it clear that his plans are not just for global events but are very personal to each individual: "The word of the LORD came to me, saying, 'Before I formed you in the womb I knew you, before you were born I set you apart; I appointed you as a prophet to the nations'" (Jeremiah 1:4-5, NIV). And yet, following God's perfect plan doesn't mean we won't be impacted by the actions of others. People go against God's will and do hurtful things that cause us to suffer—Jeremiah was called the "weeping prophet" for a reason. Hard-hearted people caused Jeremiah much grief. We still live in a world in which God's plans and people's free-willed choices seem to collide. And this is where it gets confusing.

SOVEREIGNTY INCLUDES FREE WILL

Our choices matter. God declares through Moses, "Today I have given you the choice between life and death, between blessings and curses. Now I call on heaven and earth to witness the choice you make. Oh, that you would choose life" (Deuteronomy 30:19). Jesus also taught that we have a free will with real consequences: "Anyone who chooses to do the will of God will find out whether my teaching comes from God" (John 7:17, NIV). Many NDErs see a book in heaven with all their choices and deeds recorded, just as Scripture reveals: "Your eyes saw my unformed body; all the days ordained for me were written in your book before one of them came to be" (Psalm 139:16, NIV). The apostle John "saw the dead, great and small, standing before the throne, and books were opened. Another book was opened, which is the book of life. The dead were judged according to what they had done as recorded in the books" (Revelation 20:12, NIV). So clearly, God's sovereignty *includes* our choices, and we are responsible before God for the choices we make. The confusion comes with trying to understand how our free-willed choices and God's sovereign plans work together.

While he was present with God in his NDE, Dr. Mark McDonough had no doubt that God's plan was perfect. However, what he still had to go through when he returned to earth would make anyone question God's plan: thirty surgeries, constant pain, life as a teenage burn victim without a mother. "I got angry," Mark admits. "I questioned God: 'I know you're real. I know you're there. But why me? Why am I picked for this? Why does it have to be this burn injury? Why did my mom have to die?' And as soon as I get in the 'whys,' I can easily get frustrated and challenged."[6]

And that wasn't the end of his suffering. After the fire, his father plunged into alcoholism. Mark soon followed, feeling the numbing effects of beer on the PTSD that he later discovered. Ten years after the NDE, Mark was working as a physical therapist when he admitted he was an alcoholic. After going through recovery, Mark realized that with God's help he had the discipline and desire to do more. That led him to medical school to become a reconstructive surgeon.

Was Mark somehow predestined to become addicted to alcohol so that his recovery would lead him to medical school? Or did he make choices against God's will due to his struggles, yet God used them for good as Mark turned back to God? And how do we make sense of the painful choices others make and the sufferings caused by the chaos of life which Mark experienced?

Three years before Mark entered medical school, his brother Packy took his own life. When Mark was just thirty, he had a stroke on the anniversary of his mother's death. Years later, congestive heart failure led to an open-heart surgery that eventually brought an end to Mark's work as a full-time surgeon. In 2016, Mark and his wife, Joan, were at a concert performed by their three musically talented sons, and the opening singer, a close friend, was shot by an obsessed fan. Mark attempted to save her with CPR, but she passed away after EMS arrived. How could anyone in Mark's circumstances not be confused or wonder about God's plan? Yet, here is how Mark sums up his perspective on everything he's been through:

> God wants us to know we can do anything with His help. He will help us through anything, but He doesn't just dump stuff on us so we can prove how strong we are. He does that so we can be sculpted and molded and forged into the being and character He'd like us to be. . . . I want people to realize the joys far outweigh the pain, and it's worth it. . . . I've had such a good life.[7]

How could someone who has suffered so much say, "I've had such a good life?" Could it be that this is the goal through it all? That God would grow us spiritually to the point that absolutely nothing—not even the worst suffering or circumstances—can rob us of God's joy and love and peace as we closely follow him? I think that's what it means to be conformed to the image of his Son.

Even if that's the case, we're still left with internal dissonance and unanswered questions. If God knows all that will happen, then isn't God *responsible* for all that happens—including evil? Does God "cause" or "predetermine" suffering or evil? Or is it that God has sovereignly allowed other forces to rule earth for a time in order to teach us our need for God's rule? Jesus told his followers that Satan rules this world for now (John 12:31). We live behind enemy lines. For a time, God has allowed evil to reign on earth, and if we don't understand this, we will misinterpret much of what happens to us.

Kevin Zadai came back from his NDE with this reminder from Jesus:

> He showed me all the things that are happening against people down here. I said, "Lord, you know, it's hard down there." He said, "Yeah, but it's not about you, Kevin. It's about the people that I'm sending you to. If you tell people what you saw, it's going to help them and reroute their life." He said, "I am going to send you back, and I want you to tell your story, and [I] want you to start to reroute people's lives so that they finish right." . . . Jesus wanted to show me how we can walk in the Spirit, we can walk in love, and finish right. . . .
>
> Jesus told me, "The Father and I love everyone. We aren't doing any of these terrible things that are happening to people on the earth. That's the devil doing that. Go back and tell people that it's the god of this world doing all these things."[8]

NDE testimonies such as Kevin's highlight why God's sovereignty and human free will might feel like a contradiction: God is revealing two truths from two different perspectives, one beyond time as we know it (God's foreknowledge) and one within time (human free will). God is *sovereign* (in control of all things), and God is *immutable* (unchanging). Through the prophet Malachi, God said to his people, "I the LORD do not change. . . . Return to me, and I will return to you" (Malachi 3:6-7, NIV). God's *immutability* and *sovereignty* allow us to exercise free will: "Return to me" is an invitation to make a choice. The mystery is that while our free choices are not predetermined, God's perfect and sovereign plan will prevail.

Maybe instead of trying to resolve the tension, we should embrace both revealed truths—God is sovereign, and we have free will. However, understanding God's multidimensional time versus our one-dimensional time can give us a new perspective on the tension.

GOD'S TWO-DIMENSIONAL TIMELINE

Astrophysicist Hugh Ross helps us imagine two- and three-dimensional time.[9] He points out that earth time is one-dimensional and sequential. Picture it moving in one direction along a line. If you know with absolute certainty what I will do tomorrow, I cannot have a choice. Either my choice has been predetermined, and I have no free will; or I can choose, but then you can't know my choice with certainty. That's our one-dimensional experience of time. But if we existed in more than one dimension of time, all that changes!

If God, who is beyond time, functions in two dimensions of time, then at each "moment" on our timeline, there would be an infinite amount of time to experience that moment. Picture a horizontal line numbered 1 to 100 for the years of your life (one-dimensional time). A second dimension of time would look like a perpendicular line intersecting each moment and extending each moment infinitely upward on another timeline (see below).

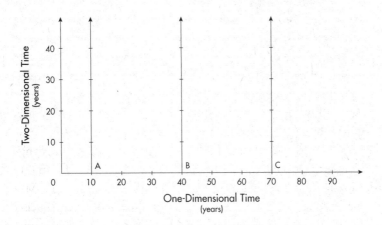

Just as NDErs indicate, each moment of one-dimensional time would feel like an infinite amount of time experienced, or no time at all. Father Cedric Pisegna said, "I'm not sure how much time I stood before God and Jesus. . . . When you come before God, time stands still."[10] Other NDErs say they were aware of time moving, but nothing was rushed.

I believe the Bible implies two-dimensional time when it says, "A day is like a thousand years to the Lord, and a thousand years is like a day" (2 Peter 3:8). I got some unique insights into this concept when Gregg Rickert reached out to me to tell me about his near-death experience.

Gregg had grown up Catholic and still believed in Jesus as an adult, but he also felt his life lacked direction. He built high-end custom homes for many extremely wealthy people, and he had all the trappings of success, yet still felt that something was missing. Gregg had prayed for God to help him turn his life in a better direction.

One night on his way home from a disappointing singles event at a bar, he rounded a bend and saw an oncoming car cross the median into his lane. He quickly tried to swerve around it but was hit head-on. Gregg's face and ankle were shattered in the collision, and he had to be life-flighted to the hospital. The doctors told Gregg's parents, "Your son is going to die. If he survives, he will be both brain dead and blind. We'd like to take his organs." After denying repeated requests for his organs, his parents said they wanted to try surgery, so Gregg was put into a medically induced coma.

While in the coma, Gregg says he "woke up," floating out of his body toward "beautiful glass doors in front of me with the nicest grain wood I've ever seen." Isn't it just like God, with his personal touch, to craft an entrance to heaven that a custom home builder would appreciate? Gregg looked back and saw his body in the hospital bed. He noticed a soccer ball and a poster with "I love you Gregg" written in his sister's handwriting. That's when Gregg realized that his soul was alive, and he was actually seeing his body in his hospital room.

> I floated through the doors and the next thing I know, I'm in this huge glass hall, like a glass dome with a glass floor, and under the floor I can see stars. I'm thinking, *This is amazing!* I see two people in front of me. One is Jesus and the other is my guardian angel. I always thought it was BS that you have a guardian angel, but I did. He was twelve feet or so—huge, big. And I just knew the other person was Jesus. There was no doubt in my mind. When you're in front of God, you have absolute comprehension and understanding. There's no questioning or reasoning; it's pure knowledge.

Jesus was a person, the form of a human being. He gestured
to a four-foot circle to the side of him, like a round window,
but it was like an interdimensional time portal. I realized that
we were somehow outside of time and space. A three-foot
book opened under the portal, and I started to see my book of
life displayed in the portal.

We were reviewing the things written down in my life's
book. He showed me good things and bad things. I realized
I had been striving for the wrong things—earthly perfection,
the nicest house, the coolest car, or the most beautiful wife.
None of it holds any weight or has any meaning once you're
in heaven. I felt welcoming, caring, loving feelings from him.
I was in the absolute understanding of my life and experienced
how important little things truly are. What really matters.
You're being judged in that moment by being allowed to see
the importance of what we do and how we live, and how our
choices matter. It's very humbling to see life so clearly.[11]

As Gregg's experience continued, Jesus took Gregg to heaven, where
he witnessed two-dimensional time in action.

The next thing I know, I'm in heaven. I'm looking at my new
body, at my arms and legs. My body is translucent but glowing
with this golden light* and vibrating with the joy coming
out of everything around me, which was worship of God!
Everything was brilliant. In the distance there was a waterfall
flowing, but it was like a river of golden perfection flowing.
Everything was golden, but amazing, gorgeous. I used to do
custom homes for super wealthy people and some celebrities,
where everything had to be perfect. But anything here on this
earth just has no comparison to the beauty I saw there, the joy
I felt there—nothing even in the same ballpark. . . .

I was shown a timeline of two-dimensional time. I saw

---

* See Matthew 13:43.

a beginning and end, but was outside of it. In heaven you're allowed to see through these portals, and I watched some kind of battle. It appeared to be in Egypt, and two armies were going against each other with pyramids in the background—but I was watching it in reality. I was actually experiencing what was happening in their time. What significance that moment had, I don't know, but I experienced it. I experienced it like watching a movie, but so much more real, even feeling what people were feeling or thinking. As I was watching that timeline at a point in time, I somehow knew that you were not allowed to go through that portal back into time, but I was allowed to see it. But when in heaven, you're experiencing it as it is actually happening.

I saw through another portal that an angel beckoned me to look through, and I was looking at a guy with blond hair, skinny guy, with a weird-looking haircut, and a girl. I said, "Oh, she's a pretty girl," and I saw this orb, this glowing, one-foot round ball that was reverberating with excitement and energy, and I was told, "This is their child. . . ." It was awesome. It was joy and excitement—just amazing. After seeing the child [with] her parents, I found myself in the throne room of God. I see this glowing, bright white, unexplainably powerful bright light shining from his face. All the music is going to him—it's joy, peace, perfection—you know it's God the Father.[12]

Jesus sent Gregg back to his body on earth. Gregg said, "I had about eight doctors say, 'You're a miracle.'" He wasn't supposed to ever see, talk, walk, or run, but now he does all of those things. And one more twist was the confirmation Gregg later received that he had, in fact, seen history in two-dimensional time.

So, two-and-a-half years later, I meet this guy and this girl who were friends of our family, but I'd never met them. They had a little blonde girl, about two-and-a-half years old, who looks up at me with so much excitement and joy. The mom said, "I don't know why she loves you so." And suddenly, it hit me—this is the mom. This is the woman I saw with the skinny guy, and this must be the little unborn girl I saw in the portal.[13]

Remember what God said to the prophet Jeremiah? "I knew you before I formed you in your mother's womb. Before you were born I set you apart" (Jeremiah 1:5). God has a plan, and his plan includes the free-willed choices of people and angels. For time-bound humans, this may always seem like a contradiction, yet God reveals these truths more as a paradox—both equally true in God's multidimensional time.[14] And yet, there is another twist to consider. What if God functions not just in two dimensions of time but in *three* dimensions of time? I believe that would resolve the seeming contradiction or paradox between God's sovereignty and human free will.

RESOLVING THE TIME PARADOX

Imagine the illustration of two-dimensional time wrapped around a third dimension of time. Hugh Ross pictures it as a globe, where each moment of our timeline runs horizontally along the equator.

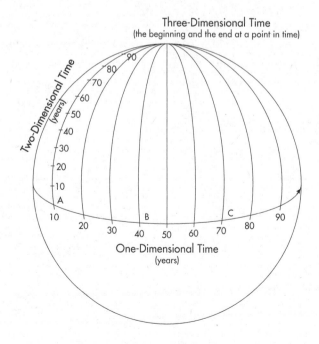

God experiences each moment of our latitudinal timeline (horizontal, one-dimensional time) on a longitudinal (vertical, two-dimensional) timeline, extending up to a single point (similar to the North Pole). That's how God attends to billions of prayers being prayed at the same moment—each moment of our time extends his experience of that moment into a second dimension of time, as Gregg described.

In three-dimensional time, God experiences each moment on north-south longitudinal timelines that all converge at a third dimensional point in time (where the North Pole is on a globe). God would experience the beginning and ending of our timeline in the eternal *now* of a single point of third dimensional time.

I believe this is exactly what God revealed to the prophet Isaiah: "I am God, and there is none like me. I make known the end from the beginning, from ancient times, what is still to come. I say, 'My purpose will stand'" (Isaiah 46:9-10, NIV). And Jesus affirms this when he declares, "I am the Alpha and the Omega, the First and the Last, the Beginning and the End" (Revelation 22:13, NIV).

The reason there's been such a debate about God's sovereignty and human free will is our unwillingness to accept the tension of living in one-dimensional time while God lives in multiple dimensions of time. God's sovereign plan and foreknowledge is truth revealed from *God's dimension of time*. Our free will is a truth God assures us we possess and must exercise in *our dimension of time*. Both can coexist because God exists beyond the limits of our timeline.

OFF-ROADING AND REROUTING

Can you miss God's plan and purpose for you? No, not if you walk with God's Spirit like we've discussed. The problem is people can choose against God's intended purpose. Through the Old Testament prophets, God foretold that Jesus, the Messiah, would die for our sins. The Pharisees (religious rulers) instigated Jesus' death. Yet, Scripture says, "the Pharisees and experts in the law rejected God's purpose for themselves" (Luke 7:30, NIV).

It was not God's purpose for each individual Pharisee to be hard-hearted and demand Jesus' Crucifixion (and not all Pharisees did).

In other words, they were not forced by God to choose evil and go against God's will. Yet, God's perfect plan (God's sovereign will) still happened through their free-willed choices. Could one or more of the Pharisees have chosen differently without foiling God's plan to save humanity through Jesus' sacrifice? I believe so. Could another besides Judas have betrayed Jesus to fulfill prophecy? I think so. God's *providence*—his outworking of his plan through history—is so grand and so magnificent, it can adjust to endless iterations of human decisions, perfectly.

Diana Shepherd received insight into this after she had a massive panic attack in the gym at USC; doctors later said her heart had stopped. She instantly found herself in another world.

But this was real, more real than anything here by an exponential amount. I walked up a gradual incline of a hill on a dirt path, but the dirt of the path was golden with flowing, short green grass all around. The colors were unlike anything you've ever seen. Here we have 4K [resolution]; there it was 10K. There were millions of colors that don't even exist here. Up on the hill, a man waited for me. He was around six feet, [with] brownish, wild, shoulder length hair and beard, healthy appearance, olive Mediterranean skin, dressed in a white robe. He looked a lot like my dad, as he's also Middle Eastern.

He placed his hand on my shoulder, gently coaxing my eyes to his. When my eyes met his, It. Was. Incredible. Like the Mediterranean Sea—greens, blues, like swimming in his eyes, and the entire rest of Heaven faded. Like when you stare into the eyes of the one you love, nothing else matters, all else fades.[15]

Jesus sent Diana back, but later, in a time of prayer, she felt Jesus give her an analogy about God's sovereignty and our choices:

When we choose Jesus, we also have choices to make within his plan. He works with us; however, he guides it overall. Like a mobile navigation app. The navigation app would be like the Holy Spirit you've decided to download. Jesus decides on locations but gives you routing options. The routing options all end in the same place, but there are different things you'll see along the way—different obstacles, different paths, all leading to the destination. You make the choice of which route.

Think of all the choices we make throughout the day. Jesus knows of alternate routes and plans for them all, depending on your choice. Now multiply that by billions of people. That is a snapshot of just how incredible and smart, brilliant, really, our God is![16]

I hope this analogy gives all of us some reassurance when it comes to our mistakes. Just as GPS can reroute you to your destination when you make a wrong turn on a road trip, God's Holy Spirit has an infinite number of ways to reroute you when you get lost or hit a dead end in life. In both cases, as long as you don't throw out the "GPS" but keep following where it leads, you'll get there.

We can all make wrong turns on our path in life, just as Dr. Mark McDonough did when he chose to drown his pain in alcohol. That was not God's will for Mark's life (see Ephesians 5:17-18). However, Mark was willing to change course when he got into recovery and admitted his need for God's help and guidance. God used the disciplines Mark developed in recovery to reroute him to medical school. This allowed Mark to be a conduit of God's healing for burn victims and show compassion borne of his experience.

It's never too late to reroute in life. If you make a detour or hit a dead end because you chose to go against God's will, admit it. Then return to God for his guidance and allow him to put you back on course to accomplish your purpose. You may miss some of the beautiful sights God originally had planned. You may have to power through some rocky terrain on the new path, but God's plan for your life will still be accomplished, and it will be for a good and hope-filled future. And don't forget, God's plans center around relationship.

GOD'S PLANS ARE RELATIONAL

Dr. Colin Perry, a college professor in Melbourne, Australia, experienced how important it is to stay relationally connected to Jesus, because God's plans for us are relational at the core. While gardening one day, Colin felt his heart failing. He called an ambulance, but on the ride to the hospital, Colin died. At first, he found himself in a dark void, starting to drift downward. He became afraid, and he cried out for Jesus to help him.

> I felt this vicelike grip on my forearm just grab me and start to pull me upwards. And he said to me, "You don't want to go that way." And he started to pull me up, and we were traveling at enormous speed over an enormous distance, and we came to settle in a place that had a dim glow, and as I adjusted to it, I realized I was surrounded by half a dozen angels, as well as the One who had pulled me up. . . . I asked, "Who are you?" He said, "I'm the one you call Lord."
>
> And then it really hit me where I was, and it was such a beautiful experience. No experience even comes near it. . . . I did get a very good look at the face of Jesus. A fairly slight face, he had a beard. He had longish hair, and he was wearing a robe. He just looked like an average Middle Eastern male. There was nothing particularly remarkable about his features; that's not what is remarkable. . . . What's remarkable is his heart and who he is. It's how they're communicating and what you're feeling, and the soul-to-soul connection is what really struck me. This warmth that was massively powerful— like the power of love was just exploding within my chest. He said to me at that point, "You're not in heaven, you're not in paradise, we've come out to meet you. I'm going to give you the choice of whether you come on with us to paradise or whether I send you back to your life. The choice is yours."[17]

Colin thought about his life. He had grown up a Christian but had turned away from God while touring with a rock band, smoking pot, and occasionally doing hard drugs. Eventually, he left that lifestyle behind, got married, settled down, and even got his PhD. But he also experienced a great deal of hardship. His first wife left him, and then three years later, his seven-year-old daughter was struck by a car and left brain-damaged, unable to walk or talk.

> I was there considering my life and my daughter in her wheelchair. I also had two [more] beautiful girls, and a young boy, and an older son. And my youngest son was eight at the time, and I thought, "Gee, I don't feel good about leaving my children behind," and I didn't feel my life's journey was complete.
>
> Jesus said, "Okay, we will do that." And Jesus looked at one of the angels and said, "Go check the vessel," by which, he [meant] my body. And one of the angels took off and drifted down, and I could see, in the far distance, the ambulance driver working on me, and I could see this angel float down there.
>
> And I looked back to Jesus because I couldn't take my eyes or attention off him. I wanted to know more, and he said to me, "I need to do some work, some healing, on you. You've been through a lot of trauma." He then started to . . . I don't know how to explain this . . . it was like Jesus' whole being just came into me and began to shift things around, break down barriers, rearrange things within me. And I could feel, literally feel, things within my soul restoring and healing. It was a beautiful and amazing sensation.
>
> As he did that, I got a real direct line into his awareness. I didn't truly understand who Jesus was until this moment. Jesus was not limited by time. He was aware of all the things in the universe that were happening. I understood that he was seeing through time, through space; he was seeing through all those dimensions infinitely. I could have been aware of a bug on a rock. I could have been aware of the dust on the moon. He had an awareness of the whole universe going on—as if he was just connected to all things, and I just felt for a few seconds probably,

the immensity of who he is and what sort of power he has. And what sort of love underlies all that power. It was overwhelming, it was magnificent, so beautiful—nothing has compared since, and I won't really be happy until I'm back in his presence. And that is something I will never forget, [something] that explained to me all those words like *omniscient* and *omnipotent* and *sovereign*—all those big words we use to describe God, but to actually feel some small aspect of it was an amazing thing.

The angel returned and said, "The vessel is good," that my body is okay. And at that point, Jesus started to describe a couple of things that I was likely to encounter when I came back. And the fact that I had to be careful, that I had to make choices that would keep in line with him, because there was potential, there was risk for me, to turn away.

Interestingly, he took me aside and let me look through the veil; it was as if I was watching a video of the future. It was quite incredible, and he was discussing with the angels things that were going to happen in the future, people who I was going to meet, and different aspects of my life that were coming up. And it was as if he was informing them of how things were going to pan out, and how they would play in my life, which was just amazing. And there were moments when Jesus said, "No, don't let him see that," and there were moments when he said, "Come and see this." And it was all about different people that I was going to meet, some I had not yet met, but later did.[18]

When we think of God's plan or purpose for our lives, we usually think first about careers or accomplishments that would seem noble or important. I'm convinced that although that matters, it's not central to God's plan for your life. As Colin discovered, much of God's plan appeared be about the *people* he would meet *along his path*.

NDEs confirm what the Scripture teaches: God's plan seems to first center around who you become in relationship to God and how you impact those around you. Secondarily, God's plan is about what you do to serve humanity through your gifts, time, and resources. In her

NDE, Erica McKenzie heard God say he was giving her new gifts and old gifts, and as she maintained her connection to God, he would lead her to fulfill her relational mission.

> God made it clear He had a plan for everyone and that we are not to judge someone else's journey. . . . We are here to help each other. Our experiences, even the most tragic and painful, are opportunities to remain in the state of love, grow our compassion and kindness, and maintain our connection to God. I felt God smile and then He said, "You're not staying, child. I'm sending you back because your mission has just begun. You work for Me now, remember? And Erica, when you go back, you must be quiet and listen to the people I put into your life. Then when you do, you will take [My gifts of] patience, beauty, and now knowledge and wisdom, and when you speak you will change millions of lives."[19]

God has a plan for your life. It's a plan that's as unique as you are. Follow the leading of the Holy Spirit day by day, and you won't miss it—and one day, he will show you the ripple effect that your faithfulness had on millions of lives. Remember that no matter the circumstance, situation, or challenge, God's plan for you is good—a plan for hope, a prosperous future, and definitely for joy. Joy no matter what!

14

THE JOY AND LAUGHTER
OF GOD

REBECCA SPRINGER LIVED IN THE LATE 1800S, long before NDEs were globally recognized. She had traveled hundreds of miles from home when she became ill, possibly with pneumonia. Alone with only an attendant watching over her, she asked Jesus to be with her if she was indeed passing from this life. In 1898, after miraculously reviving, Rebecca wrote about leaving her body behind as her deceased brother-in-law, Frank, came to escort her to heaven.

> I turned my head and looked back into the room. . . . The attendant sat by the stove at the farther end, comfortably reading a newspaper; and on the bed, turned toward the window, lay a white, still form, with the shadow of a smile on the poor, worn face [her face]. My brother drew me gently, and I yielded, passing with him through the window, out on the veranda, and from thence, in some unaccountable way, down to the street . . . .

"You are so weak I think I had better carry you"; and without waiting for a reply, he stooped and lifted me in his arms . . . . The next I knew, I was sitting in a sheltered nook, made by flowering shrubs, upon the softest and most beautiful turf of grass, thickly studded with fragrant flowers, many of them the flowers I had known and loved on earth.[1]

Rebecca's experience more than a century ago confirms many of the common experiences of heaven I've heard NDErs relay today.[2] What marks Rebecca's NDE are the varied joys of heaven she experienced, which remind us that God is the God of all joy. Though Rebecca's nineteenth-century language feels different, consider the similarities of joy she experienced in God's presence:

Away, away—far beyond the limit of my vision, I well knew—stretched this wonderful sward of perfect grass . . . not a single blade was any color but the brightest green. The air was soft and balmy, though invigorating; and instead of sunlight there was a golden and rosy glory everywhere. . . . And out of [the grass] grew equally wonderful trees, whose drooping branches were laden with exquisite blossoms and fruits of many kinds. I found myself thinking of . . . "the tree of life" that grew in the midst of the garden. . . .

Beneath the trees, in many happy groups, were little children, laughing and playing, running hither and thither in their joy, and catching in their tiny hands the bright-winged birds that flitted in and out among them, as though sharing in their sports, as they doubtless were. All through the grounds, older people were walking, sometimes in groups, sometimes by twos, sometimes alone, but all with an air of peacefulness and happiness. . . .

Look where I would, I saw, half hidden by the trees, elegant and beautiful houses of strangely attractive architecture, that I felt must be the homes of the happy inhabitants of this enchanted place. I caught glimpses of sparkling fountains in many directions, and close to my retreat flowed a river.[3]

Rebecca became overwhelmed with awe and wonder and felt unworthy to be in such a pure, holy place, so Frank led her into the nearby river where she soon discovered new surprises. She could breathe and communicate under the water, and she was not wet when she came out of this mystical water.

"Frank, what has that water done for me?" I said. "I feel as though I could fly."

He looked at me with earnest, tender eyes, as he answered gently, "It has washed away the last of the earth-life, and fitted you for the new life upon which you have entered."

"It is divine!" I whispered.

"Yes, it is divine," he said. . . .

The verandas and steps of the homes we passed were full of their happy inmates; glad voices could be constantly heard, and merry shouts of laughter . . . .

"Frank, where are we going?" at length I asked.

"Home, little sister," he answered tenderly.

"Home? Have we a home . . . ?"

"Come and see," was his only answer, as he turned into a side path leading toward an exquisitely beautiful house.[4]

After Frank showed Rebecca this gorgeous house crafted just for her, decorated with the familiar tastes she loved combined with enchanting new wonders too, another joyful surprise awaited.

Advancing up the long room to meet me, I saw my dear father and mother, and with them my youngest sister. With a cry of joy, I flew into my father's outstretched arms, and heard, with a thrill of joy, his dear, familiar "My precious little daughter!"

"At last! At last!" I cried, clinging to him. "At last I have you again!"

"At last!" he echoed, with a deep-drawn breath of joy. Then he resigned me to my dear mother, and we were soon clasped in each other's embrace. . . . Oh, what an hour was that! I did not dream that even heaven could hold such joy.[5]

Rebecca explained, "There was no measurement of time as we measure it here, although many still spoke in the old-time language of 'months' and 'days' and 'years.' I have no way of describing it as it seemed to me then. There were periods . . . for happy duties, hours for joyful pleasures, and hours for holy praise. I only know it was all harmony, all joy."[6] So it was on another "day" when Mae, Rebecca's niece who died before her, came to show her more of heaven's wonders.

Before us spread a lake as smooth as glass, but flooded with a golden glory caught from the heavens, that made it like a sea of molten gold. The blossom- and fruit-bearing trees grew down to its very border in many places, and far, far away, across its shining waters, arose the domes and spires of what seemed to be a mighty city. Many people were resting upon its flowery banks, and on the surface of the water were boats of wonderful structure, filled with happy souls, and propelled by an unseen power. Little children, as well as grown persons, were floating upon or swimming in the water. . . .

[Mae] led me into the water, down, down into its crystal depths, and when it seemed to me we must be hundreds of feet beneath the surface, she threw herself prostrate and bade me do the same. I did so, and immediately we began to slowly rise. Presently I found that we no longer rose, but were slowly floating in mid-current, many feet still beneath the surface. Then appeared to me a marvel. Look where I would, perfect prismatic rays surrounded me. I seemed to be resting in the heart of a prism; and such vivid yet delicate coloring, mortal eyes never rested upon. Instead of the seven colors, as we see them here, the colors blended in such rare graduation of shades as to make the rays seem almost infinite. . . . As I lay watching this marvelous panorama, for the colors deepened and faded like the lights of the aurora borealis, I was attracted by the sound of distant music.[7]

Rebecca recognized the song. Several times, she had been delightfully surprised to hear songs she knew and loved on earth. As she swam in the water, enjoying both new and old surprises, she reflected on what Frank told her about heaven:

> One of the delights of this rare life is that no occasion is ever overlooked for reproducing here the pure enjoyments of our mortal life. It is the Father's pleasure to make us realize that this existence is but a continuance of the former life, only without its imperfections and its cares.[8]

Just before they came out of the water, dry, Rebecca noticed a "strange sense of invigoration and strength . . . dissimilar to that experienced during a bath in the river." Mae explained, "One takes away the last of the earth-life, and prepares us for the life upon which we enter; the other fills us to overflowing with a draught from the Celestial Life itself"[9] (see Revelation 7:17; 22:1-2). They stood watching as children "climbed the trees that overhung the water, with the agility of squirrels, and dropped with happy shouts of laughter into the lake." It hit Rebecca what misconceptions we have of God's life. It is the life we enjoy, and abundantly more!

> Not far from our home we saw a group of children playing upon the grass, and in their midst was a beautiful great dog, over which they were rolling and tumbling with the greatest freedom. As we approached he broke away from them and came bounding to meet us. . . .
> "Do you not know him, auntie?" Mae asked brightly. "It is dear old Sport!" I cried, stooping and placing my arms about his neck. . . . "Dear old fellow! How happy I am to have you here!". . . "He understands every word we say," said Mae. "Of

course he does; he only lacks speech to make him perfect. I somehow hoped he might find it here." "He would not be half so interesting if he could talk," said Mae.[10]

After returning, Rebecca went to visit a friend. While she was there, a guest arrived.

He was tall and commanding in form, with a face of ineffable sweetness and beauty. Where had I seen him before? . . . I thought . . . "it is St. John, the beloved disciple." He had been pointed out to me one morning by the river-side.

"Peace be unto this house," was his salutation as he entered. . . . "Sit thou awhile beside me," he continued. . . . "You have but lately come?" he said.

"Yes, I am here but a short time. So short that I know not how to reckon time as you count it here," I answered.

"Ah, that matters little," he said with a gentle smile. "Many cling always to the old reckoning and the earth-language. It is a link between the two lives; we would not have it otherwise. How does the change impress you? How do you find life here?"

"Ah," I said, "if they could only know! I never fully understood till now the meaning of that sublime passage, 'Eye hath not seen, nor ear heard, neither have entered into the heart of man, the things which God hath prepared for them that love him' [1 Corinthians 2:9, KJV]. It is indeed past human conception." I spoke with deep feeling.

"'For them that love him'? Do you believe that all Christians truly love him?" he asked. "Do you think they love the Father for the gift of the Son and the Son because of the Father's love and mercy? Or is their worship ofttimes that of duty rather than love?" He spoke reflectively and gently.

"Oh," I said . . . "how can you doubt the love he must inspire in all hearts who seek to know him?" A radiant glow overspread the wonderful face, which he lifted, looking directly at me—the mist rolled away from before my eyes, and I knew him! With a low cry of joy and adoration, I threw myself at his feet, bathing them with happy tears. He gently stroked my bowed head for a moment, then rising, lifted me to his side. "My Savior—my King!" I whispered, clinging closely to him.

"Yes, and Elder Brother and Friend," he added, wiping away tenderly the tears stealing from beneath my closed eyelids.[11]

Rebecca later reflected that compared to earth's joys, "there is a depth, a mystery to all that pertains to the divine life, which I dare not try to describe. . . . Suffice it to say, that no joy we know on earth, however rare, however sacred, can be more than the faintest shadow of the joy we there find."[12]

JOY IS YOUR BIRTHRIGHT

There is one attribute of God often overlooked by theologians, miscalculated by most people, yet clearly revealed in Scripture—God's eternal joy! Failing to imagine God as the source of all our joy and laughter, fun and games, pleasures and enjoyments of life has led many people to turn away from God. But we should be running toward God if we desire to enjoy life fully! As one of my favorite authors C. S. Lewis declared, "Joy is the serious business of Heaven."[13] NDErs agree!

When Jesus asked Dr. Colin Perry if he wanted to continue on to heaven or go back, Colin felt fear and anxiety creep in. The angels' reactions shocked him:

The response was really quite amazing. The angels all came towards me and started to calm me. And they said, "We're not used to that emotion [fear/anxiety] here, [it] is not in place here, it's out of place here, so please, be calm, be still, and don't be afraid. And they were talking me out of my fear into a state of peace and joy, which for them is the norm. I could hear their thoughts directly in my thoughts, so it was a very direct link. I could feel the fear subside. I could feel that beautiful sense of peace and joy welling up inside me, and I knew that Jesus and the angels were the source of that celebratory feeling—that I'm so happy to be here. That was the norm for them.[14]

If you follow Jesus, joy is your birthright. You are a child of the king of all joy! Joy is where you are headed, joy is what you'll inherit, joy is the norm, and God's joy is available to you, even now. In fact, you can experience the eternal now of God's joy regardless of trials, through tribulations, no matter what circumstances surround you. As a child of God, joy is available because God is with you, and God *is* joy.

During his last night on earth, Jesus promised joy to his disciples. After explaining the simplicity of staying connected to him like branches to a vine, he said, "I have told you these things so that you will be filled with my joy. Yes, your joy will overflow!" (John 15:11). God wants us to have his overflowing joy—*now*. And yet, while we remain on earth, joy is also a choice.

Happiness comes from happenings—when circumstances go our way—but joy comes from God as we seek his ways. Do you realize that you can choose to seek God's joy, even when circumstances around you are anything but happy? The prophet Habakkuk wrote, "Even though the fig trees have no blossoms, and there are no grapes on the vines; even though the olive crop fails, and the fields lie empty and barren . . . yet I *will rejoice* in the LORD! I *will be joyful* in the God of my salvation!" (Habakkuk 3:17-18, emphasis added). His external life was falling apart, yet Habakkuk made a choice to seek a joy that comes from God—and so can we. God gives a joy that comes from within, a genuine happiness that no circumstance can take away. But maybe you've never imagined God as very joyful, so you don't really look to God for your joy. NDEs reveal an encouraging truth.

Derry from Finland recalls sitting with Jesus in a heavenly garden as Jesus looked deep into her eyes. "The joy radiating from his eyes filled my heart with joy, and the memory of it makes my mind happy now even as I write this."[15] When Randy Kay walked with Jesus in his NDE, he experienced the joy of Jesus:

I viewed a promenade with columns taller than I could see. From column to column hung lavish garments made of white fabric finer than silk. The same peace permeated the space all around me; however, here I sensed tremendous joy. Figures frolicked through petals of soft linen that cushioned their feet as they walked. Angelic beings harmonized with worshipful music more grandiose, more awe-inspiring than anything in the world. The enchanting sounds exceeded twenty symphonies. . . . Joy exuded from every sight and sound causing my heart to leap with excitement . . . . "You see my joy?" Jesus asked. I guessed that the more you serve others unselfishly in the world, the greater your joy in heaven.[16]

The dancing, celebrating, music, and singing of angels and people are *his joy*. As Jesus said to Randy, "You see *my* joy?" God is the most joyful being in all of creation. Yet joy is a characteristic of God that we don't often imagine. How could we miss it? All our enjoyments and pleasures are in fact *his creations*. And God wants us to include him in the enjoyments of life he has provided. One of the greatest lies of evil is the upside-down idea that laughter and fun, pleasure and thrills, and all the really fun parties are found apart from God. We need to infuse our imaginations with truth—no one enjoys life with his children more than God.

Does God also grieve, suffer with those who suffer, and get angry at our injustices? Yes! But all of those are temporary reactions to an evil world. Joy is God's eternal default state! God tells us, "Be glad and rejoice forever in what I will create, for I will create Jerusalem [heaven's New Jerusalem] to be a delight and its people a joy. I will rejoice over Jerusalem and take delight in my people; the sound of weeping and of crying will be heard in it no more" (Isaiah 65:18-19, NIV).

THE LAUGHTER OF GOD

Not only does God experience joy, but it may also surprise you to realize that God laughs. In fact, Jim Woodford discovered in his NDE that joy and laughter are related. "The tall warrior angel described joy as living on the edge of a huge laugh motivated by a constant awareness of the presence of God. . . . I experience that feeling even today as I recall my experience in Heaven," Jim says.[17]

When Jesus gave Heidi Barr her life review, they shared a humorous moment together, as often seems to happen in life reviews. Remember, Heidi was just sixteen at the time.

> I saw my life all at once. . . . I saw him there, teaching me. He sat beside me, chatted with me, when I was an infant in my playpen. In fact, at one point he "paused the tape" at a silly scene. Every event was still playing all around me, but he and I focused on this event.
>
> There I was, an infant of four or five months. I could already sit up. I was in my playpen, shaking a plastic rattle. There was a knock at the door and my mother went to open it. I watched, both through my baby eyes and my sixteen-year-old eyes, as a couple entered. The woman carried a baby in her arms. He was my age. The mother set him down right in the playpen, right where Jesus was sitting. The first thing that baby did was grab the rattle from my hand and use it to whack me over the bridge of my nose. I opened my mouth and screamed until my mother came and lifted me out of the playpen.
>
> Rewatching this, Jesus and I began to whoop with laughter. I could see that he'd chuckled even when it had originally happened. The baby me wasn't hurt, just indignant. No, Jesus doesn't want anyone to be hurt, but honestly, this was just plain funny. My baby face was beet red with anger and indignation. Jesus and I floated side by side in the air, watching this replay and laughing our heads off.[18]

Gregg Rickert told me that during his life review, "There were moments where Jesus laughed at the funny things that I did or that happened. Not making fun of me, but just laughing with me about a funny situation."[19] Another NDEr, Leonard, declared, "God has a fantastic sense of humor; I never laughed so much in all my life!"[20]

God *laughs*? There's laughter in heaven? Jokes or funny things we say are also funny to God? Many NDErs report so. Does this seem hard to believe? If so, who do we think created us with the ability to laugh or see humor in things? Dr. Ron Smothermon described humor as a characteristic of God that exploded into his understanding: "Humor was a quality transmitted instantly with the light, plus all these other qualities—kindness, compassion, love, joy—but also humor like you would feel after laughing doubled over from a joke. But there's no joke—there's just this characteristic of delightful humor!"[21]

We are made in the image of God. Of course God laughs! We are the lesser; he is the greater. Psychologists tell us humor is a complex form of communication that bonds people and improves health—something the Bible acknowledged three thousand years ago: "A cheerful heart is good medicine, but a broken spirit saps a person's strength" (Proverbs 17:22).

It's worth noting that often when the Bible refers to God's laughter, God is laughing at the absurdity of humans. God laughs when people think they can thumb their noses at him or pretend he isn't there in order to get away with evil. Psalm 2 describes God's response to future rulers (Caiaphas, Pilate, Herod) who would one day plot against God's Messiah: "But the one who rules in heaven laughs. The Lord scoffs at them" (Psalm 2:4). God's plans for Jesus could not be thwarted. The psalmist continues, speaking prophetically of the coming Messiah: "The LORD said to me, 'You are my son. Today I have become your Father. Only ask, and I will give you the nations as your inheritance'" (Psalm 2:7-8). When God laughs at the absurdity of human behavior, it is a cue to those who love God that evil *will* be conquered: "But what joy for all who take refuge in him!" (Psalm 2:12).

Jesus reminds us that laughter is God's blessing: "God blesses you who weep now, for in due time you will laugh" (Luke 6:21). We so underestimate how relatable and "normal" God is in the sense of understanding and enjoying the nuances of life, including laughter. Why wouldn't he laugh and enjoy life? He invented it all.

GOD HAS FUN?

After Heidi's life review with Jesus, she experienced the thrill of her life. Heidi told me she loved adventure and the speed of horseback riding. She recalls,

[Jesus] looked into my eyes, and his love for me was palpable. He knew everything about me, and he loved me anyway. And I loved him. And we were best friends. And he was my brother. And he was my dad. He was all those things, all at once. And it's so hard to explain, but his eyes are filled with humor, and laughter, and gaiety, and joy. And I couldn't look away from his eyes.

Jesus took my right hand, and we held hands like Superman and Lois Lane. And he gets this big, mischievous smile on his face. And we took off. It wasn't quite flying, although I did stretch out my left arm like a bird's wing. Jesus took me surfing, on a wave of light! We surfed. It was like body surfing on this wave of light. It was the most fun experience in the history of the world! I looked down, and I could see a wave of light rolling beneath our bare feet, pushing us forward, faster and faster. The light was made of all colors. I laughed as I felt it tickling the bottoms of my feet. I could look down and see both of our bare feet with this wave of light under them. Jesus was grinning from ear to ear. As I stretched out my arm, I could feel the light flow through my fingers like water. This was great. Jesus was great. He and I were laughing out loud as we surfed.

His smile was so wide and there was such a mischievous sparkle in his eyes. His sense of fun was contagious! He loved having the ability to gift this experience to me, to share this experience with me. I was awed by his power and his laughter and his joy as we journeyed together. He said into my mind, "This is so cool, don't you think this is so cool?" It was the greatest thing I have ever done.

This wave of light was pushing us faster and faster, but I could see individual things as we surfed. At first, trees, buildings, mountains, things on earth passing by. But then we left earth, and I could see stars and galaxies passing behind Jesus, but I was still just looking at him—enthralled with him. Jesus was all that mattered to me. I've never felt so much joy and happiness and love.[22]

Jesus eventually took Heidi back to earth. Heidi always believed in Jesus, even as a Jewish woman. Several years after her NDE, during college, she took an astronomy course from the famous Dr. James Van Allen, discoverer of the Van Allen radiation belts. One night, the class visited an observatory. They peered through the massive telescope at the moon, then Jupiter, and Saturn, and eventually the professor aimed the giant telescope at the next spiral galaxy, the Andromeda Galaxy. Heidi stepped up to take her turn:

> When it was my turn to look, I did, and I was stunned. I was so stunned I nearly fainted. The professor ran to grab a chair. He shoved me back into it and pushed my head between my knees. The room was spinning and for a few moments, I didn't know where I was. Jesus and I had passed that galaxy on our journey, and I remembered the awe I'd felt at the time, thinking out loud, "This is what God sees when he wakes up in the morning." Jesus had smiled at me. He'd been so pleased I'd recognized God's immensity![23]

When Heidi first told me about surfing with Jesus, I had a doubtful reaction. I thought, *That can't be. It doesn't even seem right—God doesn't "play."* And then I started to reason, *Why not?* The Scriptures are filled with admonitions toward joy, promises of good things, and gladness forever. King David declared to God, "You will fill me with joy in your presence, with *eternal pleasures* at your right hand" (Psalm 16:11, NIV, emphasis added). Jesus said to his disciples, "Let the children come to me. Don't stop them! For the Kingdom of God belongs to those who are like these children" (Luke 18:16). Maybe author G. K. Chesterton was right when he reflected: "It may be that [God] has the eternal appetite of infancy; for we have sinned and grown old, and our Father is younger than we."[24]

BASEBALL IN HEAVEN

Luke Siegel was a healthy, active, athletic nine-year-old boy who loved to play baseball. He and his dad, Tim, would play catch for hours. Tim told me that baseball was Luke's first love, second only to sitting down to watch the New Orleans Saints play football. All that changed that year, when Luke was on a golf cart and it tipped over, causing head and chest trauma. For seven years, Luke fought hard through rehab to regain mobility and speech, but in August 2021, Luke contracted COVID-19. His body could not overcome it. Tim approached me after church one Sunday, telling me how my book *Imagine Heaven* had helped his grief, and he shared his story of hope.

Ty Marshall was a twenty-one-year-old with Down syndrome doing rehab at the same facility as Luke. Though Ty and Luke never met, their parents met and had a few conversations three months before Luke got COVID-19. One month after Luke's death, Ty had a nine-hour surgery on his brain. After the surgery, when his mom, Darcy, came to see him, Ty said, "Mom, I've been crying for you." Then the words kept coming, which was uncharacteristic of Ty. "Mom, I saw Hannah singing and dancing." Hannah Grace was Ty's friend who had died six years prior in 2015. "And I saw Luke Siegel with a baseball in his hand." Darcy was shocked as Ty continued, "The three of us walked away to throw the baseball."

Tim explained to me that Sunday, "Ty Marshall had never met Luke. Never talked to him. Ty never knew that Luke had a love for baseball!" Tim takes great consolation in knowing there's nothing lost on earth that God won't restore in heaven. As Jesus said, blessed are the children for the Kingdom of God belongs to such as these (see Matthew 19:14). So it makes perfect sense that father and son will play baseball again because God created us to play like children forever!

What if God wants far more for us than we imagine? Maybe God wants us to be more carefree, trusting, playful, unburdened—like his little children living on earth inside a bigger Kingdom perspective. Yes, we must work, be responsible, deal with life's challenges. But in the end, joy, laughter, and playfulness will endure eternally. What if God wants to teach us to live with more of heaven's joy coming to earth through us, right now? With the psalmist we can call out to God, "Satisfy us each morning with your unfailing love, so we may sing for joy to the end of our lives" (Psalm 90:14). Will you ask him for that?

THE DESIRES OF YOUR HEART

All that we love here on earth and all we can imagine enjoying in heaven come from God. This life and the next are continuous! In heaven, Rebecca Springer, who lived during the 1800s, experienced playing with her dog, music, and the games of children, but also flying, diving hundreds of feet deep in a lake with no air tanks, and even "self-propelled" boats, which were not common in her day.

In heaven, we will experience old pleasures and joys, and new ones too—exploring the deepest wonders of God's universe—thrills and adventures like we've only imagined in our wildest sci-fi novels, fairy-tales, or fantasies. Maybe all those imaginative desires are actually signs pointing us homeward?

The promise of Scripture is that God wants to give us what we long for most: "Take delight in the LORD, and he will give you the desires of your heart. Commit your way to the LORD; trust in him and he will do this: He will make your righteous reward shine like the dawn" (Psalm 37:4-6, NIV). Many NDErs testify that those in heaven literally "shine like the dawn" with God's light and love and that God does fulfill their deepest desires. In fact, you may recall from chapter 10 that God told Dr. Richard Eby, "I only give them the desires of their heart."[25]

Jim Woodford, the airline pilot, said, "I was looking down on this golden city, and instantaneously I knew I was looking down on God's celestial home . . . and I wondered if this was for me because I was a pilot." God knew Jim would love to experience heaven just as he loved to experience earth—from a pilot's perspective. Jim saw the layout of the city—massive concentric circles of golden boulevards separated by greenbelts. "Interspersed here and there [were] cascades of sparkling crystal waterfalls with softly meandering waterways," Jim said.[26]

Isn't it fascinating that two commercial airline pilots, Jim Woodford and Dale Black, were both given a pilot's "airborne view" of the city of God! It shows us how the Father delights in delighting us. God knows all our deepest desires, and he enjoys meeting them—in heaven, but also on the earth. As Jim walked with the angels, he smelled tapioca pudding, a smell that reminded him of his favorite place as a child—his grandmother's cozy home. Then to his surprise, he came upon one of his greatest earthly loves:

> We walked along the path, and I saw birds and deer, trees
> of incredible size and beauty, all of it having this light of
> God coming out of it. We came to this split-rail fence, just
> like you'd see here on earth. The angel took my elbow and
> motioned, saying, "James, look." And across the grass trotted
> three of the most beautiful horses I've ever seen, and the grass
> was lighting up under their feet as they trotted toward me.
> And just as the smell of tapioca had come to me, making me
> instantly feel at home, now I see my earthly love—horses. I
> love Arabian horses. There was a magnificent Arabian that
> also seemed to have a greater size than an Arabian, and it was
> white. I had never studied the Bible, and I didn't know Jesus
> is coming back riding a white horse. I put my hand through
> the gate to stroke its mane, and in its eyes it was like it was
> thanking me for the kindness I had shown toward horses on
> earth. The fence and the horses were for me to find familiarity
> with the things I loved on earth.[27]

Karina Martinez from Colombia also experienced Jesus giving her the desire of her heart, and more. At first, she felt unworthy to enter heaven. Jesus told her she *was* worthy (she had just prayed to him for forgiveness, by which *he* makes us worthy). He said, "Look!"

> I saw my Max, my beautiful dog Max, that I had lost the day
> before getting my pacemaker. And I saw my other dog, Tasha,
> who had died. And I opened my eyes fully and was so full of
> joy, I just went right in. I was so happy. I ran after my dog,
> and then I started just flying. When I was there, I was flying,
> flying, and flying. And I saw this tree, this beautiful, beautiful
> tree with purple flowers, with this radiant white light going
> through the roots. It was by a river. I flew above this beautiful
> garden, and I could see golden streets, but light coming out of

them, so they looked like shiny glass almost. And there was a city with structures—gorgeous. I was home. I knew this was my true home, and it filled my heart with joy.[28]

The apostle Paul told the Greeks in Lystra, God is the one who "fills your hearts with joy" (Acts 14:17, NIV). James said, "Every good and perfect gift is from above, coming down from the Father of the heavenly lights" (James 1:17, NIV). Think about all the joys, thrills, and pleasures of life—everything we would call good or fun, delightful, or enjoyable. Who do we think made the enjoyments of life that way? God thought up every pleasurable, fun, thrilling experience and created us with the ability to enjoy it all.

Can we abuse God's good gifts? Absolutely. We can choose to use them in ways or for reasons that go against what God intended. But we can also learn to enjoy them fully in relationship with God. And guess what—he enjoys you enjoying his good gifts.

I play soccer, and I love competition. I've learned I can let it get the best of me and say or do things I regret, or I can enjoy the rush of friendly competition (without taking myself too seriously), enjoy working with a team, and have an attitude of gratitude to God for this fun.

The same is true with whatever you enjoy. As long as it's not violating God's intended purpose, when you invite him in to enjoy life with you, thanking him, it increases your enjoyment. And I have no doubt he smiles and enjoys you enjoying his gift. Try it! Invite him into those things you love, thanking him, imagining his smile, enjoying God enjoying you. God told the prophet Zephaniah, "For the LORD your God is living among you. He is a mighty savior. He will take delight in you with gladness. . . . He will rejoice over you with joyful songs" (Zephaniah 3:17).

GOD'S ETERNAL PARTY

God is *the Life* of the party. Literally. Whenever people gather together to enjoy each other, what we are enjoying is the very life God created. In fact, God commanded Moses and all the people to hold celebrations—giant street parties—three times per year. "*Rejoice* before the LORD your

God at the place he will choose as a dwelling for his Name. . . . *Celebrate* the Festival of Tabernacles for seven days. . . . *Be joyful* at your festival. . . . *For seven days celebrate* the festival to the LORD your God . . . and your joy will be complete" (Deuteronomy 16:11, 13-15, NIV, emphasis added).

God enjoys it when we gather and celebrate and laugh and deepen relationships. God created parties of celebration for his people because he wants us to rejoice, celebrate, and be joyful together while also recognizing God in our midst. NDErs say that's what the Kingdom of God is like. Recall what Rebecca Springer said as she passed the homes of heaven, "Glad voices could be constantly heard, and merry shouts of laughter."[29] Dr. Mary Neal said, "My arrival was joyously celebrated and a feeling of absolute love was palpable as we hugged, danced, and greeted each other."[30] During her NDE, Linda went through a life review with God, and then, "All these people showed up—hundreds of them, as though they were having a party. . . . We were so happy to be there."[31]

Evil's great lie is that God frowns on our merriment. The truth is that God created us with the ability to enjoy life and be merry. Of course, we can abuse alcohol, or use drugs, or use each other sexually. We can elevate coarse joking and tearing others down when we gather—we can use our free will to destroy what God intended. Or we can learn to invite God into our gatherings, increasing our enjoyment and his enjoyment. God wants an invitation to your party. After all, you're invited to his party for eternity. The least you and I could do is return the favor!

The other night, my neighbor had a party and about fifty people on our street came. It looked like the United Nations gathering as I talked to my neighbors from India, Pakistan, Israel, Korea, China, and from across the United States. It was a wonderful time, great food, fun, and laughter. Nobody got drunk (as far as I could tell), and my wife and I had some awesome conversations, even sharing about writing this book and how God is better than any of us could ever begin to imagine.

Did everyone invite God to the party? No, but Kathy and I did. And you can too. I imagine God is pleased when our neighbors get to know each other, when they learn to care more about one another, and when someone tells them of God's immense love for them. My prayer since that party has been, *God, move the party to heaven! I want all my neighbors to come to your eternal party.* Will you invite God into your gatherings, thanking him, loving those he puts in your path, telling them how much God cares for them? Invite them to his party!

His last night on earth, Jesus told his closest friends that they would celebrate and feast together again, but "I will not drink wine again until the day I drink it new with you in my Father's Kingdom" (Matthew 26:29). Jesus described heaven as a celebratory feast:

> The Kingdom of Heaven can be illustrated by the story of a king who prepared a great wedding feast for his son. . . . "Come to the banquet!" [the servants of the king declared]. But the guests he had invited ignored them and went their own way. . . . And he said to his servants, . . . "Now go out to the street corners and invite everyone you see." So the servants brought in everyone they could find, good and bad alike, and the banquet hall was filled with guests.
> MATTHEW 22:2, 4-5, 8-10

God's Kingdom is an open party—everyone is invited. Regardless of what we've done, good or bad, he is the one who makes us worthy of his eternal party. But not all accept his invitation. Have you accepted his invitation to heaven's party? You are invited!

What God began four thousand years ago when he announced his plan to bless all nations, he will bring to fulfillment with a grand and joyful celebration of people from all nations who accept his invitation: "Look to Abraham, your father, and to Sarah, who gave you birth. When I called him he was only one man, and I blessed him and made him many. . . . [Now] everlasting joy will crown their heads. Gladness and joy will overtake them, and sorrow and sighing will flee away" (Isaiah 51:2, 11, NIV).

God is infinitely greater than you or I can imagine, in every way. His grand love story will never end but truly begins with all nations united with God in a joyful celebration like earth has never seen.

All nations will come to your light;
   mighty kings will come to see your radiance.

Look and see, for everyone is coming home!
   Your sons are coming from distant lands;
   your little daughters will be carried home.
Your eyes will shine,
   and your heart will thrill with joy. . . .

I will make you beautiful forever,
   a joy to all generations. . . .
You will know at last that I, the LORD,
   am your Savior and your Redeemer. . . .

No longer will you need the sun to shine by day,
   nor the moon to give its light by night,
for the LORD your God will be your everlasting light,
   and your God will be your glory.

ISAIAH 60:3-5, 15-16, 19

Trust in Jesus, do life with God's Spirit, enjoy the Father's good gifts. God's everlasting promise is that his joy and glory will be yours, now and forever.

A Prayer to Pray from the Heart

AS YOU FINISH THIS BOOK, I hope you've not only read about God; I hope you've connected with the lover of your soul. Here is a prayer to help you begin doing just that. Remember, God knows your heart, and that's what he cares about most.

God, thank you for the many ways you've demonstrated your love for me. I realize how you feel about me, and I see the good things you desire for me. I need your forgiveness, God. I want what Jesus did on the cross to count for me so that I know I'm forgiven. Thank you for restoring me into your family forever. I invite you to come do life with me—leading me, loving me, guiding me in your ways—so that I daily become more and more the person you created me to be, now and forever. Amen.

Acknowledgments

EVERY BOOK IS A TEAM EFFORT but *Imagine the God of Heaven* has been a labor of love for many. Many people poured their hearts and souls into this project, going far beyond what is normally required. There are so many people I need to thank.

First and foremost, I want to thank all the courageous people who have shared their NDE stories with me. Thank you for the hours you spent allowing me to interview you. You have inspired my walk with God in more ways than I can tell you, and I know others will be blessed by your stories as much as I have been blessed. This book is really God's story, told through the Scriptures and through you, to encourage all of us.

My wife, Kathy, who has helped me on all the books I've written, was intricately involved in every aspect of shaping this book, from concepting ideas to interviewing to editing drafts and securing permissions. It would not have happened without her. She's amazingly gifted. Thank you for your tireless endurance, Kathy.

Christine Anderson did a heroic job editing, fact-checking, and helping shape the flow of the book—thank you so much! I know this was a very complicated project, requiring way more than normal, and I know you did it with dedication and service to Christ.

I'm so grateful to the whole team at Tyndale House, Jon Farrar and Kim Miller especially, who shepherded this massive project forward. Thanks also to Elizabeth Czajkowski, who gave valuable editorial input.

And thank you to Don Gates, my agent, who has been a friend and partner in ministry, dedicated to every facet of this project. I'm also grateful to Dom Steinmann who created the hand graphics in chapter 8, to Kayla Covington for her research, to Mary Lou Covington for her generous help, and to all those who read early drafts and gave me feedback: Jack Kuhatschek, Mark Norton, Vince Antonucci, Ashley Burke Steinmann, Justin Burke, Lauren Main. Your input was invaluable. I'm grateful to all of you. And above all, I'm grateful to my Heavenly Father, who, for whatever reason, chose me to compile and report what is only a small glimpse of God's infinite wonders.

Appendix

What about Those Who Have Never Heard?

JESUS SAID, "I am the way, the truth, and the life. No one can come to the Father except through me" (John 14:6). But what does that mean for those who have never heard about Jesus? That is a commonly asked question. The real concern for most seems to be about God's fairness. C. S. Lewis comments on this in *Mere Christianity*:

> Is it not frightfully unfair that this new life should be confined to people who have heard of Christ and been able to believe in Him? But the truth is God has not told us what His arrangements about the other people are. We do know that no man can be saved except through Christ; we do not know that only those who know Him can be saved through Him.[1]

I'm confident God is not only fair, but he also cares about all people much more than we do. I'd like to expound on this same sentiment C. S. Lewis expressed and relate it to NDEs and God's work of salvation through Jesus.

To start, I believe NDEs are God's gift to us, providing even more evidence from around the world of God's reality, identity, and great love for all people. But why do people from all faiths and religious backgrounds so often see God or Jesus? Does this mean all will be saved and that all paths lead to heaven? No, I don't believe it does. And many

NDErs I've interviewed say the same. Just because NDErs briefly experience God or a taste of heaven does not mean they are right with God. I may be invited to visit Buckingham Palace, but that doesn't mean the king or queen of England has adopted me to move in permanently as part of the royal family. NDEs are visits, they are not permanent residency.

So experiencing an NDE does not mean heaven *or* hell is determined for that person. Remember, NDErs do not cross over the border or boundary that separates this life from eternal life. They say crossing that border would mean never returning to earth. Instead, the NDE happens *between* life on earth and eternal life. Thus, Scripture does not negate NDEs when stating, "Each person is destined to die once and after that comes judgment" (Hebrews 9:27).

Since NDErs have not crossed permanently into death, they can still make temporal decisions for or against God. We see that some NDErs who experience Jesus in heaven come back and seek to follow him, but some do not. Others may change their ways, but they don't really seek the God they encountered in their NDE. Having an NDE does not remove free will, nor do NDEs determine that people will make the best spiritual decisions once they are back.

Regarding people who have had NDEs, we should hope all will be saved. To not have that hope would be counter to God's will. God is "not wanting anyone to perish, but everyone to come to repentance" (2 Peter 3:9, NIV). And Scripture is clear that salvation comes only through Jesus: "Jesus is the one referred to in the [Old Testament] Scriptures. . . . There is salvation in no one else! God has given no other name under heaven by which we must be saved" (Acts 4:11-12). But does this mean that *only* those who have heard about Jesus will be given eternal life? I agree with C. S. Lewis—we won't know the answer for certain this side of eternity, but we can know some things for certain.

God is fair and just and does not favor some people over others. Around 1000 BCE, God declared, "The eyes of the LORD search the whole earth in order to strengthen those whose hearts are fully committed to him" (2 Chronicles 16:9). In the New Testament, the Lord saw the heart of a God-seeking Gentile named Cornelius and sent Peter to tell him about Jesus. When Cornelius responded in faith, Peter declared, "I now realize how true it is that God does not show favoritism but accepts from every nation the one who fears him and does what is right" (Acts 10:34-35, NIV).

We also know from Scripture that salvation has always been a free gift of God, received by faith. All it takes to be saved is a humble heart, turning to God in faith, and calling on his name. Around 500 BCE, the prophet Joel wrote, "Everyone who calls on the name of the LORD will be saved" (Joel 2:32). God forgave and restored relationships with people from Old Testament times who called on his name. Why? Because, as the apostle Paul wrote,

> [Jesus'] sacrifice shows that God was being fair when he held
> back and did not punish those who sinned in times past
> [before Jesus], for he was looking ahead and including them
> in what he would do in this present time [through Jesus].
> ROMANS 3:25-26

In the Old Testament, there are many examples of salvation given to non-Jewish people (and, therefore, non-Christian people). For example, Rahab, the Gentile prostitute, is mentioned as a person of faith in the New Testament (Hebrews 11), along with Abraham and Moses. The African queen of Sheba came seeking God in Jerusalem and was saved (1 Kings 10), and most notably the Ninevites—whom God calls "wicked"—were saved (Jonah 3). God sent Jonah to tell them to repent, and they responded with faith in Almighty God. Clearly, non-Jewish people were saved (made right with God) when God saw their faith and repentant hearts, and he credited to them what Jesus would do in the future. He applied their faith *forward* to the cross, just as today he applies our faith *back* to the cross. Jesus himself acknowledged this when he said to the Pharisees who would crucify him,

> The queen of Sheba will stand up against this generation on
> judgment day. . . . The people of Nineveh will also stand up
> against this generation on judgment day and condemn it, for

they repented of their sins at the preaching of Jonah. Now someone greater than Jonah is here—but you refuse to repent.

LUKE 11:31-32

So being religiously Jewish or Christian does not make someone right with God. God looks at the heart to see if the person repents and turns to God in faith. All the Old Testament heroes of faith (Abraham, Moses, Rahab, and others chronicled in Hebrews 11) were made right with God by faith only because of what Jesus would ultimately do on the cross. Yet, they never knew the name of Jesus. Paul points out that this same salvation is available for people of all nations:

> What did he [Abraham] discover about being made right
> with God? If his good deeds had made him acceptable to
> God, he would have had something to boast about. But
> that was not God's way. For the Scriptures tell us, "Abraham
> believed God, and God counted him as righteous because of
> his faith. . . . Now, is this blessing only for the Jews, or is it also
> for uncircumcised Gentiles [all nations]? . . . It is given as a free
> gift. And we are all certain to receive it, whether or not we live
> according to the law of Moses, if we have *faith like Abraham's*.
> For Abraham is the father of all who believe. That is what the
> Scriptures mean when God told him, "I have made you the
> father of many nations."
>
> ROMANS 4:1-3, 9, 16-17, EMPHASIS ADDED

So can people be saved *through* Jesus without knowing until eternity *the means* by which they are saved? Well, clearly that's how God saved many Ninevites, Rahab the Canaanite prostitute, and all the Old Testament Jewish and Gentile people who had "faith like Abraham's."

Does God do the same for people today who have never heard the name of Jesus? We aren't told for sure in Scripture either way. But think about it logically. Up until Jesus came, Jewish people and Gentile people around the world could seek God, and everyone who called on his name was saved (Joel 2:32). "Everyone" would mean that no one is geographically excluded from the ability to call out to God and be saved. That happened through what Jesus would do in the future.

So when Jesus came and paid for all humanity's sins (the means by which all can be saved), did access to salvation suddenly narrow? The day after the resurrection of Jesus, did salvation go from all who "have faith like Abraham's" to only those few thousand in Israel who knew the name of Jesus and believed? That seems to contradict the heart of God who does not favor one nation over another but searches "the whole earth in order to strengthen those whose hearts are fully committed to him" (2 Chronicles 16:9).

Having said all of that, people do need to hear about Jesus. Paul quoted the prophet Isaiah in relation to spreading the message of Jesus, "How beautiful are the feet of those who bring good news!" (Romans 10:15, NIV). Jesus commanded his followers to tell all nations (Matthew 28:18-20), and he declared, "The Good News about the Kingdom will be preached throughout the whole world, so that all nations will hear it" (Matthew 24:14). So clearly, God's desire is that all people will hear about Jesus. We must also know that if people hear the message, yet persistently reject it, Jesus himself says, "Anyone who rejects me is rejecting God, who sent me" (Luke 10:16).

Jesus reminds us of the necessity of sharing the gospel message so that all people hear of the forgiveness and freedom offered to them. God wants all people to know they are right with him and to be confident in their relationship with him. I've spent my adult life helping people understand this great love and forgiveness God offers through Jesus. Without hearing and trusting the message of Jesus, we remain locked up in condemnation and fear because all have sinned, and we know it. God wants all of us to know we can be forgiven, safe and secure with him, so we can live purposeful and abundant lives with him today and forever.

Notes

WHY IMAGINE GOD?

1. In his book *The Knowledge of the Holy*, author A. W. Tozer put it this way: "What comes into our minds when we think about God is the most important thing about us."

2. John Burke, *Imagine Heaven: Near-Death Experiences, God's Promises, and the Exhilarating Future That Awaits You* (Grand Rapids, MI: Baker Books, 2015).

3. This illustration was inspired by Edwin A. Abbott's satirical novella *Flatland: A Romance of Many Dimensions*.

CHAPTER 1: THE GOD OF ALL NATIONS

1. Santosh Acharjee, phone interview with John Burke, November 15, 2022. Used with permission.

2. Santosh (Sandy) Acharjee, *My Encounter with Jesus at Heaven's Gates: A Life-Changing Near Death Experience* (Bloomington, IN: AuthorHouse, 2016), loc. 600–650, Kindle. Used with permission. The last sentence in this paragraph is taken from Acharjee, phone interview with John Burke.

3. Acharjee, phone interview with John Burke. See also Santosh Acharjee, "Near-Death Experience: Hindu Man Dies and Faces Gate to Heaven and Hell," video interview by Randy Kay, Randy Kay Ministries, April 24, 2022, https://www.youtube.com/watch?v=Utcf052XGx8.

4. Acharjee, *My Encounter with Jesus at Heaven's Gates*, loc. 600–650, Kindle.

5. Acharjee, *My Encounter with Jesus at Heaven's Gates*, loc. 696–700, 1256, Kindle.

6. Acharjee, "Near-Death Experience," video interview by Randy Kay.

7. "Near-Death Experiences Illuminate Dying Itself," *New York Times*, October 28, 1986, https://www.nytimes.com/1986/10/28/science/near-death-experiences-illuminate-dying-itself.html.

8. Daniel Kondziella, Jens P. Dreier, and Markus Harboe Olsen, "Prevalence of Near-Death Experiences in People with and without REM Sleep Intrusion,"

PeerJ 7, (August 27, 2019):7585, https://peerj.com/articles/7585/. The study reported 10 percent claiming to have an NDE. I think 10 percent is high. This study included people who had elements of an NDE but who were not in life-threatening situations. This is not equivalent to NDEs I'm reporting, in which clinical death did occur. Fifty-five percent of NDE respondents in the study were in life-threatening situations, so a better approximation would be about 5.5 percent. Still, that suggests that there are millions and millions across the globe who died, came back, and had NDEs.

9. "René Hope Turner NDE," Near-Death Experience Research Foundation (NDERF), accessed January 12, 2023, https://www.nderf.org/Experiences /1rene_hope_turner_nde.html. NDERF excerpts used with permission of Jeffrey Long and Jody Long, founders and administrators of the Near Death Experience Research Foundation.

10. Throughout my book *Imagine Heaven*, I compare the commonalities of how NDErs experience heaven with what the Bible says about heaven.

11. "Mario NDE," Near-Death Experience Research Foundation (NDERF), accessed January 13, 2023, https://www.nderf.org/Experiences/1mario_nde.html.

12. Kenneth Ring and Sharon Cooper, *Mindsight: Near-Death and Out-of-Body Experiences in the Blind*, 2nd ed. (Bloomington, IN: iUniverse, 2008), chap. 3, "Case 3: Marsha." Used with permission.

13. Ring and Cooper, *Mindsight*, chap. 3, "Case 3: Marsha."

14. Ian McCormack, quoted in Jenny Sharkey, *Clinically Dead: I've Seen Heaven and Hell* (self-pub., CreateSpace, 2012, 2013), loc. 599–600, Kindle.

15. "Nan A NDE," Near-Death Experience Research Foundation (NDERF), accessed January 14, 2023, https://www.nderf.org/Experiences/1nan_a_nde .html. See also Atif Khalil, "Science, Religion, and the Challenge of Near-Death Experiences," *Renovatio*, June 19, 2020, https://renovatio.zaytuna .edu/article/science-religion-and-the-challenge-of-near-death-experiences.

16. "Mary NDE," Near-Death Experience Research Foundation (NDERF), accessed January 14, 2023, https://www.nderf.org/Experiences/1mary_nde .html.

17. "Mary NDE," Near-Death Experience Research Foundation (NDERF).

18. "Mary NDE," Near-Death Experience Research Foundation (NDERF).

19. Howard Storm, personal interview with John Burke, Austin, Texas, February 25, 2016. Used with permission.

20. "Dr. Bell C NDE," Near-Death Experience Research Foundation (NDERF), undated, https://www.nderf.org/Experiences/1bell_c_nde.html.

21. At the time of Abraham, 2000 BCE, some of today's religions claim to have existed, but their sacred scriptures had not been written. Hinduism as a formal religion was not yet established (as the Vedas were written 1500–500 BCE); nor were Judaism (1500–1400 BCE), Zoroastrianism (1000 BCE), Buddhism and Confucianism (500 BCE), Taoism (300 BCE), Christianity (50–90 CE), or Islam (600 CE). Note that all dates are approximate. See Joshua J. Mark, "The Vedas," *World History Encyclopedia*, June 9, 2020, https://www.worldhistory

.org/The_Vedas/; "Hinduism," Internet Sacred Text Archive, https://www
.sacred-texts.com/hin/, and "List of Founders of Religious Traditions,"
Wikipedia, last updated December 29, 2022, https://en.wikipedia.org/wiki
/List_of_founders_of_religious_traditions; and "Jewish History," Wikipedia,
last updated January 4, 2023, https://en.wikipedia.org/wiki/Jewish_history.

CHAPTER 2: SCIENCE, SKEPTICS, AND NDES

1. Rajiv Parti with Paul Perry, *Dying to Wake Up: A Doctor's Voyage into the Afterlife and the Wisdom He Brought Back* (New York: Atria Books, 2016), 4.
2. Parti, *Dying to Wake Up*, 5.
3. Parti, *Dying to Wake Up*, 6.
4. Parti, *Dying to Wake Up*, 70–71.
5. See Maureen Fiedler, "Debating the Meaning of Near Death Experiences," March 23, 2017, *Interfaith Voices* podcast, audio, 32:59, https://interfaithradio .org/Story_Details/Debating_the_Meaning_of_Near_Death_Experiences.
6. Jeffrey Long, MD, personal interview with John Burke, Austin, Texas, October 2, 2019.
7. Jeffrey Long, MD, with Paul Perry, *Evidence of the Afterlife: The Science of Near-Death Experiences* (New York: HarperCollins, 2010), 44.
8. Brian Duigan, "Occam's razor," *Encyclopedia Britannica*, last updated December 1, 2022, https://www.britannica.com/topic/Occams-razor.
9. Jeffrey Long, MD, "Near-Death Experiences: Evidence for Their Reality," *Missouri Medicine* 111, no. 5 (September-October 2014): 373, accessed via NIH National Library of Medicine, https://www.ncbi.nlm.nih.gov/pmc /articles/PMC6172100/#b9-ms111_p0372.
10. J. Steve Miller, *Near-Death Experiences as Evidence for the Existence of God and Heaven: A Brief Introduction in Plain Language* (Acworth, GA: Wisdom Creek Press, LLC, 2012), loc. 8, Kindle.
11. Michael Shermer, "Why a Near-Death Experience Isn't Proof of Heaven," *Scientific American*, April 1, 2013, https://www.scientificamerican.com/article /why-near-death-experience-isnt-proof-heaven/.
12. Michael Sabom, MD, *Light and Death: One Doctor's Fascinating Account of Near-Death Experiences* (Grand Rapids, MI: Zondervan, 1998), 14.
13. Gerald M. Woerlee, "Could Pam Reynolds Hear? A New Investigation into the Possibility of Hearing During This Famous Near-Death Experience," *Journal of Near-Death Studies* 30, no. 1 (Fall 2011): 3–25, https://digital.library.unt.edu /ark:/67531/metadc461684/m1/5/.
14. Pam Reynolds, "Decoding the Mystery of Near-Death Experiences," interview by Barbara Bradley Hagerty, *All Things Considered*, NPR, May 22, 2009, https://www.npr.org/templates/story/story.php?storyId=104397005.
15. Sabom, *Light and Death*, 39.
16. "Pam Sees God," excerpted from the documentary "The Day I Died," BBC, aired February 5, 2003, YouTube video, April 7, 2009, https://www.youtube .com/watch?v=WNbdUEqDB-k.

17. "Pam Sees God."
18. "Pam Sees God."
19. "Pam Reynolds: NBC Interview about Her Near-Death Experience," excerpted from "Back from the Dead," MSNBC, aired April 11, 2001, YouTube video, August 10, 2016, https://www.youtube.com/watch?v=gd3Vtn8WiVE.
20. "Pam Sees God."
21. J. E. Geshwiler, "Pam Reynolds Lowery, Noted for Near-Death Experience," Atlanta Journal-Constitution, May 28, 2010, https://www.ajc.com/news/local/pam-reynolds-lowery-noted-for-near-death-episode/0pAo5DxNyyVmF09WAmN4vN/.
22. Sabom, *Light and Death*, chap. 3.
23. Pim van Lommel, "Non-Local Consciousness: A Concept Based on Scientific Research on Near-Death Experiences during Cardiac Arrest," *Journal of Consciousness Studies* 20, no. 1-2 (January 1, 2013): 18, https://pimvanlommel.nl/wp-content/uploads/2017/10/Pim-van-Lommel-Nonlocal-Consciousness-article-JCS-2013.pdf.
24. Penny Sartori, *The Near-Death Experiences of Hospitalized Intensive Care Patients: A Five-Year Clinical Study* (Lewiston, NY: Edwin Mellen Press, 2008), cited in: *The Handbook of Near-Death Experiences: Thirty Years of Investigation*, ed. Janice Miner Holden, Bruce Greyson, and Debbie James (Santa Barbara, CA: Praeger, 2009), loc. 2861, Kindle, and https://www.neardeathexperience.us/wp-content/uploads/2015/01/Rousseau_Journal_of_the_Society_for_Psychical_Research_75.1_902_47-49.pdf.
25. Janice Miner Holden, "Veridical Perception in Near-Death Experiences," in *The Handbook of Near-Death Experiences*, loc. 2788, Kindle.
26. Van Lommel, "Non-Local Consciousness," 18. Dr. van Lommel asked that the last sentence be added to his quote.
27. Bruce Greyson, "Varieties of Near-Death Experience," *Psychiatry* 56, no. 4 (November 1993): 390–399, https://pubmed.ncbi.nlm.nih.gov/8295976/; Daniel Kondziella, Jens P. Dreier, and Markus Harboe Olsen, "Prevalence of Near-Death Experiences in People with and without REM Sleep Intrusion," *PeerJ* 7 (August 27, 2019):e7585, https://peerj.com/articles/7585.
28. In my book *Imagine Heaven*, I show how all the above elements correlate to Scripture's expectations of heaven, which I believe is even more evidence of its reality.
29. This list includes data collected from studying 613 NDEs on NDERF.org and reported in Long, *Evidence of the Afterlife*, loc. 6–17, 59 (vision), 61 (hearing), 177 (life change), Kindle. Encountering the God of Light and Love (48 percent) comes from Dr. Long's 2023 study of 834 NDEs, which he sent to me via email, January 28, 2023. Life review (32 percent) comes from Raymond A. Moody, MD, with Paul Perry *The Light Beyond: Explorations into the Afterlife* (New York: Bantam Books, 1988; Paradise Valley, AZ: SAKKARA Productions Publishing, 2016), 5. Citations refer to the SAKKARA edition. For others, see Jeffrey Long, MD, with Paul Perry, *God and the Afterlife: The Groundbreaking*

New Evidence for God and Near-Death Experience (New York: HarperCollins, 2016), 37, 41. All percentages have been rounded to the nearest whole number.

30. Long, *Evidence of the Afterlife*, 8.

31. Mally Cox-Chapman, *The Case for Heaven: Near Death Experiences as Evidence of the Afterlife* (Windsor, CT: Tide-Mark Press, 2012), loc. 471–484, 488–494, Kindle.

32. Long, personal interview with John Burke.

33. Why would only 18 percent of cardiac arrest patients report NDEs? There does not appear to be any correlation between NDEs and the length of time a person was clinically dead, or any other factor. It may be that NDEs are simply gifts from God that provide further evidence of his existence and a life to come.

34. Van Lommel, "Non-Local Consciousness," 12–14. See also Dr. Pim van Lommel, Ruud van Wees, Vincent Meyers, Ingrid Elfferich, "Near-Death Experience in Survivors of Cardiac Arrest: A Prospective Study in the Netherlands," *Lancet* 358 (December 15, 2001): 2039–2045, https://www.thelancet.com/pdfs/journals /lancet/PIIS0140-6736(01)07100-8.pdf.

35. Kenneth Ring and Sharon Cooper, *Mindsight: Near-Death and Out-of-Body Experiences in the Blind*, 2nd ed. (Bloomington, IN: iUniverse, 2008), chap. 4. Used with permission.

36. Ring and Cooper, *Mindsight*, chap. 4.

37. Ring and Cooper, *Mindsight*, chap. 4.

38. Van Lommel, "Non-Local Consciousness," 21.

39. "Dr. Rajiv Parti's NDE," *Present!*, KMVT15 Community Media, interview, November 25, 2013, YouTube video (recorded three years after his NDE in 2010), https://www.youtube.com/watch?v=7l-nbk_8EII.

40. Tricia Barker, phone interview with John Burke, April 10, 2019. Used with permission.

41. Raymond A. Moody, MD, with Paul Perry, *The Light Beyond: Explorations into the Afterlife* (New York: Bantam Books, 1988; Paradise Valley, AZ: SAKKARA Productions Publishing, 2016), 16. Citations refer to the SAKKARA edition.

42. Van Lommel, "Non-Local Consciousness," 22.

43. Van Lommel, "Non-Local Consciousness," 13, 28.

44. Sam Parnia, quoted in Pim van Lommel, "Getting Comfortable with Near-Death Experiences: Dutch Prospective Research on Near-Death Experiences During Cardiac Arrest," *Missouri Medicine* 111, no. 2 (March–April 2014): 126–131, https://www.ncbi.nlm.nih.gov/pmc/articles/PMC6179502/. See also Sam Parnia et al., "A Qualitative and Quantitative Study of the Incidence, Features and Aetiology of Near Death Experiences in Cardiac Arrest Survivors," *Resuscitation* 48, no. 2 (February 1, 2001), 151, https://pubmed.ncbi.nlm.nih.gov/11426476/.

45. Van Lommel, "Non-Local Consciousness," 15–16.

46. "Jang Jaswal's Near-Death Experience," *Present!*, KMVT15 Community Media, interview, November 25, 2014, YouTube video, https://www.youtube.com/watch ?v=eobvYMNPmRc.

47. "Jang Jaswal's Near-Death Experience."

CHAPTER 3: THE GOD OF LIGHT IN HISTORY

1. Heidi Barr, "Your Life Is in Good Hands," (unpublished manuscript), PDF. Used with permission.

2. Heidi Barr, personal interview with John Burke, April 7, 2020. Used with permission. Some quotes also taken from Barr, "Your Life Is in Good Hands."

3. All dates are approximate. The Jewish Torah (the first five books of the Hebrew Bible) dates between 1500–1400 BCE. Genesis in the Torah dates the history of God with Abraham and Sarah to approximately 2000 BCE. The Vedas of Hinduism have no clear date of writing, though it's estimated they were written around 1500–500 BCE. Zoroastrian scriptures were written around 1000 BCE. The scriptures of Jainism were written in the 800s BCE. The sacred texts of Buddhism, Confucianism, and Taoism were written between 500–300 BCE. The books of the New Testament were written approximately 50–90 CE, and the Koran of Islam around 600 CE.

4. Bibi Tahereh and Saeed Edina Abedini, personal interview with John Burke, Austin, Texas, April 19, 2019. Tahereh and Edina, phone interview with John Burke, March 7, 2022. Used with permission.

5. Tahereh and Edina, personal interview with John Burke.

6. Bryan Windle, "Top Ten Discoveries Related to Moses and the Exodus," Bible Archaeology Report, September 24, 2021, https://biblearchaeologyreport.com /2021/09/24/top-ten-discoveries-related-to-moses-and-the-exodus/.

7. "Arvind B NDE," Near-Death Experience Research Foundation (NDERF), accessed January 17, 2023, https://www.nderf.org/Experiences/1arvind_b_nde .html.

8. Wendy Doniger, "Kali," *Encyclopedia Britannica*, last updated January 4, 2023, https://www.britannica.com/topic/Kali.

9. "Neha S NDE," Near-Death Experience Research Foundation (NDERF), accessed January 17, 2023, https://www.nderf.org/Experiences/1neha_s_nde .html.

10. "Neha S NDE," Near-Death Experience Research Foundation (NDERF).

11. Editors of *Encyclopedia Britannica*, "Durga," *Encyclopedia Britannica*, last updated November 1, 2022, https://www.britannica.com/topic/Durga.

12. The inspiration of Scripture by God does not mean God said, "Isaiah, take a note," and dictated the text word for word. The inspiration of Scripture claims God used the uniqueness of each human author—personality, writing style, and genre—to convey his message to a particular culture. Interpretation of Scripture requires exegeting (or drawing out) the timeless message from the particular genre of writing or cultural situation to which the author was writing. However, God's inspiration implies that, just as humans can create different colored pencils with which to write or draw, God can create different individuals through whom to faithfully record God's message for all generations.

13. In *Truth in Religion*, Dr. Adler concluded that only three religions—Judaism, Christianity, and Islam—claim their sacred texts to be divine revelation from

God. With Islam, Muhammad was a human historical figure whose claim was not direct revelation from God, but that an angel gave him the words of the Koran. Dr. Adler's research eventually led him to faith in Jesus. See "Mortimer J. Adler," Wikipedia, https://en.wikipedia.org/wiki/Mortimer_J._Adler.

14. A Biblegateway.com search for the terms "the nations," "all nations," "all peoples," "all mankind," "all creation," "every creature," "every knee," "every tongue," "every language," and "the world," generates well over five hundred references.

15. Hugh Ross, "Fulfilled Prophecy: Evidence for the Reliability of the Bible," Reasons to Believe, August 22, 2003, https://reasons.org/explore/publications /articles/fulfilled-prophecy-evidence-for-the-reliability-of-the-bible.

16. Jesus, the promised Messiah, lived on earth almost seven hundred years after Isaiah wrote this. The week before his Crucifixion, Jesus foretold the reason for the second scattering of Israel: "As [Jesus] approached Jerusalem and saw the city, he wept over it and said, 'If you, even you, had only known on this day what would bring you peace—but now it is hidden from your eyes. The days will come upon you when your enemies . . . will not leave one stone on another, because you did not recognize the time of God's coming to you" (Luke 19:41-44, NIV). Jesus later reiterated that the Jewish people would be scattered to all nations: "They will fall by the sword and will be taken as prisoners to all the nations. Jerusalem will be trampled on by the Gentiles [non-Jewish people] until the times of the Gentiles are fulfilled" (Luke 21:24, NIV).

17. See also Jeremiah 23:1-8 and Ezekiel 36:16-38, which tell of the day Israel would be regathered from the nations.

18. Gene Currivan, "Zionists Proclaim the New State of Israel; Truman Recognizes It and Hopes for Peace; Tel Aviv Is Bombed, Egypt Orders Invasion," *New York Times*, May 15, 1948, https://archive.nytimes.com/www.nytimes.com/library /world/480515israel-state-50.html.

CHAPTER 4: THE UNCONDITIONAL LOVE OF GOD

1. Dr. Ron Smothermon, phone interview with John Burke, May 13, 2022. Used with permission. Some quotes also taken from Dr. Ron Smothermon, "My Near-Death Experience during a Murder Attempt" (unpublished manuscript), Microsoft Word file. Used with permission.

2. Smothermon, "My Near-Death Experience during a Murder Attempt."

3. Smothermon, phone interview with John Burke. Smothermon, "My Near-Death Experience during a Murder Attempt."

4. Smothermon, phone interview with John Burke.

5. "Chen M NDE," Near-Death Experience Research Foundation (NDERF), accessed January 17, 2023, https://www.nderf.org/Experiences/1chen_m_nde .html.

6. *Merriam-Webster*, s.v. "anthropomorphic," accessed January 13, 2023, https://www.merriam-webster.com/dictionary/anthropomorphic.

7. Dean Braxton, personal interview with John Burke, Austin, Texas, September 26, 2019. Used with permission.

8. Philip Yancey, *Disappointment with God: Three Questions No One Asks Aloud* (Grand Rapids, MI: Zondervan, 1988), 60.

9. "Sarah W Probable NDE," Near-Death Experience Research Foundation (NDERF), accessed January 17, 2023, https://www.nderf.org/Experiences /1sarah_w_probable_nde.html.

10. "Sarah W Probable NDE," Near-Death Experience Research Foundation (NDERF).

11. "Sarah W Probable NDE," Near-Death Experience Research Foundation (NDERF).

12. Erica McKenzie, *Dying to Fit In* (self-pub., CreateSpace, 2015), loc. 68. Kindle. Used with permission.

13. McKenzie, *Dying to Fit In*, loc. 73–74, Kindle.

14. Smothermon, phone interview with John Burke.

CHAPTER 5: THE PASSIONATE COMPASSION OF GOD

1. Santosh Acharjee, phone interview with John Burke, November 15, 2022. Used with permission.

2. Santosh (Sandy) Acharjee, *My Encounter with Jesus at Heaven's Gates: A Life-Changing Near-Death Experience* (Bloomington, IN: AuthorHouse, 2016), loc. 600–650, Kindle. Used with permission.

3. Acharjee, phone interview with John Burke.

4. Acharjee, phone interview with John Burke.

5. Acharjee, *My Encounter with Jesus at Heaven's Gates*, loc. 1259–1274, Kindle.

6. Acharjee, *My Encounter with Jesus at Heaven's Gates*, loc. 210–218, Kindle.

7. Dr. Mary Neal, personal interview with John Burke, Austin, Texas, February 22, 2016. Used with permission.

8. Kaline Fernandes, "He Gave Life and Also Took It Away," interview by Carlos Mendes, After All, What Are We?, October 16, 2021, YouTube video, https:// www.youtube.com/watch?v=o4JcqQPaoVo&list=PL3svxEC1Wa7PtzcaSBHF Jeu2UvCbhoQz-&index=24. Used with permission of Kaline Fernandes and Carlos Mendes. Includes minor edits by Kaline Fernandes.

9. Fernandes, "He Gave Life and Also Took It Away," video interview by Carlos Mendes.

10. Fernandes, "He Gave Life and Also Took It Away," video interview by Carlos Mendes.

11. "Micki P NDE," Near-Death Experience Research Foundation (NDERF), accessed January 18, 2023, https://www.nderf.org/Experiences/1micki_p_nde .html.

12. "Micki P NDE," Near-Death Experience Research Foundation (NDERF).

13. "DW NDE," Near-Death Experience Research Foundation (NDERF), accessed February 1, 2023, https://www.nderf.org/Experiences/1dw_nde .html.

14. D. S. Weiler, *Dead Is Just a Four Letter Word* (self-pub., 2007), http://www.1way 2see.com/thebook.html.

15. Bibi Tahereh and Saeed Edina Abedini, phone interview with John Burke, March 7, 2022. Used with permission.
16. Tahereh and Edina, phone interview with John Burke.
17. Wayne Fowler, Zoom interview with John Burke, November 1, 2021. Used with permission.
18. Acharjee, phone interview with John Burke.
19. This description is consistent with the account given by fourteen-year-old Sarah, whom you met in chapter 4: She said she saw twelve crystal walls or foundations, and she also saw names written on them. "Sarah W Probable NDE," Near-Death Experience Research Foundation (NDERF), accessed January 18, 2023, https://www.nderf.org/Experiences/1sarah_w_probable_nde.html.

CHAPTER 6: THE HIDDEN JUSTICE OF GOD

1. Melanie McCullough, Zoom interview with John Burke, May 28, 2019. Used with permission.
2. McCullough, Zoom interview with John Burke.
3. McCullough, Zoom interview with John Burke.
4. McCullough, Zoom interview with John Burke.
5. Dr. Ron Smothermon, phone interview with John Burke, May 13, 2022. Used with permission.
6. Erica McKenzie, *Dying to Fit In* (self-pub., CreateSpace, 2015), 85. Used with permission.
7. McKenzie, *Dying to Fit In*, 85.
8. See Nancy Evans Bush, "Distressing Western Near-Death Experiences: Finding a Way through the Abyss," in *The Handbook of Near-Death Experiences: Thirty Years of Investigation*, ed. Janice Miner Holden, Bruce Greyson, and Debbie James (Santa Barbara, CA: Praeger, 2009), 70.
9. The European Academy of Neurology presented a study done across thirty-five countries in which 10 percent reported having had an NDE, and almost 50 percent of those were "negative" or even hellish. They included people who claimed to have had an NDE but who did not experience clinical death, which may have increased the distressing experiences reported. Daniel Kondziella, Jens P. Dreier, and Markus Harboe Olsen, "Prevalence of Near-Death Experiences in People with and without REM Sleep Intrusion," *PeerJ* 7 (August 27, 2019):7585, https://peerj.com/articles/7585/.
10. I have interviewed people such as Santosh Acharjee, who knew nothing about the God they encountered, came back, searched for him, and found faith in him. I've also interviewed others who had encounters with this God of Light or even Jesus, yet they did not appear to become seekers of God or followers of Jesus upon their return; they sought instead to recreate the experience rather than seek the God of the experience. This shows the reality of what Jesus himself said about human pride and free will: "If they do not listen to Moses and the Prophets [the Bible's words], they will not be convinced even if someone rises from the dead" (Luke 16:31, NIV).

11. McKenzie, *Dying to Fit In*, 97.

12. McKenzie, *Dying to Fit In*, 97.

13. C. S. Lewis, *The Quotable Lewis*, ed. Wayne Martindale and Jerry Root (Wheaton, IL: Tyndale,1989; 2012), 292.

14. Lewis, *The Quotable Lewis*, 292.

15. When we read of God's "wrath" in the Bible, this is God's just punishment of prideful, stubborn rebellion against the Creator—to let the free will turned against God have its horrific consequences.

16. Dale Black with Ken Gire, *Flight to Heaven: A Plane Crash . . . A Lone Survivor . . . A Journey to Heaven—and Back* (Minneapolis, MN: Bethany House, 2010), 109.

17. C. S. Lewis, *The Abolition of Man: How Education Develops Man's Sense of Morality* (New York: Macmillan Publishing, 1947), 97–121. This is my summary of his key points and examples given in the appendix of this book.

18. Santosh (Sandy) Acharjee, *My Encounter with Jesus at Heaven's Gates: A Life-Changing Near-Death Experience* (Bloomington, IN: AuthorHouse, 2016), loc. 1461–1531, Kindle. Used with permission.

19. See Peter W. Flint and Eugene Ulrich, trans., "The Great Isaiah Scroll," The Digital Dead Sea Scrolls, Israel Museum, Jerusalem, accessed February 2, 2023, http://dss.collections.imj.org.il/chapters_pg.

20. Georges Bonani, et al. "Radiocarbon Dating of Fourteen Dead Sea Scrolls," *Radiocarbon* 34, no. 3 (1992): 845, https://journals.uair.arizona.edu/index.php/radiocarbon/article/download/1537/1541.

21. "The Great Isaiah Scroll MS A (1Qisa)," Israel Museum, Jerusalem, accessed January 19, 2023, https://www.imj.org.il/en/collections/198208-0.

22. Flint and Ulrich, trans., "The Great Isaiah Scroll."

23. Swidiq later changed his name to Cedric when he converted to Christianity and became an Anglican priest.

24. Cedric Kanana with Benjamin Fischer, *I Once Was Dead: How God Rescued Me from Islam, Drugs, Witchcraft, and Even Death* (Chicago: Oasis International, 2022), loc. 84–85, Kindle. Used with permission of Oasis International and Cedric Kanana.

25. Kanana with Fischer, *I Once Was Dead*, loc. 101, Kindle.

26. Kanana with Fischer, *I Once Was Dead*, loc. 106, Kindle.

27. Kanana with Fischer, *I Once Was Dead*, loc. 97–99, 109–112, Kindle.

28. Kanana with Fischer, *I Once Was Dead*, loc. 111–112, Kindle.

29. Kanana with Fischer, *I Once Was Dead*, loc. 115–116, Kindle.

30. Flint and Ulrich, trans., "The Great Isaiah Scroll."

31. People have asked me, "Why don't Jewish people see this and believe Jesus was their Messiah?" It's a complicated question historically, but rabbis normally say that Isaiah's use of terms such as "servant" and "arm of the Lord" refer to Israel, not the Messiah. In Isaiah, God does call Israel his servant, reminding his people in Isaiah 48 that he states in advance what he will do to redeem them. Then there is a shift to a new servant in Isaiah 49: "He said to me, 'You are my servant, Israel, in whom I will display my splendor.' But I said, 'I have labored

in vain'" (Isaiah 49:3-4, NIV). Another new servant appears in the next verse: "He who formed me in the womb to be his servant to bring Jacob back to him and gather Israel to himself. . . . It is too small a thing for you to be my servant to restore the tribes of Jacob and bring back those of Israel I have kept. I will also make you a light for the Gentiles, that my salvation may reach to the ends of the earth" (Isaiah 49:5-6, NIV). If this servant is Israel, how does Israel, who "labored in vain," bring itself back to God and save itself and all the nations? Clearly, a new servant, described further as the "suffering servant" in Isaiah 53, is now being talked about.

CHAPTER 7: THE UNWAVERING FORGIVENESS OF GOD

1. Rajiv Parti with Paul Perry, *Dying to Wake Up: A Doctor's Voyage into the Afterlife and the Wisdom He Brought Back* (New York: Atria Books, 2016), 13.

2. "Dr. Rajiv Parti's NDE," *Present!*, KMVT15 Community Media, interview, November 25, 2013, YouTube video, https://www.youtube.com/watch?v=7l-nbk_8EII.

3. Dr. Rajiv Parti, "IANDS Conference, Santa Barbara, Dr. Raj Parti on Near-Death Experiences," August 26, 2022, YouTube video, https://www.youtube.com/watch?v=Z4xadsz1yIs.

4. Parti, *Dying to Wake Up*, 30.

5. Dr. Rajiv Parti, "OBE: Dr. Rajiv Parti," All Reality Video, November 19, 2013, YouTube video, https://www.youtube.com/watch?v=2EFAq_aQkJc.

6. Parti, *Dying to Wake Up*, 32–34. Dr. Rajiv Parti, "Dying to Wake Up: A True NDE Story with Dr. Rajiv Parti," interview by Curry Stegen, Passion for the Paranormal, September 18, 2019, YouTube audio, https://www.youtube.com/watch?v=inHo47fYYYA&t=1076s.

7. Parti, *Dying to Wake Up*, 42.

8. Parti, "OBE: Dr. Rajiv Parti," All Reality Video.

9. Parti, *Dying to Wake Up*, 57–58.

10. Parti, "OBE: Dr. Rajiv Parti," All Reality Video.

11. Parti, *Dying to Wake Up*, 60.

12. Parti, *Dying to Wake Up*, 61.

13. Parti, *Dying to Wake Up*, 66.

14. Although the two angels Dr. Parti mentions may not be the same as those mentioned in Scripture, it is interesting to note that they are the names of archangels. The archangel Michael is mentioned in the Bible (Daniel 10:13, 21; Jude 1:9). The archangel Raphael is mentioned in Tobit, a Hebrew book preserved in Greek and included in the Catholic Bible but not the Hebrew or Protestant Bible (Tobit 3:17; 5:4; 12:15). Raphael is also mentioned in the Book of Enoch chapter 71 (see "Chapter LXXI," Internet Sacred Text Archive, https://www.sacred-texts.com/bib/boe/boe074.htm), a non-canonical Hebrew book known and quoted in the New Testament by Jude (see Jude 14-15, which quotes Enoch 1:9).

15. Parti, "Dying to Wake Up," interview by Curry Stegen.

16. Parti, "My Epiphany: Christ Consciousness and Universal Love," Raj Parti, MD, accessed January 19, 2023, https://rajpartimd.com/my-epiphany/.

17. Parti, "My Epiphany."

18. After Dr. Parti's encounter with Jesus, he says he thought maybe he was supposed to become a follower of Jesus. He admits he struggled in his soul about converting from Hinduism to follow Jesus alone. At one point, he was baptized as an acknowledgment of his faith in Jesus. But then while visiting India, he went to a temple high in the Himalayas and had another spiritual experience during a meditation. He decided not to follow Jesus solely, but to serve all religions through the message "Forgive, Love, Heal." While these three things are good values, it's very easy in this world to miss or get distracted from what Jesus said his main message was about. Interestingly, Rajiv even says that, years later, angels appeared to him to remind him of the encounter he had with Jesus during his NDE, which he said was to refocus him on Jesus.

This leads to an important point. I've encountered NDErs who write about being overwhelmed by the unconditional love and compassion of this God of Light and may even experience Jesus himself, yet they then turn away from seeking God. Some even deny Jesus or pursue other supernatural encounters, such as out-of-body experiences, or attempting to contact angels, other spirits, or the dead. These are things God warned through the prophets that we should not do, because when we go to the other side unprotected, evil is lurking to deceive us. And sometimes evil disguises itself as light (2 Corinthians 11:14), appearing to be good and helpful, only to draw us away from following and serving God. I do not think evil can disguise itself as love, however. That's why I'm trying to show through the prophets that God has given us historical evidence of who he is so that we follow the teachings of Jesus. Any time an NDE account contradicts what Jesus taught while on earth, we should always follow the words of Jesus in Scripture, not the NDEr's interpretation of their encounter.

Dr. Parti's NDE is also complex because he had life reviews while still on the hellish side, before going through the tunnel to the heavenly side, where he says he experienced past lives. The purpose of this book is to explore God's identity, not reincarnation or past lives, which I may take up in a future book. In short, I've never heard an NDEr say they were given the choice to either stay in heaven or to reincarnate into a new body; the only choice they report is the choice of whether to stay in heaven or return to their present body. I have had some tell me that time and interconnectedness in an NDE are such that you could be getting a lesson from someone else's life and feel like it's your past life, but it's just an immersive lesson—like watching a movie but from the perspective of one of the characters. Since past life experiences are not widely reported, something like this could possibly explain what NDErs are experiencing.

19. Thallus, a Roman historian writing in 52 CE, is quoted in another early work by the Roman general and statesman Africanus: "Thallus, in the third book of his histories, explains away this darkness as an eclipse of the

sun—unreasonably, it seems to me . . . it was at the season of the Paschal full moon that Christ died." Africanus also quotes Phlegon, a Greek historian who writes about the strange darkness: "[Phlegon] records that in the time of Tiberius Caesar at full moon, there was a full eclipse of the sun from the sixth hour to the ninth." These are the same hours Matthew reports the darkness. See Derek Walker, Daniel's 70 Weeks (self pub., 2009), appendix 4, https://www .oxfordbiblechurch.co.uk/index.php/books/new-book-daniel-s-70-weeks/477 -appendix-4-the-day-the-sun-stopped-shining.

20. Dr. Metherell explains the medical reason this is proof of heart attack in Lee Strobel, *The Case for Christ: A Journalist's Personal Investigation of the Evidence for Jesus* (Grand Rapids, MI: Zondervan, 1998), 199.

21. Although Father Cedric does not indicate a known cause of death, I have interviewed NDErs who died in their sleep and later were diagnosed with sleep apnea. Some NDErs have the same vivid experience yet had no cause of death (like John in the book of Revelation).

22. Father Cedric Pisegna, phone interview with John Burke, September 15, 2022. Used with permission.

23. Fr. Cedric Pisegna, *Death: The Final Surrender* (Houston, TX: Passionist Publications, 2013, 2022), 87. Used with permission. Includes minor edits and additions by Father Cedric Pisegna.

24. Father Cedric Pisegna, phone interview with John Burke.

25. Pisegna, *Death*, 102–103, 114, 93.

26. Heidi Barr, Zoom interview with John Burke, October 2, 2019. Used with permission.

27. Howard Storm, personal interview with John Burke, Austin, Texas, February 25, 2016. Used with permission.

28. Dean Braxton, personal interview with John Burke, Austin, Texas, October 2, 2019. Used with permission.

29. "Alexa H NDE," Near-Death Experience Research Foundation (NDERF), accessed January 20, 2023, https://www.nderf.org/Experiences/1alexa_h_nde .html. Used with permission. Includes minor edits and additions by Alexa Hartung sent to Kathy Burke via email, January 5, 2023.

CHAPTER 8: THE MYSTERY OF A TRIUNE GOD

1. Heidi Barr, "Your Life Is in Good Hands," (unpublished manuscript), PDF. Used with permission.

2. Heidi Barr, phone interview with John Burke, September 20, 2022. Used with permission.

3. "Kaluza-Klein Theory," Wikipedia, last updated December 8, 2022, https:// en.wikipedia.org/wiki/Kaluza%E2%80%93Klein_theory.

4. I first read about this multidimensional idea in Edwin A. Abbott's satirical novella *Flatland: A Romance of Many Dimensions*.

5. Over the years, people have come up with many analogies for the Trinity. I call them "not-half-bad," meaning the analogies are half somewhat helpful and half

not. Every analogy eventually breaks down, and it's good to understand where analogies can sometimes go wrong in imagining what God is like.

One widely used analogy for the Trinity is that God is like an egg. An egg has a yolk, a white, and a shell—three parts but one egg. Another common analogy likens God to water, which can exist as a solid, liquid, or vapor—one substance, three states. Those are helpful to a point, right? However, most analogies for the Trinity tend to fall into one of two common misconstructions—tritheism or modalism.

Tritheism denies the unity of the essence of God and holds to three distinct beings or parts of God who share a unity of purpose and endeavor. But the God of the Bible shares a unity of essence as well as of purpose and endeavor. So the parts of the egg are not equivalent to the divine essence of the Father, Son, and Holy Spirit. And my analogy of three fingers intersecting a two-dimensional plane falls short because the full essence of "me" is not resident in each finger.

Modalism holds to a Trinity of revelation but not of nature. Modalism speaks of a threefold functionality of God in the same way a person may simultaneously be an artist, a teacher, and a friend. The three "modes" of water as an analogy for the Trinity falls into the modalism category. God is not Father, Son, and Holy Spirit in different modes or roles alone, but in all modes at the same time. In its creeds, the early church tried to put finite words to what seems intuitive to NDErs—that the God at the heart of the universe is a relationship of love. God is perfect love, equality, and unity in diversity.

Leaders of the early church wrestled with how to describe the Trinity, which they captured in the form of creeds. For an example, see the Athanasian Creed of the fourth century: "Athanasian Creed," Christian Reformed Church, https://www.crcna.org/welcome/beliefs/creeds/athanasian-creed.

6. Crystal McVea and Alex Tresniowski, *Waking Up in Heaven: A True Story of Brokenness, Heaven, and Life Again* (New York: Howard Books, 2013), loc. 1, 89–91, Kindle.

7. Dean Braxton, phone interview with John Burke, August 10, 2022. Used with permission.

8. See Revelation 22:8-9 for one example of angels refusing worship.

9. Some theologians differ on what these appearances represent. For more Old Testament examples and to learn more about theophanies, see Vern Poythress, "Theophany," Gospel Coalition, accessed January 29, 2023, https://www.thegospelcoalition.org/essay/theophany/.

10. William Smith, "In Realms of Glory," in Sid Roth and Lonnie Lane, *Heaven Is beyond Your Wildest Expectations: Ten True Stories of Experiencing Heaven* (Shippensburg, PA: Destiny Image, 2012), loc. 136–137, Kindle.

11. Santosh Acharjee, phone interview with John Burke, November 15, 2022. Used with permission.

12. Bibi Tahereh and Saeed Edina, phone interview with John Burke, March 7, 2022. Used with permission.

13. Nancy Botsford, *A Day in Hell: Death to Life to Hope* (Tate Publishing and Enterprises, LLC, 2010), loc. 203-209, Kindle.
14. Dean Braxton, phone interview with John Burke.

CHAPTER 9: AWESOME GOD AND FATHER

1. Susanne Seymoure, Zoom interview with John Burke, February 28, 2022. Used with permission.
2. Susanne Seymoure, *My Secrets from Heaven: A Child's Trip to Heaven and Back* (White Birch, LLC, 2017), 56. Used with permission.
3. Seymoure, Zoom interview with John Burke. Susanne Seymoure, phone interview with John Burke, August 5, 2022. Used with permission.
4. Seymoure, Zoom interview with John Burke.
5. Quoted in Pim van Lommel, *Consciousness Beyond Life: The Science of the Near-Death Experience* (New York: HarperCollins, 2010), 34–35.
6. *Eternity in Their Hearts* by Don Richardson is an excellent book showing how missionaries to indigenous peoples in the Americas or to other people groups in Indonesia, India, and Africa found traces of this one true God in their cultures, just as Paul did with the Athenian "Unknown God" described in Acts 17.
7. See Revelation 20:13-15.
8. Fr. Cedric Pisegna, *Death: The Final Surrender* (Houston, TX: Passionist Publications, 2013, 2022), loc. 78–79, Kindle. Used with permission.
9. Father Cedric Pisegna, phone interview with John Burke, September 15, 2022. Used with permission; Pisegna, *Death: The Final Surrender*, loc. 65–66, Kindle.
10. Richard Feynman, *The Character of Physical Law* (Cambridge, MA: MIT Press, 2017), 130.
11. In his book *Flight to Heaven*, Dale includes photos of the wreckage that were printed in the *Los Angeles Times*.
12. Dale Black with Ken Gire, *Flight to Heaven: A Plane Crash . . . A Lone Survivor . . . A Journey to Heaven—and Back* (Minneapolis, MN: Bethany House, 2010), 99.
13. Captain Dale Black, personal interview with John Burke, Austin, Texas, September 26, 2019. Used with permission.
14. Black with Gire, *Flight to Heaven*, 100, 102.
15. Richard Sigmund, "A Picture of Life in Heaven" in Sid Roth and Lonnie Lane, *Heaven Is beyond Your Wildest Expectations: Ten True Stories of Experiencing Heaven* (Shippensburg, PA: Destiny Image, 2012), loc. 118–119, Kindle.
16. Matthew 17:1-5 (when Jesus was transfigured) and Exodus 24:16 (when God appeared on Mount Sinai) both refer to a cloud accompanying God.
17. Dean Braxton, phone interview with John Burke, August 10, 2022. Used with permission.
18. Dr. Ron Smothermon, "My Near-Death Experience during a Murder Attempt," (unpublished manuscript), Microsoft Word file. Used with permission.
19. Karina Martinez, Zoom interview with John Burke, April 28, 2022. Used with permission.

CHAPTER 10: JESUS, OUR BROTHER AND FRIEND

1. Randy Kay, personal interview with John Burke, April 7, 2020. Used with permission. Randy Kay, personal journal (unpublished), Microsoft Word file. Used with permission.

2. "Pepi NDE," Near-Death Experience Research Foundation (NDERF), accessed January 22, 2023, https://www.nderf.org/Experiences/1pepi_nde.html.

3. Adam Frank, "200,000 Years of Holidays: Where Do You Fit In?," NPR, December 20, 2016, https://www.npr.org/sections/13.7/2016/12/20 /506304087/200-000-years-of-holidays-where-do-you-fit-in. The current world population exceeds 8 billion according to "Current World Population," Worldometer, accessed January 22, 2023, https://www.worldometers.info /world-population/.

4. Some think the significance of mentioning the first seven "sevens" of years is that it took forty-nine years (7 x 7 = 49) to rebuild the city of Jerusalem (see Nehemiah). Some contest it was not quite forty-nine years, so it must refer to the first Year of Jubilee (year of rest) after forty-nine years.

5. There are three good reasons to assume these are sevens of years. First, Daniel 9:24 gives the context of the seventy "sevens" as the time when all transgressions are finished (which still has not happened). Second, for a Jewish person, seven years would clearly refer to the sabbatical year, God's command to let the land rest every seven years. And third, the Year of Jubilee came every seven sabbatical years (or 7 x 7 = 49 years). So a Jewish person would know the first seven of "sevens" of Daniel's years as the reinstatement of the first Jubilee of sabbatical years (forty-nine years). Then sixty-two more "sevens" of sabbatical years = 483 years until Messiah. In this view, the seventieth "seven-year period" (Daniel 9:24 and 9:27) does not come until after Messiah is killed and after the sabbatical year cycle is reinstated, which cannot happen until the Temple in Jerusalem is rebuilt (recall that the Temple was destroyed in 70 CE). So the Jewish people will have one last act in prophetic world history during the seventieth "seven-year" period.

6. Wikipedia and other secular sources consistently claim the Book of Daniel is a made-up history, written after the rebuilding of Jerusalem, around 160 BCE. Why? Because there is so much prophetic history foretold and fulfilled. Their assessment is based on the assumption that there is no God who foretells the future, therefore, the Book of Daniel must have been written after the fact. But they fail to account for so much evidence to the contrary—such as an Aramaic decree using language consistent with the sixth century BCE, not the second century BCE. Or the value of coins Daniel mentions, which fits the 500s BCE, not the 100s. A modern-day equivalent in the US would be reading a document that says "a Coke costs 5 cents," which would date the document to between 1886–1959, because Coke sold for a nickel during that time period—but not today!

7. Editors of *Encyclopedia Britannica*, "Artaxerxes I," *Encyclopedia Britannica*, last updated April 3, 2020, https://www.britannica.com/biography/Artaxerxes-I.

8. For extensive scholarly work on the subject, see Rick Lanser, "The Daniel 9:24-27 Project: The Framework for Messianic Chronology," Associates for Biblical Research, March 4, 2019, https://biblearchaeology.org/abr-projects -main/the-daniel-9-24-27-project-2/4760-daniel-9-24-27-the-sixty-ninth-and -seventieth-weeks. For a less technical overview, see William H. Shea, "When Did the Seventy Weeks of Daniel 9:24 Begin?," Seventh-day Adventist Church, originally published in the *Journal of the Adventist Theological Society* 2, no. 1 (1991): 115–138, https://www.adventistbiblicalresearch.org/materials/when -did-the-seventy-weeks-of-daniel-924-begin/. There are two camps of dating, and there is debate about which is correct. Both make a case that they land within the timeline of Jesus' last years, but I think the case I presented makes more sense. For the alternative dating, see "What are the seventy sevens in Daniel 9:24–27?," Got Questions, accessed February 6, 2023, https://www .gotquestions.org/seventy-sevens.html.

9. "Micki P NDE," Near-Death Experience Research Foundation (NDERF), accessed January 22, 2023, https://www.nderf.org/Experiences/1micki_p_nde .html.

10. Jeremy, email message to John Burke, February 10, 2021. Used with permission.

11. Jeremy, email message to John Burke.

12. "Julie H Probable NDE," Near-Death Experience Research Foundation (NDERF), accessed January 22, 2023, https://www.nderf.org/Experiences /1julie_h_probable_nde.html.

13. Kevin Zadai, "What Jesus Warned Me about in Heaven Will Shock You," Supernatural Stories, October 8, 2020, YouTube video, https://www.youtube .com/watch?v=CyYHlYPEpfQ&list=PLWqRBgNjtFbdrqLTICgh_6gHJDJUs 589j&index=2&t=2s. Used with permission.

14. Dr. Mary Neal, personal interview with John Burke, Austin, Texas, February 22, 2016. Used with permission.

15. Richard Eby, "Experiencing Heaven, Experiencing Hell," in Sid Roth and Lonnie Lane, *Heaven Is beyond Your Wildest Expectations: Ten True Stories of Experiencing Heaven* (Shippensburg, PA: Destiny Image, 2012), loc. 1669, Kindle.

16. Gary Wood, *A Place Called Heaven* (Kingswood, TX: RevMedia Publishing, 2014), loc. 436–453, Kindle.

17. Dr. Ron Smothermon, phone interview with John Burke, May 13, 2022. Used with permission.

CHAPTER 11: GOD'S SPIRIT SPEAKS

1. Penny Wittbrodt, Zoom interview with John Burke, September 28, 2022. Used with permission.

2. Wittbrodt, Zoom interview with John Burke.

3. Wittbrodt, Zoom interview with John Burke.

4. Wittbrodt, Zoom interview with John Burke.

5. Randy Kay, personal journal, (unpublished), Microsoft Word file. Used with permission.
6. Kay, personal journal.
7. "Jeff S NDE," Near-Death Research Foundation (NDERF), accessed January 22, 2023, https://www.nderf.org/Experiences/1jeff_s_nde.html.
8. Santosh Acharjee, phone interview with John Burke, November 15, 2022. Used with permission.
9. Kaline Fernandes, "He Gave Life and Also Took It Away," interview by Carlos Mendes, After All, What Are We?, October 16, 2021, YouTube video, https://www.youtube.com/watch?v=o4JcqQPaoVo&list=PL3svxEC1Wa7PtzcaSBHFJeu2UvCbhoQz-&index=24. Used with permission of Kaline Fernandes and Carlos Mendes.
10. Erica McKenzie, *Dying to Fit In* (self-pub., CreateSpace, 2015), loc. 74, 76, 79, Kindle. Used with permission.
11. Kevin Zadai, "What Jesus Warned Me about in Heaven Will Shock You," Supernatural Stories, October 8, 2020, YouTube video, https://www.youtube.com/watch?v=CyYHlYPEpfQ&list=PLWqRBgNjtFbdrqLTICgh_6gHJDJUs589j&index=2&t=2s. Used with permission.
12. Zadai, "What Jesus Warned Me about in Heaven Will Shock You."

CHAPTER 12: HOW PRAYER WORKS WITH GOD
1. Jim Woodford, phone interview with John Burke, December 9, 2022. Used with permission. The last line taken from Jim Woodford with Dr. Thom Gardner, *Heaven, an Unexpected Journey: One Man's Experience with Heaven, Angels, and the Afterlife* (Shippensburg, PA: Destiny Image, 2017), 18.
2. Woodford with Gardner, *Heaven, an Unexpected Journey*, 138.
3. Woodford, phone interview with John Burke.
4. Woodford, phone interview with John Burke.
5. Woodford, phone interview with John Burke.
6. Woodford with Gardner, *Heaven, an Unexpected Journey*, 110.
7. Gary Wood, *A Place Called Heaven* (Kingswood, TX: RevMedia Publishing, 2014), loc. 322–332. Kindle.
8. Steve Kang, Zoom interview with John Burke, November 9, 2022. Used with permission.
9. Jenny Sharkey, *Clinically Dead: I've Seen Heaven and Hell* (self-pub., CreateSpace, 2012, 2013), loc. 16, Kindle.
10. Ivan Tuttle, personal interview with John Burke, Greenville, South Carolina, March 18, 2022. Used with permission.
11. Dean Braxton, phone interview with John Burke, August 10, 2022. Used with permission.
12. Santosh Acharjee, phone interview John Burke, November 15, 2022. Used with permission.
13. Karina Martinez, Zoom interview with John Burke, April 28, 2022. Used with permission.

14. Martinez, Zoom interview with John Burke.
15. "Douglas D NDE," Near-Death Experience Research Foundation (NDERF), accessed January 27, 2023, https://www.nderf.org/Experiences/1douglas_d _nde_3107.html.
16. Randy Kay, personal interview with John Burke, April 7, 2020. Used with permission. Randy Kay, personal journal, (unpublished), Microsoft Word file. Used with permission.

CHAPTER 13: THE PERFECT PLANS OF GOD

1. Mark McDonough, "House Fire Kills Family and Burns Most of Surgeon's Body as Teen. Next, He Meets Them in Heaven," interview by Randy Kay, Randy Kay Ministries, September 3, 2022, YouTube video, https://www .youtube.com/watch?v=DVdkjJA-Ycc&t=843s. Used with permission of Mark McDonough. Includes minor edits by Dr. Mark McDonough.
2. Mark D. McDonough, *Forged through Fire: A Reconstructive Surgeon's Story of Survival, Faith, and Healing* (Grand Rapids, MI: Revell, 2019), 75.
3. McDonough, "House Fire Kills Family," video interview by Randy Kay. Includes minor edits by Dr. Mark McDonough.
4. McDonough, *Forged through Fire*; McDonough, "House Fire Kills Family," video interview by Randy Kay. Includes minor edits by Dr. Mark McDonough.
5. Dr. Mary Neal, personal interview with John Burke, Austin, Texas, February 22, 2016. Used with permission.
6. McDonough, "House Fire Kills Family," video interview by Randy Kay. Includes minor edits by Dr. Mark McDonough.
7. Cheri Henderson, "Dr. Mark McDonough: Burn Victim Turned Plastic Surgeon," *Orlando*, August 7, 2020, https://www.orlandomagazine.com/dr -mark-mcdonough-burn-victim-turned-plastic-surgeon/.
8. Kevin Zadai, "What Jesus Warned Me about in Heaven Will Shock You," Supernatural Stories, October 8, 2020, YouTube video, https://www.youtube .com/watch?v=CyYHlYPEpfQ&list=PLWqRBgNjtFbdrqLTICgh_6gHJDJU s589j&index=2&t=2s. Used with permission.
9. Hugh Ross, *Beyond the Cosmos: The Transdimensionality of God*, 3rd ed. (Covina, CA: RTB Press, 2017), 168.
10. Father Cedric Pisegna, phone interview with John Burke, September 15, 2022. Used with permission.
11. Greggory Rickert, phone interview with John Burke, July 20, 2022. Used with permission.
12. Rickert, phone interview with John Burke.
13. Rickert, phone interview with John Burke.
14. Although one chapter isn't enough to cover all the Scriptures that declare God's foreknowledge, predestination, and providence over history, or the equal number of passages that declare human free will as real, I put a list of both in appendix B of my book *Unshockable Love: How Jesus Changes the World through Imperfect People* (Grand Rapids, MI: Baker, 2014).

15. Diana Shepherd, Zoom interview with John Burke, February 24, 2022. Used with permission.

16. Shepherd, Zoom interview with John Burke.

17. Dr. Colin Perry, Zoom interview with John Burke, October 5, 2022. Used with permission. For more, see C. Thomas Perry, *Dying to Be Alive* (self-pub., Xlibris, 2015).

18. Perry, Zoom interview with John Burke.

19. Erica McKenzie, *Dying to Fit In* (self-pub., CreateSpace, 2015), loc. 90, Kindle. Used with permission.

CHAPTER 14: THE JOY AND LAUGHTER OF GOD

1. Rebecca Ruter Springer, *Intra Muros* (Elgin, IL: David C. Cook Publishing, 1898), 9–10.

2. To learn more about this, see my book *Imagine Heaven* (Grand Rapids, MI: Baker, 2015), in which I examine all the commonalities in NDE accounts of heaven compared with what the Bible says about heaven.

3. Ruter Springer, *Intra Muros*, 11–12.

4. Ruter Springer, *Intra Muros*, 15–17, 120.

5. Ruter Springer, *Intra Muros*, 30–31.

6. Ruter Springer, *Intra Muros*, 126.

7. Ruter Springer, *Intra Muros*, 60–61.

8. Ruter Springer, *Intra Muros*, 120.

9. Ruter Springer, *Intra Muros*, 62–63.

10. Ruter Springer, *Intra Muros*, 64–65.

11. Ruter Springer, *Intra Muros*, 71–73.

12. Ruter Springer, *Intra Muros*, 91.

13. C. S. Lewis, *Letters to Malcolm: Chiefly on Prayer* (New York: Harcourt, Brace and World, 1963; New York: HarperCollins, 2017), ch. 17.

14. Dr. Colin Perry, Zoom interview with John Burke, October 5, 2022. Used with permission.

15. "Derry KRK," Near-Death Experience Research Foundation (NDERF), undated, https://www-nderf-org.translate.goog/Finnish/derry_krk.htm?_x_tr_sl=fi&_x_tr_tl=en&_x_tr_hl=en&_x_tr_pto=sc. Translated from Finnish.

16. Randy Kay, personal journal (unpublished), Microsoft Word file. Used with permission.

17. Jim Woodford with Dr. Thom Gardner, *Heaven, an Unexpected Journey: One Man's Experience with Heaven, Angels, and the Afterlife* (Shippensburg, PA: Destiny Image, 2017), 81–82.

18. Heidi Barr, "Your Life Is in Good Hands," (unpublished manuscript), PDF. Used with permission.

19. Greggory Rickert, phone interview with John Burke, July 20, 2022. Used with permission.

20. Jeffrey Long, MD, with Paul Perry, *Evidence of the Afterlife: The Science of Near-Death Experiences* (New York: HarperCollins, 2010), loc. 131–132, Kindle.

21. Dr. Ron Smothermon, phone interview with John Burke, May 13, 2022. Used with permission.
22. Heidi Barr, phone interview with John Burke, September 20, 2022. Used with permission.
23. Barr, "Your Life Is in Good Hands."
24. G. K. Chesterton, "The Ethics of Elfland," in *Orthodoxy*, Christian Heritage Series (New York: John Lane, 1908; Moscow, ID: Canon Press, 2020), 61.
25. Richard Eby, "Experiencing Heaven, Experiencing Hell," in Sid Roth and Lonnie Lane, *Heaven Is beyond Your Wildest Expectations: Ten True Stories of Experiencing Heaven* (Shippensburg, PA: Destiny Image, 2012), loc. 1672, Kindle.
26. Jim Woodford, phone interview with John Burke, December 9, 2022. Used with permission.
27. Woodford, phone interview with John Burke.
28. Karina Martinez, Zoom interview with John Burke, April 28, 2022. Used with permission.
29. Ruter Springer, *Intra Muros*, 120.
30. Dr. Mary Neal, personal interview with John Burke, Austin, Texas, February 22, 2016. Used with permission.
31. Mally Cox-Chapman, *The Case for Heaven: Near Death Experiences as Evidence of the Afterlife* (Windsor, CT: Tide-Mark Press, 2012), loc. 420–422, Kindle.

APPENDIX: WHAT ABOUT THOSE WHO HAVE NEVER HEARD?

1. C. S. Lewis, *Mere Christianity* (New York: HarperCollins, 1952, 1980), 64.

About the Author

JOHN BURKE is the author of the *New York Times* bestseller *Imagine Heaven*, along with *No Perfect People Allowed*, *Soul Revolution*, and *Unshockable Love*. He and his wife, Kathy, founded Gateway Church, a multisite church based in Austin, Texas, that helps people explore faith. As an international speaker, John has addressed hundreds of thousands of people in thirty countries on topics of leadership, spiritual growth, and the exhilarating life to come. John and Kathy have two children and two grandchildren. To keep up with John, visit JohnBurkeOnline.com.

JOIN JOHN BURKE AND DISCOVER THE GOD WHO LOVES YOU DEEPLY AND IS CLOSER THAN YOU COULD EVER IMAGINE.

What nearly seventy near-death experiences reveal about the God of heaven

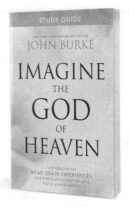

Great for small group or individual study

DVD to accompany the study guide with teaching from John Burke

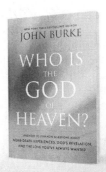

A concise guide to commonly asked questions about near-death experiences

TO CONNECT WITH

JOHN BURKE

SEARCH ONLINE FOR
"AUTHOR JOHN BURKE"

SPEAKING EVENTS

BOOKS

CONTACT

OTHER FREE RESOURCES

CP1903